Transactions
of the
American Philosophical Society
Held at Philadelphia
For Promoting Useful Knowledge
Volume 90, Pt. 4

KOS BETWEEN HELLENISM AND ROME

Studies on the Political, Institutional and Social History of Kos from ca. the Middle Second Century B.C. Until Late Antiquity

Οἱ ἑκασταχόθεν μέγιστοι καὶ δυνατώτατοι
τὰς ἑαυτῶν πατρίδας ὑμῖν φυλάττουσιν
(Ael.Arist., Εἰς Ῥώμην, 64)

KOSTAS BURASELIS

American Philosophical Society
Independence Square ▪ Philadelphia
2000

ISBN:0-87169-904-4
US ISSN:0065-9746

Library of Congress Cataloging-in-Publication Data

Buraselis, Kostas.
    Kos between Hellenism and Rome : studies on the political, institutional, and social history of Kos from ca. the middle second century / Kostas Buraselis.
        p. cm. -- (Transactions of the American Philosophical Society ; v. 90, pt. 4)
    Includes bibliographical references and index.
    ISBN 0-87169-904-4 (pbk.)
        1. Kos Island (Greece)--Civilization. 2. Greece--History--146 B.C.-323 A.D. 3. Kos Island (Greece)--Relations--Rome. 4. Rome--Relations--Greece--Kos Island. I. Title. II. Series.

DF261.C7 B87 2000
949.5'87--dc21

                                                                            00-036252

The Editor wishes to thank the following people for assistance with the Greek text: Ralph Hancock for providing the font; Richard Rosen for suggesting a proofreader; Sarah Burges Watson for expert assistance in proofreading and correcting Greek passages.

Κῴοις   ἥρωσιν

William Paton

Ἰακώβῳ Ζαρράφτῃ

Rudolph Herzog

Mario Segre

καθιεροῦται

CONTENTS

Abbreviations of Lexica, series and similar works[1]

AnÉp : L`Année Épigraphique

BMC : British Museum Catalogue of the Greek coins of...

Bull. : Bulletin Épigraphique

Dessau : H.Dessau, *Inscriptiones Latinae Selectae*, I-III (1892-1916)

LSJ : H.G.Liddell-R.Scott-H.S.Jones-R.McKenzie, *A Greek-English Lexicon*[9].
Oxford 1940 (with the Revised Supplement, by P.G.W.Glare-A.A.
Thompson, Oxford 1996)

OCD[3] : *The Oxford Classical Dictionary*[3], ed. by S.Hornblower and An.
Spawforth. Oxford 1996

OGIS : W.Dittenberger, *Orientis Graeci inscriptiones selectae,* I-II, Lipsiae 1903-
5.

Sel.Pap. : A.S.Hunt-C.C.Edgar, *Select Papyri*, I-II, Loeb Classical Library. Cam-
bridge(Mass.) 1932-1934

SNG : Sylloge Nummorum Graecorum

Staatsv. : Die Staatsverträge des Altertums: II. H.Bengtson, *Die Verträge der
griechisch-römischen Welt von 700 bis 338 v.Chr.*[2] München 1975; III.
H.H.Schmitt, *Die Verträge der griechisch-römischen Welt von 338 bis 200
v.Chr.* ibid., 1969.

Syll.[3] : W.Dittenberger et al., *Sylloge Inscriptionum Graecarum*[3], I-IV, Lipsiae
1915-24

---

[1]Periodicals have been cited according to the system of *L`Année Philologique* and classical
authors usually according to the abbreviations given in *LSJ* and C.T.Lewis-C.Short, *A Latin
Dictionary,* (Oxford 1879, repr. 1966).

Foreword

Kos has often inspired interesting case studies in its ancient Aegean context. This may be explained thematically first by the island's belonging to that eastern Aegean chain of islands from Lemnos in the north to Rhodes in the south that form the "nearest bridge" to Asia Minor. These islands' fortunes have always depended on their relations to—and the strategic, political and economic balance between Europe and the Asiatic coast opposite. In addition, the connection of Kos with the cult of Asklepios and the tradition of Hippokrates has helped the island acquire in the Hellenistic period a special aura of holiness and medical wisdom, thus effectively claiming a relative inviolability and consequent protection from external vicissitudes. Nevertheless, Rome's involvement, gradual predominance, and subsequent domination in the Greek East rendered also the fortunes and status of Kos totally dependent on its relations to the new suzerain. How Kos developed with regard both to its Hellenistic past and traditions on the one side and the need to adapt itself into its new role of a properly smoothed stone in the great mosaic of the Roman Empire on the other, is a fascinating subject. It has formed a part of Susan Sherwin-White's *Ancient Kos* (1978), a still basic synthesis of the political, institutional, and socioeconomic history of the island from its "Dorianisation" until the late antiquity.[1]

The opportunities for research on ancient Kos have always been considerable, despite human setbacks and an unforgettable tragedy. Kos has been lucky enough to have produced an especially large number of inscriptions that throw invaluable light on many points of its ancient course and sometimes decisively supplement the rudimentary ancient literary tradition on it. William Paton and Edward Hicks first assembled these inscriptions about a century ago. Later, Rudolph Herzog, with some help from the dedicated local antiquary, Iakobos Zarraphtis, greatly contributed to the knowledge of ancient Kos not only by his finding and excavating the Asklepieion but also with the systematic publication of many inscriptions. Under Italian rule on the Dodecanese since 1912 Koan history has been especially associated with the systematic, devoted study of the inscriptions of Kos (and Kalymna, a part of the Koan polis-state) by Mario Segre, a victim of inhumanity at Auschwitz. The posthumous publication of Herzog's and Segre's extensive *Nachlass* of

---

[1] Some aspects have been also treated in the later, special study by Höghammar.

Koan inscriptions has advanced only sporadically since the Second World War. Segre's collection of Koan inscriptions, in the first and last version of his manuscript, was finally published in 1993. This rich new material and the access to some important inscriptions originally found and noted by Herzog seem to offer a new base for the study of the subject.

A full synthesis seems premature, however, (see below), and I have preferred to present here mainly a series of partial studies in the political, institutional, and social history of Kos between ca. the middle of the second century B.C., and the end of the second century A.D., that is, aspects of the subject on which I believe I have reached some original conclusions. These studies (and some similar, already drafted ones on Samos, Chios and Lesbos) originate from my broader, ongoing work to prepare a fascicle of the *Tabula Imperii Romani* covering the area of the Aegean islands. These I offer as modest contributions to the research of the Greek East under the Roman hegemony and empire.

I have been lucky enough to further my research, first during a three-month stay at the Universität Würzburg (summer 1995), facilitated by a grant of the Gerda-Henkel-Stiftung; second during February 1996 in London as British Academy Visiting Professor, and finally as a member of the Institute for Advanced Study at Princeton/N.J. in the academic year 1996/97, during my sabbatical from the University of Athens.

Many people have offered advice, help and encouragement, and I am grateful to them all. I may cite as representatives of this whole circle of colleagues and friends Dieter Timpe, Erika Simon and Karlheinz Dietz (Würzburg), Walter Ameling (now Jena), Michael Crawford and Andrew Burnett (London), Christian Habicht and G.W.Bowersock (Princeton,N.J.), Kerstin Höghammar (Uppsala). Klaus Hallof (Berlin) generously made texts and other data from Herzog's *inedita* accessible to me;[2] my Athenian colleague Georgia Alevra shared with me a common seminar on "Hellenistic and Roman Kos" (spring 1995); Ersi Bruskari allowed me to present here the new honorary text for Sabinianus; the *ephoros* Ioannis Papachristodulu as well as Dimitris Bosnakis and his colleagues in the Archaeological Service on Kos have tried to facilitate my work there and, more generally, my study of Kos in every possible way. Maria Tulanta and Basilis Chatzigiakumis have offered me generous hospitality—almost turning the Athenian scholar into a Koan

---

[2] A first, considerable part of Herzog's unpublished Koan texts have now appeared: C.V.Crowther-C.Habicht-L.&K.Hallof,"Aus der Arbeit der"Inscriptiones Graecae." I. Drei Dekrete aus Kos für δικασταγωγοί," *Chiron* 28(1998): 87-100; L.&K.Hallof-C.Habicht, "Aus...II. Ehrendekrete aus dem Asklepieion von Kos," ibid., 101-142; eidem, "Aus...III. Unedierte koische Epidosis-Listen," ibid., 143-162. None of these texts touches directly on the subjects treated here, cf. below.

metic; an anonymous reader and Anne Ramu-Chapsiadi read the whole manuscript through with friendly diligence and corrected mistakes; Paschalis Paschidis patiently initiated his teacher into the informatic mysteries; Paulina Grigoriadi greatly contributed to the preparation of the indices; Carole Le Faivre-Rochester has kindly and effectively aided an obstinately Hellenizing manuscript.

International collaboration is perhaps one of the most humanizing aspects of what we call (perhaps sometimes undeservedly) humanities. I have enjoyed such collaboration as often as I could in preparing these studies, and the dedication of this book somehow expresses the same spirit retrospectively.

Athens/K.Iliupoli, August 2000.

Plates 1A and 1B

A. The historical interpretation of Segre, *I.Cos,* ED 229 and the perils of Koan security and free status from the Second Cretan War (ca. 155-153 B.C.) to the aftermath of the First Mithridatic War (89-85 B.C.).

Introduction

Kos managed to survive the period of Hellenistic history up to ca. 200 B.C. without any serious detriment to its full local sovereignty—before the blatant Roman intrusion in the Eastern Mediterranean. This was greatly due to the island's early affiliation with the Ptolemaic dynasty. This relationship, resting on quite personal, original bonds (Philadelphos' birth on Kos in 309/8 B.C.)[1] and variously fostered thereafter by both sides,[2] had adopted a form similar to that between Egypt and Rhodes in the same period. Kos was certainly a faithful ally (as well as a useful source of manpower and commercial link) and no direct dependency of the Lagids. Loyalty to Alexandria in external policy was the guarantee of Egyptian support for the island's full internal liberty. Antigonid influence on Kos may have also built a minor rival tradition, but it cannot have amounted to more than temporary breaks in the long line of the Koan-Ptolemaic *entente cordiale.*

The decline of Ptolemaic power in the Aegean after ca. 245 B.C.[3] seems to have brought the island into closer political collaboration with its great nesiotic neighbor, Rhodes. In the years of the so-called First Cretan War (ca. 205-201 B.C., cf. below) Kos and Rhodes found themselves equally exposed to the assaults of Cretan pirates, which they bravely resisted, probably in common.[4] It was clear by then, however, that the absence of a real naval master of the Aegean, more precisely: the renewed rivalries of powers aspiring to such a role (as Rhodes and Philip V) left islands like Kos without a steady and effective protection of their security. The policy of exclusive loyalty, such as to the Ptolemies in the third century B.C., seemed insufficient to cover the needs of a new age.

---

[1] Marmor Parium (*FgrHist* 239) B19. Cf. Theokritos 17.58ff.; Kallimachos, Hymn. IV.160ff.

[2] Cf. esp. the overview in Sherwin-White, *Cos,* 90 ff., which remains fundamental.

[3] See Buraselis, *HM&A,* 176 and recently Reger, *Kyklades.*

[4] Useful reconstructions of the relevant events in Brulé, 29-56 (on a point of disagreement cf. below) and more recently Baker.

The actual successors of the Ptolemaic naval presence in the Aegean were Rhodes and the Attalids. With the latter, we find Koan relations prospering.[5] The main new affiliation was with Rome, however, the power that now began to exert political influence, aid and control, gradually ascending in Greek eyes from a single anti-Macedonian role to an imperial one.

Thanks to new epigraphic evidence, some aspects of this period of transition from 200 B.C. to the final establishment of Roman control in this area by Sulla may now emerge. We shall see some late application of the Koans' prevalent diplomatic agenda, that is relying on the Ptolemies, in the third century B.C. and their growing effort (and difficulties) to comply with the Roman wishes and strict definition of loyalty.

a. Segre, *I.Cos*, ED 229 is a fragment of a Koan honorary decree: it concerns a local *euergetes* from a family whose distinguished service of their home city vividly and succinctly emerges from the text. Christian Habicht has drawn scholarly attention to this document, "ein schönes Beispiel," as he wrote, "für die in die Ehrung eines Mannes eingeflochtenen Würdigungen der Verdienste seiner Vorfahren."[6] Segre himself noticed here that his restorations were meant to indicate the sense that the text should give, and that he intended to study elsewhere in more detail this "notevolissimo documento." Cucuzza has recently touched on the historical interpretation of the text in a study of religious connections (cult of Artemis Toxitis) between Kos and Crete.[7] I was myself able to rediscover the inscription and study it in the courtyard of the magazine of antiquities inside the Knights Castle of Kos in May 1997. Thus my study of the text rests also on a useful personal inspection of the stone.

The extant decree had been inscribed on an orthogonal block of blue-grey marble (Plate 1 A). The thickness of the stone is given by Segre as 0,355 m. This, however, is the measurement of the base; the upper surface is a polished strip of 0,11 m width from the inner edge of which the stone slopes down to the base. This sloping surface is only coarsely worked (Plate 1 B) so that one gets the impression that the stone could have been part of an outer wall of a building or some sort of pedestal. The lettering of the inscription fully supports, I think, Segre's dating: "I sec. a.C.." There are clear but light apices, alpha has the cross

---

[5] Sherwin-White, *Cos*, 132f. offers a concise picture of the main relevant evidence.
[6] Habicht, *I.Kos*, 89.
[7] Cucuzza (he kindly allowed me to consult his article while still unpublished). See below on his views.

bar curved, sigma has the top and bottom strokes parallel, the mu has the outer strokes slightly sloping, pi the right stroke slightly shorter and the horizontal bar projecting on both sides, theta is as tall and omicron just slightly smaller than the other letters, omega also slightly smaller and closed, that is, consisting of a circle and a more or less tangent horizontal line below it. I have the general impression that the letter forms are approximately one style-phase older than those in documents of the Augustan age (e.g. *PH* 81) and some of the private dedications for Nikias (e.g. *PH* 76, 77). They seem to come closer, I think, to the style of e.g. *PH* 61= Höghammar 36 (50-40 B.C.) and ibid. 48 (ca. 70-30 B.C.). A personal inspection of Segre, *I.Cos*, ED 7 (Sulla's letter to the Koans) shows that some of its letter forms (alpha with broken cross bar, omega distinctly opening below; on the other side, sigma with the top and bottom strokes still distinctly divergent) are more advanced than those of ED 229 while the letters of the latter are more distinctly apicated. The lettering of ED 236, which is dated by Segre to the first century B.C. and cannot be at any rate earlier than ca. 150 B.C. (ὑ[πο]δοχᾶς ʽΡωμαίων in ll.18/19!), certainly looks older than that of ED 229.[8]

The text was arranged in columns, from which the preserved fragment offers only a large part of one column and a tiny, upper left part of the next. One has only about ten lines, each comprising about seven words of continuous text with which to work, an additional difficulty being that the beginnings of eight of these lines have to a larger or smaller degree to be restored. However, this fragment is important since it obviously belongs to the justificative part of the decree, in which the benefactions of the unknown honorand (we may call him "the son of Chairylos") and notable elements of his family history are related. We gain through these "personal entries" precious glimpses of the island's history in a span of approximately one century—as we are going to see.

b. The first lemma of this family history preserved concerns an ancestor of the honorand, Diogenes. The exact form of relationship (grandfather of the honorand? more remote relative?) cannot be established: it stood at the beginning of l.1, restored by Segre as [ἔκγονος ὤν], which is very probable.[9] Further glorious ancestors of the

---

[8] I have also noticed the following, minor corrections to Segre's text of ED 229 on my study of the stone: γενηθεῖσαν (not γεννηθεῖσαν), l. 2; there is an uninscribed space of about two letters length before ὅς in l.5, so that the text should read here υυ ὅς; the first preserved letters after the second gap of l. 10 are IAN, see below; in l. 12 there is no mistake (alpha instead of lambda) of the scribe, the stone has ΠΟΛΙΤΗΑΝ, only that the alpha is a little damaged.

[9] [ἔγγονος ὤν] would be also a possible restoration. ἔκγονος means properly "descendant" (e.g. *Syll.*[3] 845) and ἔγγονος "grandchild" but the meaning of the two terms often

honorand—either antedating or postdating Diogenes—must have existed as the decree itself goes on to mention (ll.4-5); their acts/honors may have even exceeded the importance of those by/for Diogenes.[10] The latter's own mark of service to Kos, however, and obviously a memorable and permanent accolade of the whole family in the eyes of the city, was his diplomatic intervention with the Ptolemies and the preservation of Koan liberty in a phase of hostile relations between the island and the Cretan League.

The published text says that Diogenes "had established friendly relations to the kings [then reigning] in Egypt, and put this friendship into the service of his homecity's liberty in the critical situation that had occurred between the city and the Cretan League ἐπὶ πολεμωτάτοις.[11] At first sight this last expression means simply "being in a fierce war" Habicht has already connected the events referred to with the well-known involvement of the island in the so-called First Cretan War (ca. 205-201 B.C.), when Kos became the target of repeated attacks by Cretan pirates and had to mobilize all its forces and meticulously organize its defense, as we know from various epigraphic texts (especially honorary decrees for benefactors ad res) of the period.[12] The "kings in Egypt" would then be Philopator and Epiphanes succeeding each other on the throne, and our text would reveal for the first time, as Habicht concluded, an energetic Ptolemaic support of Kos during this war.

There remain some problems by this admittedly straightforward solution that seem to me to point strongly to another direction, however. First, we should attribute the proper importance to the mention of the

---

overlaps (see the examples in *LSJ*, s.vv.). However, the term of relation to be restored here should apply both to Diogenes and ἄλλων τε ἀνδρῶν ὑπὲρ/[..]ατι τετειμαμένων ἐπ' ἀρετᾶι...(ll.4-5). So the more general meaning of "descendant" should be rather conveyed by whatever term we restore here, although this does not exclude that the exact relation of Diogenes to the honorand could be that between grandfather and grandson. Cucuzza assumed the latter without reserves.

[10] At the beginning of l. 5 there is space for ca. 4 letters on the stone. So I would restore the passage as following: ἄλλων τε ἀνδρῶν ὑπὲρ / [ταῦτ]ά τι τετειμαμένων ἐπ' ἀρετᾶι, "also descended from other men who have achieved even some higher honor for their worthiness."

[11][ἔκγονος ὢν] Διογένους, ὃς τὰν πρὸς τοὺς ἐν Αἰγύπτῳ βασιλεῖς/[τότε ὄντας] φιλίαν γενηθεῖσαν κατεχρήσατο ἐς τὰν τᾶς/ [πατρί]δος ἐλευθερίαν ἐν τοῖς συστᾶσι τᾷ πόλει πρὸς Κρη/[ταιέ]ας ἐπὶ πολεμωτάτοις καιροῖς...(col.I.1-4).The theoretically alternative restoration [Πτολεμαίους] would seem too long for the space available on the stone.

[12] Habicht, *I.Kos*, 89. The same dating of these events has also been subsequently adopted by *Cucuzza* and G.Reger, *AJA* 100(1996), 623. On Diokles, son of Leodamas, and his contribution to the defense of Kos during the First Cretan War, see now also the new evidence published by the Hallofs and Habicht (p. 2, n.2 above), 117ff. G.Alevra is also going to publish a new honorary decree for him from her excavations at Halasarna.

Cretan League. To be on safe ground on this point, let us first note that Segre's restoration Κρη/[ταιέ]ας (ll.3-4) is certainly correct. The last alpha of the word can be clearly discerned on the stone (and the published photograph), and the lacuna before it cannot have been filled by just one letter, thus excluding the theoretically alternative possibility Κρῆ/[τ]ας. Consequently, the hostile relations were not only between Cretans and Kos but between the Cretan League (for which this was the official and technical term)[13] and Kos. What we know about the so-called First Cretan War (appearing simply as Κρητικὸς πόλεμος in the contemporary sources) makes clear that, whatever the secret motives and (possibly Macedonian) instigation of this war, there are no signs of its having been more than a series of operations carried out by separate Cretan cities against the Koan (and parts of the Rhodian) state.[14] Only Hierapytna was expressly mentioned as the aggressor in *Syll.*[3] 567. A collective assault of the Cretan League on Kos and other islands is in this case neither attested nor probable. If one assumes its having been launched in accordance with the plans of Philip V, who had secured a hegemonial role in the Cretan League about ten years before,[15] one can see that it would have been unwise for Philip to reveal his plans by openly inciting the League's forces into a conflict with the nesiotic cities off the Carian coasts. Neither historical tradition nor probability allow an interpretation of that "First Cretan War" as one officially and publicly connected with the entire Cretan League. In contrast, Κρηταιεῖς as aggressors in the same area appears expressly in the decree of the Karpathian *ktoina* for Hiero published and persuasively connected by Segre[16] with the so-called Second Cretan War, half a century later than the first (see below).

The mention of the "kings in Egypt" and Diogenes' friendship (φιλίαν γενηθεῖσαν) with them seem also to indicate a later date. First,

---

[13] On Κρηταιεῖς and the nature, beginnings and development of the Cretan League, see most recently Chaniotis, *KV,* 30ff., 99ff. with the older literature.

[14] The most recent and systematic presentations of the First Cretan War are those by Brulé, 29-56 and Chaniotis, *KV,* 38-41. I am not convinced by Brulé's thesis, however, that this was openly and officially a war of the Cretan Koinon against the territory of Rhodes, Kos, and possibly other adjacent islands. The picture offered by the surviving sources (esp. *Diod.,* 27.3 and 28.1) is rather that of expressly piratical operations, separately undertaken by Cretan cities than that of a common war of the Cretan League against those islands. It is also with such a setting (*contra* Brulé) that the declaration of the war by Rhodes, not the Cretans operating, the initial number of the latter's ships engaged (just seven), and Dikaiarchos' help to the Cretan pirates organized by Philip V (not a direct, official Macedonian support!) may naturally fit. Cf. also the argument in the text.

[15] *Pol.,* 7.11.9. Cf. *Chaniotis, KV,* 441(no.76) with the older bibliography.

[16] Segre, *KP.ΠΟΛ.,* 379ff.

the impression one gets is that a friendly relation with simultaneously reigning kings, not successive ones, is meant here. The aorist of γενηθεῖσαν implies rather a common date of affiliation with these kings. A similar difficulty in recognizing them as Philopator and Epiphanes is that we should rather see in this "friendship," as in many similar cases, the result of a personal contact between the important Koan and the kings. This was something very difficult in the case of Epiphanes who ascended the throne as a child (204 B.C.) during the period of the First Cretan War, and was tutored by various successive regents in his first regnal years (Sosibios and Agathokles, then Tlepolemos and Sosibios II, still later Aristomenes).[17] Thus if we attributed the mention of the kings to Philopator and Epiphanes, we should understand Diogenes' friendship with Philopator as merely and formally "inherited" by Epiphanes, which does not seem to be conveyed by the wording of the passage.

Moreover, it is historically improbable that Philopator, shortly before his death, or the regents of Epiphanes, none of whom has been able to protect properly the Ptolemaic possessions in this area during this period, would have had the authority to force the Cretan cities—already engaged in war and plunder on Koan land during the first Cretan War— to respect of Koan liberty.[18] As mentioned before, the only Cretan aggressor known with certainty was Hierapytna, an official Macedonian ally since Doson, so that it would be at least difficult to assume some important influence of the Ptolemaic court here.[19]

---

[17] See conveniently H. Volkmann, *RE* XXIII.2(1959), s.v. Ptolemaios (23), 1692-3.

[18] The famous restitution of the incorporation of Kalymna into the Koan state (ἀποκατάστασις τᾶς ὁμοπολιτείας) under conditions of friendship and alliance with a Ptolemy (Segre, *TC*, Test.XII=*Staatsv*.III.545) should most probably be dated under Epiphanes while the conception and the initial act of this union under Philopator: the correct historical context already recognized and analyzed by Sherwin-White, *Cos*, 124-129. Cf. more recently Höghammar, 88-93 with further specifications and bibliography. Philopator's care of Kos and Kalymna in his later years cannot have actually exceeded an intense encouragement of their collective self-defense against imminent Aegean dangers. This fits well what else we know about his Aegean policy: cf. Huß, *Pt.IV*, esp. 132ff., 213ff.

[19] Hierapytna as Doson's ally: *Staatsv*. III. 502; cf. Chaniotis, *KV*, 35f. with the more recent bibliography. Certainly, diplomatic contacts between Alexandria and Philip V in Philopator's/Epiphanes' times are known (cf. the mission of Ptolemaios the son of Sosibios in *Pol.*,15.25.13 ; *ib.* 15.20.1) but it would be undoubtedly an exaggeration to suppose on the basis of them any serious indirect influence of Egypt on the actions of Cretan cities allied with Macedonia. On the evidence of a diplomatic dialogue, which never reached the level of a real dynastic rapprochement, between Egypt and Macedonia in this period cf. Huß, *Pt.IV*, 127-9.

The focus is better when we switch to a later context during the Second Cretan War (ca. 155-153 B.C.).[20] The kings reigning at that time in Alexandria were Philometor and his sister and consort, Cleopatra II, the first Ptolemaic queen officially recognized as sole co-regent with her brother and husband after 163 (Philometor's restoration).[21] Thus Diogenes' affiliation with "the kings" could simply be his special friendly relationship at Philometor's court to the co-regnants of Egypt in that period. But what weighs decisively, I think, in favor of Philometor is his well-known close relationship with, and real influence at, the Cretan Koinon. We may first recall that Philometor's mediation was instrumental in ending a war between Knossos and Gortyn ca. 168 B.C., thus reconstituting the Cretan Koinon, which then recognized the Ptolemaic protectorate of Itanos and concluded a formal treaty with Philometor.[22] The Koan, Aglaos, son of Theukles, whom the League even named their *proxenos* in Alexandria is a concrete example of an influential figure at Philometor's court (he was probably *dioiketes*). He was connected with the allied troops that the Cretan League had put under the latter's orders in somewhat earlier years, that is during Philometor's expedition against his brother Euergetes II on Cyprus (ca. 158-154),[23] Thus a lively political triangle Kos-Crete (League)-Ptolemaic court under Philometor is already demonstrated.

We may add that Philometor's era seems to have more generally coincided with a last flash of Ptolemaic influence in the Aegean, one that has left traces not only on Crete but also on Thera, Methana/Arsinoe,

---

[20] On this war see the most recent accounts by Brulé, 61-66 and Chaniotis, *KV*, 49 with the relevant sources and bibliography.

[21] See T.C.Skeat, *The Reigns of the Ptolemies*, (Munich 1954) 14; G.H.Hölbl, *Geschichte des Ptolemäerreiches*, (Darmstadt 1994) 160 (cf. 77). An example of Philometor and Cleopatra II jointly mentioned as βασιλεῖς in the Greek papyri: *P.Lond.* VII (T.C.Skeat, The Zenon Archive, Oxford 1974), 2188.32. The demotic documents expressly speak of them together as "Pharaohs": P.W.Pestman, *Chronologie égyptienne d'après les textes démotiques (332 av.J.-C. - 453 ap.J.-C.)*, (Leiden 1967) 50. Cf. also the joint mention of Philometor and Cleopatra II as rulers of Egypt in the story of Onias: *Jos., Ant. Jud.*, 12.388;13.63 and the Parian decree published by G.Despinis, *AD* 20 A(1965), 119 (ll.4-5).

[22] See most recently Chaniotis. *KV*, 45-49. The treaty between Knossos and Gortyn ibid.,no.43 (pp.289ff.); cf now also Ager, no.128 (pp.356ff.). The recognition of Philometor's *prostasia* of Itanos by the Koinon is attested in the epigraphic dossier of the longstanding territorial differences between Itanos and Hierapytna: *Syll.*[3] 685.107 (cf. Ager, no. 158). The existence of a treaty of alliance between Philometor and the Koinon may be concluded from the decree for Aglaos (next note).

[23] Honorary decree of Philometor's Cretan *symmachoi* for this Aglaos on Delos: Durrbach,*Choix*,no.92. Aglaos' post as *dioiketes* may be concluded from the Parian inscription cited above (n. 21), l. 4.

Paros, Argos and, of course, Athens.[24] With the death of Philometor all military presence or decisive political influence of the Lagids in this area disappears. Thus this king's intervention as mediator between Kos and the Cretans and protector of the former from the inimical attitudes of the latter during the Second Cretan War best fits the historical evidence we have to date. One should specify, in view of all the preceding argument, that it seems more preferable to accept an eventually deterred attack of the Cretan League on Kos under Philometor—this would completely explain the silence of our sources on any involvement of Kos in the Second Cretan War—rather than to suppose an improbably dynamic intervention of Egypt under Philopator or Epiphanes *in medias res* of the Koan struggle against intense Cretan assaults in the First War.

Even a minor textual problem of the inscription can be thus better solved. I refrained so far from examining the expression ἐπὶ πολεμω-τάτοις in Segre's text. As πόλεμος is always a substantive and not an adjective, one could first think of restoring ἐπὶ πολεμ(ι)ωτάτοις . The meaning would then be as much as: "in very warlike mood (on both sides)," and could, of course, be referred to actual warfare. The superlative might also point, however, to a climax just reached or to be reached: "while the relations (between the Cretans and Kos) had reached/were reaching the highest point of tension." By either meaning the text itself leaves room for questions: there is no other case in the inscription where the engraver would have omitted a letter, and the old maxim *lectio difficilis potior* should be overlooked. A smoother text structure and a completely satisfactory variant of the latter meaning may be restored, I think, if we read: ἐπιπολεμωτάτοις (καιροῖς), and translate: "while war was really imminent, seemed unavoidable." That the adjective ἐπιπόλεμος has not been found in any other text so far may be balanced by the existence of numerous parallels of similar composite adjectives (ἐπί + x) also meaning the local or temporal proximity of their respective second component.[25] We may conclude that the decree simply

---

[24] The evidence on Thera and Methana collected and discussed in Bagnall, 123-136 (cf. esp. his remarks, 134, on the relatively rich representation of Philometor's reign on Thera); on Paros see the decree cited above (n.21); on Argos: *SEG* 32(1982), 371; on the Ptolemaic relations to Athens in Philometor's age: Habicht, *Athens & P*, 78-83.

[25] The syntactic structure from which the formation of these adjectives actually originates is the use of ἐπί + dative of a substantive to express again such an idea of nearness: e.g. Ἀντιόχεια ἡ ἐπὶ Δάφνη, ἐπὶ τελευτῆ ("near death," in *Xen., Mem.*, 1.5.2; *Hipp., Epid.,* VII.20,35). A selection of relevant adjectives on the basis of the entries in *LSJ* (from there also the quoted translations): ἐπιθαλάμιος (ὕμνος/ᾠδή), "bridal song, sung in chorus before the bridal chamber"; ἐπιθαλάσσιος, "lying or dwelling on the coast"; ἐπιθανάτιος/ἐπιθάνατος, "sick to death, hard at death's door," so for example in *D.,* 50.60: Ἡ ...μήτηρ ἔκαμνε καὶ ἐπιθάνατος ἦν...; ἐπικίνδυνος (bringing, resulting in

emphasized here how Diogenes managed to bring on the scene of the Second Cretan War, in regard to Kos, the *deus ex machina* of Ptolemaic influence just before the outbreak of real hostilities. The sun of Egypt was still strong enough to dissolve the Cretan clouds over Kos.

c. The element of conscious ancestral models is a fundamental one in the psychology of the honorand's family as depicted in the decree. Chairylos, his father, imitated Diogenes' and many other illustrious ancestors' examples by following a similar patriotic course up to his death. One of the intriguing points in his own entry is that he was acting as an envoy of Kos in Rome when death ended a career of merit towards his homecity.[26] It is extremely important to ascertain the date and reason(s) for Chairylos' presence in Rome. It obviously belongs to a later date than Diogenes' activity, that is, after the middle of the second century B.C. as we concluded before. The end of his entry makes it at least clear that a result of his embassy was a letter from the senate (see below). Any hint at some higher, real source of power in Rome is absent, so it seems safe to conclude that Chairylos came to Rome in the Republican period—otherwise the emperor(s), not just Rome or the senate would have been mentioned.[27] This is now the more surprising as the decree expressly states that Chairylos had gone to Rome, and probably had to remain there for some time, to take care of the Koan cause expressed as νόμοι and πάτριος πολιτήα. The terms used have real importance: "the laws and the ancestral constitution" is a well-known synonym, more precisely: a periphrasis, for what a Greek city was

---

danger), e.g. in *Thuc.*, IV.92.5: (a *boeotarch* speaking of the Athenians) τοσούτῳ ἐπικινδυνοτέραν ἑτέρων τὴν παροίκησιν τῶνδε ἔχομεν; ἐπίνοσος, "subject to sickness, unhealthy"; ἐπίκηρος, "subject to death, perishable, mortal"; ἐπίπονος, in the sense: "sensitive to fatigue, easily exhausted," so for example in *Thphr.*, *Sens.*, 11: καὶ ὧν μὲν μανὰ καὶ ἀραιὰ κεῖται τὰ στοιχεῖα νωθροὺς καὶ ἐπιπόνους, ὧν δὲ πυκνά...ὀξέως φερομένους καὶ πολλοῖς ἐπιβαλλομένους..., or in the sense: "portending suffering" (of omens), as in *X.*, *An.*, 6.1.23: ...μέγας μὲν οἰωνός καὶ ἔνδοξος, ἐπίπονος μέντοι; ἐπίτεκνος, "capable of bearing children, fruitful" as in *Hp.*, *Aph.*, 5.62: ...αἱ τοιαῦται ἐπίτεκνοι γίνονται ; ἐπίμαχος (naturally exposed to the prospect of an attack) as in *Thuc.*, IV.31.2: ... ἔκ τε θαλάσσης ἀπόκρημνον καὶ ἐκ τῆς γῆς ἥκιστα ἐπίμαχον ; ἐπίκαρπος (having the prospect of bearing fruits, fruitful) as in an inscription from Kaunos, *JHS* 74(1954), 87: ...τὸν φυτεύσαντα ἐ[πί]/καρπα φυτά... Cf. also *LSJ*, s.vv. ἐπινέφελος (II), ἐπώλεθρος, ἐπισινής, ἐπίγαμος, ἐπίδικος.

[26] Segre's text (col. I.5-9) of Chairylos' entry: ὃς καὶ μειμησάμε/[ν]ος Χαιρύλος, ὁ πατὴρ αὐτοῦ, πρεσβεύων περὶ τῶν νόμων καὶ / τᾶς πατρίου πολιτήας ἐν Ῥώμᾳ, μετάλλαξεν ἄξιον ἐπαίνου/ καὶ βίον καὶ θάνατον, καὶ παρὰ τᾶι συγκλήτωι γράμμασιν ἐσχή/[θη (?) χρη]ματισθείς.

[27] Compare for example the phrase πρεσβεύσαντα...ἐς Ῥώμαν ποτὶ τὸς Σεβαστὸς καὶ τὰν σύγκλητον, in the decree (of slightly post-Claudian date) Maiuri, *NS*, 462.13-15.

especially fond of preserving in relation to Rome (and the Hellenistic monarchies before it): its internal liberty (ἐλευθερία).[28] This fitted very well into the traditional values with which the Koan family identified itself: Diogenes had also exerted all the power of his influence to preserve Koan *eleutheria* from any Cretan peril.

What this small fragment of a decree here unequivocally reveals, however, contrasts with a commonly held element of Koan history until the time of Augustus. S.Sherwin-White's valuable monograph presents the case, for example, that the free status of Kos was never altered during the period of the Roman Republic, no reasons for that ever having appeared.[29] Modern scholars have further inferred that Kos, with the end of M.Antonius and his eastern satellites (that is in the aftermath of Nikias' pro-Antonian tyranny), was probably deprived of its cherished free status by Augustus, and regained it no earlier than the Flavian period (see below). Our traditional scholarly picture of Koan relations with Republican Rome leaves no room for the Koans' free status having been imperiled, let alone annulled, at some point.

Scepticism may be reasonably succeeded by a closer scrutiny of what is actually known about Kos' relations with Republican Rome. Our modern constructs must always be ready to yield to what new evidence suggests (and not, of course, vice versa). Where during the Republican period could one note a situation in which Koan policy ran contrary to Rome's will, and may have so *de facto* questioned the privileged status of the island under Roman sway?[30] We know that there was a pro-Macedonian faction on Kos during the Roman war with Perseus (171-168 B.C.). Polybios (30.7.9-10) notes, however, that its leaders did not succeed in reversing the course of Koan foreign policy towards Rome

---

[28] Cf. e.g. the phrase in *IG* XII.1.2 referring to Rhodes' recovery of free status through Nero's support under Claudius (53 A.D., see concisely F.Hiller v.Gaertringen, *RE* Suppl. V(1931), s.v.Rhodos,810 citing the rest sources): [ἀπο/δοθείσ]ας τᾷ πόλει τᾶς πατρίου πολειτείας καὶ τῶν ὑόμων (ll.12-13). On the meaning and mutual relation/combination of *nomoi, patrios politeia, eleutheria* (and similar terms) in the political vocabulary of the Greek cities in Hellenistic and Roman times, with citation of further examples see esp. Bernhardt, *Polis & RH*, 225; Quaß, *Verf.* and *Hon.*, 142-148.

[29] Sherwin-White, *Cos*, 131-145: "Cos and Roman Supremacy (c.197-32 BC)." Cf. more recently the outline of the same period in *Höghammar*, 22-31.

[30] We may easily exclude the possibility of the Koan status having been seriously questioned under Caesar because of Pompeius' use of the island as one of his shipyards in the East (known from *Cic., Ad Att.*, IX.9.2). In such a case, not only would the decree have mentioned Caesar besides the senate but also a similar fate would have struck some of the other places used by Pompeius for the same purpose as Rhodes and Chios (ibid.). However, there is no indication of such problems in the case of these two *civitates liberae*.

and Macedonia.[31] The Koan state issued an honorary decree for Athenagoras of Larissa as doctor of C.Octavius Cn.f., the commander of the Roman fleet in Greece in 168-167 B.C.[32] Moreover, if the above interpretation and date of Ptolemaic intervention for Kos sponsored by Diogenes is correct, only a later context than the middle of the second century B.C. is possible.[33]

The only substantial political aberration in Kos's relationship with Rome was the First Mithridatic War (89-85 B.C.). A brief review of what we know about the island's involvement in it is useful. Appian[34] makes clear that the Koans accepted Mithridates into their city "with pleasure": Κῴων αὐτὸν (sc. Μιθριδάτην) ἀσμένως δεχομένων. The Koans further did not object to Mithridates' confiscating part of the Ptolemaic crown treasure deposited there by Cleopatra III. Josephus also refers to this[35] and adds that[36] the same fate befell eight hundred talents the Jews of Asia Minor had brought to Kos,[37] for safekeeping from Mithridates. It is hard to believe in a genuine and widespread Koan enthusiasm for the Pontic king.[38] Most Koans probably had to pretend a welcome when he marched in victory along the coasts of Asia Minor. The island, not as mighty as Rhodes, could not oppose him with the same measure of determination and success. Kos seems to have sacrificed, through its allowance of the above confiscations, its renown as a place of neutral financial safety to appease Mithridates' need for funding his ongoing war. At any rate, this diplomatic preference of the lesser evil under the difficult circumstances of 88 B.C. could not entitle Kos to any Roman favor after Mithridates'

---

[31] ...οὐ δυνηθέντες δὲ μεταρρῖψαι τὰ πολιτεύματα (there were such tendencies both on Kos and Rhodes) πρὸς τὴν τοῦ βασιλέως συμμαχίαν.

[32] It has been now published by the Hallofs and Habicht (p. 2, n.2 above), 105ff. They leave the question open whether the honor is to be dated before or after Pydna.

[33] Cucuzza having preferred to connect Diogenes with the First Cretan War (see above) pondered placing Chairylos' mission in the aftermath of the Third Macedonian War without considering the above data.

[34] *Mith.*, 4.23, cf. 115. Cf. McGing, 112.

[35] *AJ*, 13.13.1.

[36] Ibid., 14.111-113.

[37] Cf. Sherwin-White, *Note*, 183-4 (n.3).

[38] Cf. on the attitude of the Greek cities in Asia and Greece towards Mithridates, in the same spirit, Bernhardt, *Polis & RH*, 33-64 (63: "Die Passivität der meisten Städte wurde zweifellos vom Bewußtsein ihrer militärischen Schwäche mitbestimmt, konnten doch bei weitem nicht alle Städte eine längere Belagerung überstehen"); *Kallet-Marx*, 153-158 (on the massacre of 88, which was [157] "a deliberate act of policy in accordance with an order given by a third party [Mithridates] rather than a spontaneous expression of latent but bitter hostility"). However, a certain degree of socially or otherwise restricted identification with Mithridates' cause must remain: cf G.Reger's wise remarks in his review of the latter work, *Bryn Mawr Classical Review* 97.2.6; Pohl, 143-144.

defeat. Kos had stood on the Pontic side up to Lucullus' appearance in the island's waters (see below), this was as official as undeniable.

The Koans much later, under Tiberius (23 A.D.), supported their claim of *asylia* for their Asklepieion with an attestation of loyalty towards Rome drawn from the same period of the First Mithridatic War. As Tacitus relates, in addition to the antiquity of their sanctuary, there was also "meritum ex loco: nam cives Romanos templo Aesculapii induxerant, cum jussu regis Mithridatis apud cunctas Asiae insulas et urbes trucidarentur."[39] In other words, there was by Tiberius' time the estimable tradition that Kos had refused to participate in the pogrom of Romans ordained by Mithridates in Asia Minor, and had even offered them a shelter in the Asklepieion. The usefulness of the story for Koan interests should be as clear as the partial truth it represents. For the crucial, qualifying factor here is time. A passage and the sequence of events in Appian suggest that Mithridates almost simultaneously began the preparation of his expedition against Rhodes and ordered the slaughter of Romans.[40] It was only later that he appeared at Kos and his fleet was welcomed there on the way to the expedition against Rhodes, to which many Roman refugees had already found their way.[41] Thus, as already observed,[42] the Koan valiant protection of Romans certainly antedates, and had most probably no reason to postdate, the anchorage of the Mithridatic fleet in the harbor of the island. From that point on, there could be no question of a pro-Roman stance or even neutrality by all of Kos's cherished traditions. It is equally understandable that it would be highly advantageous for the Koans to project in later periods only the humanitarian prologue to their own Mithridatic drama. What came later was an uncomfortable truth.

Despite the clever disguising of historical reality that accompanied the Koans' later request to Tiberius (the famous C.Stertinius Xenophon was probably already at work for his homecity),[43] and has been so

---

[39] *Tac., Ann.,* 4.14. The tendentious exaggeration of this claim becomes already evident in "cunctas Asiae insulas": Rhodes and Chios certainly did not belong to them.

[40] *App., Mith.,* 4.22: ... ἐν τούτῳ δὲ (during Sulla's occupation with the civil trouble in Italy) ὁ Μιϑριδάτης ἐπί τε 'Ροδίους ναῦς πλείονας συνεπήγνυτο, καὶ σατράπαις ἅπασι καὶ πόλεων ἄρχουσι δι' ἀπορρήτων ἔγραφε, τριακοστὴν ἡμέραν φυλάξαντας ὁμοῦ πάντας ἐπιϑέσϑαι τοῖς παρὰ σφίσι 'Ρωμαίοις καὶ 'Ιταλοῖς... The arrival of Mithridates' fleet at Kos is then mentioned ib., 23 after the events of the massacre. Cf. on the date of the latter McGing, 113 (n.118).

[41] *App., Mith.,* 4.24.

[42] Pohl, 143 (n. 246): "...Kos gewährte ihnen (: the Romans) den Schutz des Asklepiosheiligtums..., wobei wir freilich nicht wissen, was mit ihnen geschah, als die Stadt Mithridates aufnahm...."

[43] See below. Cf. already Herzog, *N&X,* 221f., 229.

subsequently introduced into Tacitus' work through the *acta senatus* (and our historical "knowledge"),[44] the aftermath of the First Mithridatic War must have caused grave concern on Kos in regard to the city's status. Of course, the Koans could use in their favor the argument that they were readily persuaded by Lucullus about two years after Mithridates' triumphal entry into their harbor (86/85) to change camp and join the former's fleet. This had been operating along the coast of southwestern Asia Minor, in an expedition against Samos (probably a real Mithridatic base).[45] However, a fact never properly assessed in this context is that the neighbor of Kos, Knidos, had the same timely change of allegiance when Lucullus appeared but without being apparently able to exonerate itself from its previous conduct. Knidos must have lost its free status after the First Mithridatic War and regained it under Caesar— thanks only to the Knidian poet and statesman Theopompos, who was a friend of the dictator.[46] So a rather distant relationship between Kos and Rome after the first fight with Mithridates seems very likely, and the status of the city can very well have become a matter of deliberation for the Romans and a firm patriotic effort for the Koans.

Another piece of evidence, from Aphrodisias, on the aftermath of the First Mithridatic War, is useful here. The people of this Carian city, obviously also anxious to resume valuable contacts with Roman friends from the period of the war, thus safeguarding their own status after Sulla's victory (more on this in a later context), sent an embassy to the Roman proconsul Q.Oppius. He had borne the brunt of Mithridates' march into southern Asia Minor, been captured by him in Laodikeia and

---

[44] Among Herzog's *inedita* in Berlin there is a small Koan fragment (no. *0573 in L.Hallof's catalogue) on which there seems to be a mention of the same story as in Tacitus: we read [? συμμ]αχίας, 1.5; ['P]ωμαίους, 1.7; [βασιλέ]ως Μιθριδάτου, 1.8. The lettering is reported to suggest a date in the first century A.D., and Herzog had already thought in his unpublished notes of a connection with Tacitus' passage. Of course, this might be further evidence for an early appearance of the story but not for its historical exactness.

[45] *Plut., Luc.*, 3.3: ...'Ροδίων δὲ ναῦς αὐτῷ (sc. Λουκούλλῳ) προσπαρασχόντων Κῴους ἔπεισε καὶ Κνιδίους τῶν βασιλικῶν ἀπαλλαγέντας ἐπὶ Σαμίους συστρατεύειν. Sherwin-White, *RFPE*, 243 presses this passage too much in assuming the expulsion of "royalist garrisons" from Kos and Knidos and the existence of a wide popular support for Mithridates on Samos. We should notice that: a) *basilikoi* has in Plutarch, ib. (e.g. 12.2, 15.5) also the more general sense "royal forces," and b) if Samos was (as it had long been for the Ptolemies) the main naval base of the king in this area, its "pro-Mithridatic" difference from the other islands may have simply resulted from the presence of relatively numerous Pontic troops on it.

[46] *Plut., Caes.*, 48. Cf. Bowersock, *A&GW*, 9; Bernhardt, *I&E*, 125,160 (the Knidian inscriptions on Theopompos and his family now: *I.Knidos*, 51-61). Theopompos has been also honored on Kos: Patriarca, no.13= *RA* 4.1934, p.252 (no.91)= Höghammar, no. 49; ibid., 50 (=*PH*, 134²).

freed only later, in accordance with a clause of the treaty of Dardanos.[47] A relevant and important detail here is that the Aphrodisian embassy met the general on Kos. We know this from Oppius' consequent letter to the Aphrodisians at the heading of which he appears as ἀνθύπατος Ῥωμαίων στρατηγός.[48] So he must have been on some official mission there. Reynolds remarks in her commentary on this letter:

> ...(Oppius) presumably operated there with Sulla's approval. Cos had joined Mithridates providing his base for the attack on Rhodes, and although it subsequently changed sides there was, no doubt, occasion for Roman intervention there.[49]

Although the use of Kos as a base against Rhodes is at least partly inexact, Reynolds's remark would have already merited more attention.[50] Oppius' presence there and Chairylos' mission to Rome very probably belong in the same context and show that Kos at least did not rid itself easily of its stain of disloyalty towards Rome in the face of the triumphant Mithridates.

Finally, a new inscription from Lycia shows that there was an "allied garrison" on Kos after the expulsion of Mithridates' forces, and possibly some local sympathizers/supporters as well,. This proves now that the Mithridatic "episode" naturally inspired some circumspection into Rome's policy to Kos even after the Koans rejoined the Roman side (see Appendix 1).

The text of the Koan decree discussed, however, further discloses that Chairylos died in Rome shortly after receiving some sort of letter from the senate, obviously on the question of Koan status. Before proceeding one can probably find a better restoration (and a more complete meaning) of the relevant passage. Segre had read here (ll.8-9): ...καὶ παρὰ τᾶ συνκλήτωι γράμμασιν ἐσχή/[θη (?) χρη]ματισθείς, on which Habicht succinctly remarked: "...am Ende ist die richtige

---

[47] See Reynolds, docs. 2 and 3, with the editor's commentary. Further, McGing, 108-110 (citing the rest sources).

[48] Reynolds, doc. 3, ll.13-14: ...συνέτυχόν (sc. πρεσβευταὶ ὑμέτεροι) μοι ἐν Κῷ καὶ συνεχάρησαν...Oppius' title in ll. 2-3.

[49] Ibid., p. 19.

[50] Höghammar, 29-30 dismissed Reynolds's remark on insufficient grounds but she was right in pointing out that what we know about Mithridates' operations against Rhodes suggests a main Pontic base nearer the latter. McGing, 110 (n.103) thought that Oppius' presence on Kos might have the character of a medical cure after "his ordeal" in the war: this does not exclude some parallel official activity of the general there as the arrival of the Aphrodisian embassy itself implies.

Ergänzung noch nicht gefunden."[51] To begin with, the last word, from which only the part ...μaτισθείς has been preserved, must be a participle referring to the subject of the whole clause (nominative!), Chairylos. So it must express the art of transactions Chairylos had with the senate, mentioned just before. These transactions should include the issue of some senatorial letter. Segre's choice of [χρη]μaτισθείς seems to me to have no alternative. From all verbs in -μaτίζω mentioned in Kretschmer-Locker only this gives here an acceptable meaning. Χρηματίζω was, among other uses, a terminus technicus of the Hellenistic and then Roman administrative treatment of/answer to an embassy, petition etc. The usage has then been transferred to the gods so that there are numerous examples of a person χρηματισθείς ὑπὸ τοῦ θεοῦ x, i.e. someone who received divine instructions/an oracle to do something.[52] In the active the syntax could be with a personal object in dative, e.g. χρημaτισόν μοι ("give me an answer") + indirect question clause in *P.Fay.* 137.2. Other examples of the same grammatical structure in the active, as e.g. ἐχρημάτιζε τοῖς...πρεσβευταῖς[53] can certainly have had respective passive forms (πρεσβευταὶ χρηματισθέντες et sim.) like the one we come to recognize in the text analyzed. Therefore the meaning should be that Chairylos lived and died in a way worthy of praise, and that after he had received at the senate letters (pertaining to Kos).

What then of ἐσχή[θη (?)], which obviously did not satisfy Segre's own acute sense of the Greek? A verb would be clearly redundant here, so some other expression should be sought. It may help to note that the whole text preserves many Doric forms: so ἐς instead of εἰς (ἐς τὰν...ἐλευθερίαν, ll.2-3), ὄς instead of οὖς (l.5), πολιτήας (l.7) and

---

[51] Habicht, *I.Kos*, 89 (n.33).

[52] See the various examples in *LSJ*, s.v. χρηματίζω, esp.I.3-5; *Preisigke-Kießling*, s.v. χρηματίζω, 2. Cf. also in both these works the examples of χρηματισμός with the same sense. The essence of the semantic development has been already expressed with classic clarity by L.Robert, *Noms indigènes dans l'Asie-Mineure gréco-romaine*, (Paris 1963) 381f. (n.2): "...Quant à χρηματίζειν, χρηματισμός, je vois son origine et son histoire différement; je les rattache au sens politique et administratif de χρηματίζειν, χρηματισμός: donner réponse ou décision après audience ou étude, en parlant d'un roi, de l'assemblée du peuple ou de toute autorité; les dieux font de même, et spécialement dans leurs rapports directs avec les fidèles et pour les petites affaires personnelles que ceux-ci leur soumettent." Many cases of χρηματίζω/χρηματίζομαι in a religious sense ("give/receive an oracle") have been collected by Ad.Wilhelm, *APF* 15(1953), 74 and L.Robert, *Hellenica*, I, 72 (n.1); II, 148; XI-XII,455. We encounter χρηματίζομαι (passive) in an official but different sense in Segre, *I.Cos*, ED 178 a(A).18-19 (χρηματισθείσας εἰσωμοσίας, as a part of the wedding ritual connected with the cult of Aphrodita Pandamos).

[53] *Pol.*, 3.66.6. Cf. also ibid. esp. 4.27.9; 5.24.11 and 78.6 (here the verb accepts an adverbial complement: χρηματίσας φιλανθρώπως Λαμψακηνοῖς).

πολιτήαν (l.12) instead of πολιτείας, -αν. This may lead us to the simple solution: ἐς χῆ[ρας], i.e. "into the hands."[54] The meaning could be that Chairylos died soon after he had managed to receive personally ("into his own hands") his hard-earned response from the senate.[55] Serving as personal messenger from the senate to one's homecity was another well-known function (and distinguishing prerogative) of the ideal statesman in a Greek city striving for autonomy and similar privileges.[56]

One should be, however, very cautious about the success of Chairylos' mission. The emphasis laid on the result of his rather extended efforts at the senate might mean that he was finally successful in getting the Koan status re-affirmed (or restored), although the text is tantalizingly silent on the contents of the senate's response. There is no positive characterization of those "letters" (γράμμασιν) like the one known from other similar cases.[57] Thus we should be content to have established that Kos had to go through a phase of status uncertainty, at least, after 85 B.C. How long this phase lasted and when and how it actually ended are more complex problems to be discussed later.

d. Chairylos' son, the actual honorand of the decree, is seen next but it is here exactly that great gaps in the fragment and, finally, its conclusion tax our understanding. What remains from his portrait includes, once again, the consciousness of a great family tradition (ll. 9-10, cf. below), an early appearance of some positive features (education?, ll.10-11), and very probably a devotion to the democratic form of the state (l.12: εἰς τὰν πολιτήαν, l.13: [συμφ]έροντα τῶι πλήθε[ι]). The last unrestored word used of him here (l. 15) is characteristic of his

---

[54] Cf. the examples from the Epidaurian *iamata*, *IG* IV.1².121.96 (..ἐξελὼν τὰν λόγχαν ὁ ϑεὸς εἰς τὰς χῆράς οἱ ἔδωκε), 99-100 (...τὰς δεμελέας ἐξελεῖν καὶ δόμεν οἱ ἐς τὰς χεῖρας).

[55] There are various examples of εἰς χεῖρας διδόναι (et sim.)/ ἐγχειρίζειν in the sense of "give in trust, entrust someone with the guardianship or the delivery of something": e.g. δι' ἐπιστάλματος ἐγχειρισϑέντος διά τοῦ δεῖνα, Preisigke-Kießling, s.v. ἐγχειρίζω,-ομαι; ὅν σοι μετὰ τῆς ἐπιστολῆς υἱὸν ἐγχειρίζω, Synesios, ep.119 (Hercher); ὅτῳ μ' ἔδωκας εἰς χέρας, Soph., *El.*,1348; τὸν ἀδελφὸν τὸν σὸν καταστήσασα εἰς τὰς χεῖρας τὰς Ἰφικράτους, Aeschin., 2.28.

[56] Cf. e.g. how the honorary decree of Kolophon for Menippos does not fail to mention the honorand's having brought back personally from Rome the favorable decisions of the senate: L.&J. Robert, *Claros I*, (Paris 1989) pp.63-66, col.I.33-34 (κάλλιστα καὶ συμφορώτατα δόγματα παρὰ τῶν κρατούντων ἐνηνοχώς), col.II.3 (προσγεγραμμένον ἤνεγκε τῆι ἀποκρίσει), 5-7 (ἰδιώτατον τῆι δημοκρατίαι καὶ κάλλιστον ἐνέγκας ἀπόκριμα). Further examples and discussion of this aspect of the civic statesman's role: Quaß, *Hon.*, 132-135.

[57] Cf. the examples in the previous note and those collected by Chr. Habicht, *ZPE* 84(1990), 114 (n.4).

importance: σωτήρ.[58] The letters preserved of the next column cannot help any further.

Can prosopography at least help identify this Chairylos and his esteemed family? A Koan magistrate[59] known from a Koan drachma ("Attic tetrobol") dated to the period 200-88 B.C. is Δι[ο]γένης.[60] He could well be the friend of Philometor. Chairylos' activity, however, will fall into the period antedating ca. 80 B.C., and so his son must have been active about the middle of the same century.[61] A magistrate Chairylos is known from a Koan drachm and hemidrachm found in a hoard at Pyli (Kos) all other coins of which seem to antedate ca. 200 B.C.[62] This "numismatic" Chairylos could then well be identified with one of the dedicants and father of the honorand in the inscription of the statue base now published in Segre, *I.Cos*, EV 229: [τὸν δεῖνα] Χαιρύλ[ου]/ [Χαιρύλος] τὸν υἱ[ὸν]/ [καὶ τοὶ ἀ]δελφοὶ/[---]ς καὶ Φιλῖν[ος]/ [Θεο]ῖς (dated there to the second century B.C.). While we should rather see in this man an ancestor of the ambassador to Rome, the latter is probably identifiable with Chairylos, son of Charmylos, who won in a citharistic *agon* of younger boys in *PH* 59, roughly dated by S.Sherwin-White to the second-first century B.C.[63] We should recall here that such musical activities do not seem unusual among socially prominent families on Kos.[64] "The boys who play the cithara" are also expressly mentioned as participants in the festivities connected with the cult of Zeus and the Damos in Segre, *I.Cos*, ED 146 B, 7-8. This last connection would befit the father of our unknown honorand with his democratic ideology (see above). We should further note that one more familial combination of the names Chairylos and Charmylos (also etymologically cognate!) is found

---

[58] Segre restores σωτὴρ [ὢ]ν π[άντων] but this is just one of various possibilities (e.g. [ἐ]ν π[ᾶσι]).

[59] Single names in the nominative or genitive on Koan coins and amphora handles used to be interpreted as those of *monarchoi* given the eponymous character of the Koan *monarchia*. Cf. the arguments of Sherwin-White, *Cos*, 188f. Christian Habicht and Håkko Ingvaldsen have now (Colloquium on Hellenistic Kos at Uppsala, May 2000) persuasively disputed this because the known names of *monarchoi* are very rare among the onomastic material of the above categories.

[60] *PH*, N 134, p.312.

[61] Cf. above on the lettering of the decree.

[62] First mention: *BCH* 78(1954), 98 + ib. 79(1955), 210. Cf. M.Thompson et al.(eds.), *An Inventory of Greek Coin Hoards*, (New York 1973) no.1308. Whereas in the latter publication the burial of the hoard is dated (by O. Mørkholm) to the third century B.C., H.Ingvaldsen (Oslo) in a still unpublished larger study of the Koan coinage up to ca. 150 B.C. narrows the date to 200-180 B.C. (I owe the first form of this information to K.Höghammar).

[63] Sherwin-White, *Cos*, 545. Cf. Fraser-Matthews, s.v. Χαιρύλος (9),p.480.

[64] Cf. the useful remarks by Höghammar, 99 (n.479).

in inverse order, i.e. Charmylos son of Chairylos, as the name of one of the contributors to an *epidosis* for the Koan state ca. 205-201 B.C.[65]

Thus if Chairylos the ambassador to the senate is identical with the young citharist, the latter's patronym (Charmylos) is certainly a tempting link between the important family extolled in our document with the monumentally best known family of local magnates on Kos, the Charmyleioi. These were very probably both the possessors of the famous collective burial monument, the so-called *Charmyleion*[66] at Pyli and the bearers of the parallel cult of the Twelve Gods and the hero Charmylos at the same place. The hero Charmylos seems to have been the founder of that divine cult there and common ancestor of the Charmyleioi, who added his cult to that of the Twelve Gods. The sole written testimony of this joint cult is the inscription *PH*, 349, still built into the face wall of the later, small church of the Holy Cross at the site of the *Charmyleion*. This seems datable to the early third century B.C., i.e. in a time suiting the long glorious ancestry of the family of Diogenes and Chairylos.[67]

One should add here a few points. First, the text of ll.9/10 in Segre, *I.Cos*, ED 229 is: αὐτός (: the unknown honorand) τε [τὰ]ν παρὰ τοσούτων ἀνδρῶν/[περιαίνετ]ον διαδεξάμεν[ος γενε]άν...The inspection of the stone has shown that a clear iota precedes the two last preserved letters of this passage. So instead of [γενε]άν we need a substantive ending in -ίαν, and I think the reading [οἰκ]ίαν is the only plausible one.[68] This word fits the meaning equally well. Moreover, its use to describe the family of the honorand seems to express their almost princely status on Kos. *Oikia* is in the Hellenistic period one of the technical terms to describe the royal dynasties of the age as for example the Ptolemaic House, the royal house of Macedonia (in its diachronic entirety or just

---

[65] *PH*, 10 c, 49. Cf. L.Migeotte, *Les souscriptions publiques dans les cités grecques*, (Genève 1992) no.50.

[66] This is a modern term, definitively sanctioned in scholarly literature by Schazmann's homonymous and systematic publication, but it seems to correspond to a local tradition: Schazmann, 111 noted that the site was known in his time as "τὸ χαρμύλις" and old people at Pyli attest today they always knew the place as "τὸ χαρμύλι." On the monument, the apparently earliest private *heroon* of the Hellenistic period (fourth/third cent. B.C.), Schazmann remains fundamental; see now with the later literature and in a wider context Kader, 201f.

[67] More recent edition of the text (corrected in l. 6 after *Herzog, KF*, p.139) by Sherwin-White, *I.Cos*, 207 (no.3): Ἱερὰ ἀ γᾶ καὶ ἀ οἰκία/ ἀ ἐπὶ τᾶ γᾶ καὶ τοὶ κᾶ/ποι καὶ ταὶ οἰκίαι ταὶ / ἐπὶ τῶν κάπων Θεῶν/ Δυώδεκα καὶ Χαρμύλου/ ἥρω νυ τῶν Χαρμυλέων. I find her dating, the explanation of the identity of the hero Charmylos (not a mythical figure) and the argument for the form Charmyleioi (not Charmyleis), ib. 207-217, convincing.

[68] Other possibilities as e.g. [εὐδοξ]ίαν may be excluded by the length of the lacuna.

the Antigonids) etc., or greatly influential, noble families of the Greek cities and Rome.[69] Therefore, the connotation of great local distinction and power is obvious. On the other side, the concept of an *oikia*, a "house," i.e. a conscious succession of generations as suggested here,[70] would also perfectly match the spirit reflected in the structure of the *Charmyleion*, where the graves of the (main?) family members were arranged together on the subterranean level, leaving room for the cult above.[71]

Another piece of evidence that suits this interpretation is certainly the existence of one or (more probably) two numismatically known Koan magistrates with the name Charmylos in the age of Nikias and then Augustus (see below). The family was obviously still prominent in those periods, and the honorand of the inscription could well be one of them.

Finally, if Chairylos of the statue base EV 229 (see above) actually also belongs to the same family, he may point to another prosopographical link: he appears there as brother (or father) of a Philinos. The importance of this last name here is that there are three more Koans with the same name (admittedly common on the island)[72] who are closely connected with the Ptolemies: (a) Philinos of the decree Segre, *I.Cos*, ED 17+130[73]+26+194 (fourth century B.C.), who was apparently very influential with the first Ptolemy and put this influence in the service of

---

[69] See e.g. *Syll.*[3] 685= Ager 158.II (the arbitration of Magnesia between Itanos and Hierapytna), 97: [τὴν Πτ]ολεμαϊκὴν οἰκίαν εἰς προστασίαν καὶ φυλακὴν ἑαυτοῖς...*Pol.*, 2.37.7: περὶ δὲ τοῦ τῶν Ἀχαιῶν ἔθνους καὶ περὶ τῆς Μακεδόνων οἰκίας...(cf. ibid., 5.102.1). The use of the same word to describe important families in the Greek cities begins already in the classical period: so e.g. in *Thuc.*, 8.6.3 for the family of the Spartan ephor Endios, paternal friends of Alcibiades; *Pl., Grg.*, 472 B (ἡ Περικλέους ὅλη οἰκία); *And.*, I.126: ...ἐξώλη εἶναι καὶ αὐτὸν καὶ τὴν οἰκίαν (of Kallias son of Hipponikos, one of the Kerykes). In the Hellenistic period a pertinent example is the Boeotian, pro-Antigonid *oikia* of Neon and Brachylles in *Pol.*, 20.5.12 (...τὴν οἰκίαν...τὴν περὶ τὸν Βραχύλλην). *Pol.*, 31.23.1,12 used the same word for the Scipios' family. The use of the "twin term" οἶκος has been, of course, parallel in all periods, so e.g. in *IG* IV.1[2], 84.32; 86.15 (first cent. A.D.) and, on Kos itself, in *PH*, 137.2: [φαίδι]μος οἶκος.

[70] The nearest parallels for concept and form of διαδεξάμεν[ος οἰκ]ίαν I could find are: *Eur., Alc.*, 655: παῖς δ' ἦν ἐγώ σοι τῶνδε διάδοχος δόμων...*Pol.*, 2.4.7: τὴν δὲ βασιλείαν ἡ γυνὴ Τεύτα διαδεξαμένη...*App., Ill.*, 7: ...Πύρρος ὁ τῆς Ἠπείρου βασιλεύς...καὶ οἱ τὰ Πύρρου διαδεξάμενοι.

[71] One may also notice that the same term, *oikia*, is used in the consecrative inscription quoted above (n. 67) to denote the building on the sacred land (most probably the "Charmyleion" itself) and other (similar?) structures on the sacred gardens, apparently nearby. A systematic archaeological exploration of this area could prove very productive. The concept of the grave as house of the dead (τάφος-οἶκος) is well known in ancient (and modern) Greek belief and its respective monumental expressions.

[72] There are thirty five bearers of this name in the Koan Onomastikon of Sherwin-White, *Cos*, 536f., a high record of frequency indeed if we compare it with other usual Koan names (cf. ibid. s.vv.) like Nikagoras, Diokles etc.

[73] Originally edited as Maiuri, *NS*, 433.

(i.a.) the Koan food supply; (b) the homonymous doctor and founder of the Empiric School at Alexandria (ca. second half of the third century B.C.);[74] (c) a Φιλῖνος Πύϑωνος who appears in Segre, *I.Cos*, ED 235 A (beginning of the second century B.C.) among the five ambassadors going out to escort "the king" to the city.[75] Ph. Gauthier[76] is right in thinking that the use of the definite article seems to point to one of the Ptolemies (rather than e.g. the Attalids), with whom Kos had the longest tradition of friendship. Thus the close affiliation of Diogenes with Philometor and Cleopatra II could be also on a family level another ring in a long chain.[77]

The frequency of the name Charmylos on Kos,[78] however, should ultimately lead us to end these prosopographical considerations on a notice of caution. On the other hand, it would be at least not improbable to discover some political activities and affinities of the Charmyleioi, that three-dimensionally most famous *genos* of Kos.[79]

---

[74] Cf. concisely Sherwin-White, *Cos*, 103 and now H.v.Staden, *OCD*[3], s.v. Philinus (1), 1160 with further literature.

[75] 1. 68: πρεσβευταῖς τοῖς ἐπὶ τὰν ἀπάντασιν τῶι βασιλεῖ. Philinos son of Python mentioned in l. 71 of the relevant list.

[76] *Bull.* 1995, 448 (p.503). Habicht, *I.Kos*, 91 thought of Eumenes II.

[77] One might add, for whatever it is worth, Schazmann's remark (127) that the structure of the shaft graves in the "Charmyleion" reminded him of "gewisse hellenistische Grabanlagen in Ägypten."

[78] Twenty four cases are attested in Sherwin-White, *Cos*, 547f. (cf. n. 72 above).

[79] If Philinos the empiricist belonged to the same family (see above), they could also be a branch of the Asclepiads. The Ptolemaic connection (cf. Sherwin-White, *Cos*, 102-105) and the wealth of at least some family members would then be even more understandable.

B. The evidence of the "Lex Fonteia" (Crawford, *RS*, 36) and the period of M.Antonius. Nikias' coins, inscriptions, personality and "tyranny."

a. "Lex Fonteia": Kos and M.Antonius.

Among the inscriptions Rudolph Herzog found during the excavations of the Asklepieion (1902-1904) were fragments of an opisthographic stele with a Roman decree (*lex*) in Greek translation. It pertained to the granting of Roman citizenship and accompanying privileges to a number of Greeks whose names are not preserved; nor do we know whether all or some of them were Koans. The Roman text, obviously erected there to attain the local publicity required, had been destroyed in later times, most probably on purpose. Herzog was able to report only the essentials of this inscription in his published work.[1] The full text appeared in 1996 as Crawford, *RS*, 36(pp. 497ff.): "Lex Fonteia (Cos Fragments)." In the publication of this text the collaboration of Dr. Klaus Hallof at the *IG* archive of the reorganized Academy of Berlin-Brandenburg was fundamental. There Herzog's squeezes, notebooks and other material from his Koan excavations and researches were eventually deposited and systematically examined by Klaus and Luise Hallof. It is due to Herzog's old squeezes that the text of this "Lex Fonteia" as a whole has been now transcribed, published, and studied in for the first time. I have been unable to find (or identify) any of its published fragments in the small magazine of inscriptions and other antiquities in the precinct of the Asklepieion or in the similar magazines of the Knights Castle in the city of Kos (May and December 1997).

The front face ("i") of fragments a+b of this text bears parts of the preamble: first (ll.1-3) a date was recorded of which only the words μηνὸς Παναμου δευτέ[ραι...] have been preserved. This is followed by mention of the *rogator legis* C.Fonteius C.f. Capito styled as priest (ἱερεύς)[2] and that he submitted the decree to the people in accordance with the senate's will. Next the positive vote of the Roman people in the forum on a certain day in June and details of the typical Roman voting procedure (first tribe voting and first voter) is mentioned. The reasoning

---

[1] Herzog, *N&X*, 212f. with n.3; id., Symbolae Calymniae et Coae, *RFIC* 70(1942), 19.

[2] This apparently unparalleled mention of a Roman priest as presiding over an assembly (cf. Crawford,*RS*, ib.comm.) might also be due to an otherwise missing connection of the beneficiaries of this *lex* with the cult of Asclepius, in whose sanctuary on Kos the stele had been erected.

for the decision followed, i.e. a partly preserved ἐπεί-clause, after which the grants and their contents are referred to and continue in the rest of the fragments. The privileges granted show various resemblances to points of the SC de Asclepiade (Sherk, *RDGE*, 22) of 78 B.C. and Octavian's epistle for Seleukos of Rhosos (ibid., 58). One can assume that there must have been analogous reasons for some Koans' reward here.

There are gaps at two points in the beginning of the text due to erasure of letters in antiquity: in ll. 1-2 and l. 8, i.e. respectively, just before the date inside the month Panamos and where the purpose for the decree should start. After that we have the words αὐτοκράτωρ τριῶν ἀν/[δρῶν δημοσίων πραγμάτων κατα]στάσεως...(ll.8-9). This phrase can be restored with confidence on the basis of other passages,[3] and these and the preceding *rasura*[4] leave no doubt that M.Antonius M.f., the triumvir, is the only suitable name to fill the gap. As far as one may judge based on the squeeze,[5] the approximate number of erased letters can only confirm this conclusion. Even the trace of a sigma at the end of the rasura is discernible there (the last letter of υἱὸς or Ἀντώνιος). M. Antonius was obviously instrumental in having those privileges accepted by senate and people. This is apparently the fact recorded in the latter passage: cf. the phrase τὴν Ἀντωνίου κρίσιν, "Antonius' judgment," in l.12.

In a similar *rasura* of ll. 1-2,[6] the editors of *RS* thought that there had probably been here "the name of an Antonius" (498). In the commentary on the inscription they have then specified that "the *rasura* presumably contained the name of L. or M.Antonius" and considered the chronological problems such a solution would entail, that is, that the document would bear a date during the consulate of one of the two brothers (41 and 34 B.C. respectively). They concluded (ibid.): "It is more likely that the *rasura* contained an indication that the document had been transmitted by M.Antonius and a date; our text may then belong to 39 BC, before M.Antonius returned to the East (so Münzer)."[7] In the first words preserved after this *rasura* (μηνὸς Παναμου δευτέ[ραι...) they recognized an element of the Koan calendar but commented: "Day and month will presumably have been preceded by a reference to the

---

[3] Cf. e.g. Sherk, *RDGE*, 57.1-3 and the examples of the triumvirs' Greek title quoted by Mason, s.v. κατάστασις (1).

[4] Cf. now the example of a document of M.Antonius erased in Sardeis: P.Herrmann, "Rom und die Asylie griechischer Heiligtümer: Eine Urkunde des Dictators Caesar aus Sardeis," *Chiron* 19(1989),127-158 (133, cf.138).

[5] K.Hallof kindly allowed me to consult a good photograph of it.

[6] The text of ll. 1-3 in *RS*: [[---]]/ [[---ἔτους???]] μηνὸς Παναμου δευτέ/[ραι ἐξ ἰκάδος...

[7] I would not exclude the possibility that there stood here originally a date according to the Roman and the Koan chronology. Cf. below.

Seleucid era." On the photograph of Herzog's squeeze (see above) I was unable to discern any traces of the erased letters (ll.1-2), and K.Hallof confirmed to me in a letter that no traces are visible there.

We may proceed a little further even with these data, however. There is no reason to presume that the mention of the Koan month and day would have been combined with a year of the Seleucid era. No known parallel exists for this and historical probabilities are strongly against it. Kos has never belonged to the Seleucid Empire and there is no evidence for the official use of the Seleucid era on any of the Aegean islands. It is reasonable to conclude that the Koan month and day preserved were preceded by the typical beginning of a complete Koan date: ἐπὶ μονάρχου x, that is, during the office year of a person holding the well-known Koan eponymous magistracy. The inclusion of this kind of date may be explained most probably by the need to notice the local announcement or ratification of the Roman decree concerning the Koan citizen(s)[8] —we base this conclusion on parallels from other places and periods of Roman control in the East.[9]

The next conclusion is then, quite naturally, that both the reference to an Antonius in connection with a Roman dating (or the mention of the transmission of the whole document to Kos) and the name of the local supreme magistrate by that local publication and validation of the Roman statute had to be erased. For it is certainly not accidental that the erasure stopped exactly after the "personal" part of the local date. We cannot know who that *monarchos* was. Nevertheless, the political character of the erasure itself points to two possibilities: either the position of *monarchos* was at that time occupied *honoris causa* by M.Antonius himself or the person of the *monarchos* was a well-known, and compromised, local partisan of Cleopatra's partner. Even in the latter case a previous mention of an Antonius' name (see above) is suggested by the length of the whole erased passage: there is room for ca.75 letters.

That Antonius can have been made *monarchos* by the Koans finds its parallel in the date of a funerary inscription from Sardeis: ἐπὶ Μάρκο[υ Ἀντωνίου]/ τοῦ αὐτοκρ[άτορος, μη]/νὸς Δίου ς'...[10] More generally, the practice of Greek cities to confer an honorary eponymous archonship on

---

[8] Herzog, *HG*, 51 remarked in this sense that the *lex* "wird in Kos am 2. Panamos als eingegangen registriert."

[9] Cf. for example the similar use of the local date before the text of Octavian's letters to the Rhosians on Seleukos: Sherk,*RDGE*, 58. There is also similar practice in adding a local date at the end of a letter from an extra-civic authority, as e.g. in the case of Hadrian's letter on the sale of fish at Eleusis: Oliver, *GC*, 77.

[10] W.H.Buckler & D.M.Robinson, *Sardis VII.I: Greek and Latin Inscriptions*, (Leyden 1932) 129 (p.117). The editors held that the local office born by Antonius was the

Hellenistic kings, Roman generals, and finally the emperors and members of the imperial house is known from a whole series of examples, often studied and cited by L.Robert.[11]

The second alternative, that he is a local friend of Antonius, is equally possible. What is important and certain, however, is that either alternative shows that the epoch of M.Antonius left a renewed legacy of inopportune Koan loyalties within the Augustan state of the Greek East. There were palpable traces of favor for Octavian's rival that had to be removed even if the concomitant privileges of some families might have finally been preserved. A closer Koan collaboration with M.Antonius during his overlordship in the East had been already suggested by the sacrilegious action of Turullius, which would have otherwise encountered serious difficulties (more on this in my concluding sketch of a historical synthesis), and Nikias' probable chronological and political context (see also below). It is reassuring to see these probabilities now supported by fresh and unequivocal evidence.

There are also two more points in this fragmentarily preserved *lex* that deserve notice: first, the text of the back face includes an immunity of the persons concerned (as well as their descendants and their sons-in-law) for goods imported (and exported), for personal use,[12] ...εἰς ἐπαρχεί]/αν Ἀσίαν ἢ νῆσόν τινα Ἀσίας (face ii, ll. 1-2). The reading [ἐπαρχεί]αν does not seem to have any alternative, so we must understand that the import/export of goods into the *provincia Asia* is meant. The other end of the transport implied is certainly Kos (alone or some other places of origin of the privileged, too; cf. above). Kos should then be outside the limits of the province, that is, not subjected to the provincial administration in this period and obviously enjoying the status of a *civitas libera*. On the other side, the same privilege is applied to exports/imports of the above kind (εἰς) νῆσόν τινα Ἀσίας. The existence of a category of islands apparently not seen as an integral (or original) part of, but somehow eventually connected with, the province is clearly

---

priesthood of Rome. Cf. L.Robert, *Hellenica* 2(1946), 51f. (n.6).

[11] *Études épigraphiques et philologiques*, (Paris 1938) 143-150; *Hellenica* I, 15(n.1); II, 51(n.6); VII, 35ff. (n.3); VIII, 75; *RPh* 1959, 199f., 212f., and 1974, 212; *Bull.* 1967, 383. See also C.Habicht, *Altertümer von Pergamon, VIII.3: Die Inschriften des Asklepieions*, (Berlin 1969) 151; *Chiron* 6(1976), 130ff. I would not exclude that a Flavian example of the same practice on Kos appears in the date ἐπὶ μονάρχου Τίτου in Segre, *TC*, 158.

[12] The restoration [...τῆς ἰδίας χρείας ἕνε]/κεν εἰσάγηι.. (face ii, ll.2-3) is assured by the parallels in Octavian's grant of privileges to Seleukos of Rhosos: Sherk, *RDGE*, 58.49, 51.

indicated.[13]

Another important point may be seen a little farther on in 1.6 ff.: the privilege to choose the place of procedure is here accorded to the beneficiaries of the decree in litigation. The spirit and form of the relevant clause are again familiar both from the case of Seleukos of Rhosos under Octavian (Sherk, *RDGE*, 58.53ff.) and the earlier one of Asklepiades and his fellow pro-Roman captains in the wars of the eighties (ibid., 22 Lat. 7-9, Gr.17-20). In the Lex Fonteia, however, it is clearly implied, as the legal and practical basis of this privilege, that the persons concerned are thought to be already in possession of the *civitas Romana* by the time they make use of this right: ...μετὰ ταῦτα]/ πολιτῶν Ῥωμαίων γενο[μένων...We may then further conclude that this privileged group of people had been given, or soon would be given, Roman citizenship. Thus some Koan family(-ies), exactly like Seleukos of Rhosos but differently from Asklepiades and his fellows (who were not made Roman citizens), must have earned that option in litigation together with their political Romanization through the connections of the triumviral era. Strangely at first sight, Antonii of some distinction do not appear in our extant documentation on Kos until a much later time (from ca. 60 A.D. onwards) and then exclusively with Roman cognomina.[14] Could the latter descend from Koan clients of the triumvir? If so (we are guessing), the interim of silence on their intermediate development could be connected with the fate of Antonius' memories on Augustan Kos as shown by the erasures discussed (cf. also below on the Halasarnan list of Apollo priests). On the other hand, the violent destruction of the stone bearing the Lex Fonteia cannot be safely dated in the immediately post-

---

[13] M. Dreher, "Die *lex portorii Asiae* und der Zollbezirk Asia," *EA* 26(1996), 111-127 (esp. 118ff.) has concluded from a careful study of the new "Customs Law of Asia" (*EA* 14(1989)= *AnÉp* 1989.681), of (final) Neronian date but largely going back to the Republican period, that the status of the big islands near the coast of Asia Minor regarding the "customs zone" of Asia varied in the latter period depending on individual cases and times—according to the eventual subjection of each to the Roman provincial administration. This largely distinctive status seems now to accord well with this piece of evidence in the Lex Fonteia.

[14] The four Antonii of Kos known so far were priests of Apollo at Halasarna: Herzog, *Hal.*, 4 (=IGRR IV.1101), nos. 89, 97, 103, 119, ranging from ca. 62 to 92 A.D. (on the chronology of the list cf. below). From these no. 89: Μᾶρ(κος) Ἀν[τώ]νιος Μ[άρ(κου)] υἰὸς Κό[γνι]τος appears also on Syros in *IG* XII.5, 143 (+add., p.309), cf. *Nigdelis*, 286 (n.388); no. 103: Λεύ(κιος) Ἀντώνιος Λευ(κίου) υἰὸς Βάσσος is also *napoas* of Apollo at Halasarna in a dedication to Titus quoted in Carratelli, *Rom.Cos*, 819. Of course, one may also not exclude a descent of these Antonii from members of the same family that was active on Republican Delos. Cf. Sherwin-White, *Cos*, 252; Holtheide, 37 (against the rest evidence on Antonii in the *provincia Asia*).

Antonian period,[15] so one may not discern here any further indication on the aftermath of Actium on Kos.

b. Nikias (I): Coins, inscriptions and the "heroic portrait."

These observations should be correlated with what has been written about M.Antonius' connection with Kos and its people. As noticed above, only now may we safely assume the existence of a decidedly pro-Antonian regime on Kos before Actium. Thus old theories about this period and its protagonists are actually substantiated.

The crucial personality here is Nikias the Koan, the tyrant of our scanty historical tradition. Herzog has earned the singular merit of having reconstructed, from a whole range of disparate sources, the history of this person, especially the activities and connections of the Greek grammarian Curtius Nicias with Pompeius, C.Memmius, Cicero, Dolabella and other dignitaries of the Republic in the period ca. 60-44 B.C.[16] These sources fall broadly into four categories: a) literary texts on Nikias' career in high political and literary circles of Rome before the period of the Second Triumvirate, b) other literary fragments mentioning him in direct connection with his later political role on Kos, c) inscriptions, d) and coins. It is useful to re-examine the evidence of the three latter groups here, beginning with the last one as it may permit a fresh and more precise look at Nikias' official position on Kos.

After a period of about forty years (ca. 88 B.C.- ca. 50 B.C.) during which the previous silver coin production on Kos seems to have continued in an unsystematic way[17] we come upon a series[18] of

---

[15] Herzog, *N&X*, 212f., n.3 supposed that this happened "nach der Katastrophe des Antonius." Crawford, *RS*, p.498 is right to be more cautious : "...this need not have been in antiquity."

[16] Herzog, *X&N*, 190-216 (with full citation of the ancient sources, cf. also below). Some further prosopographical combinations, esp. explaining Nicias' gentilicium in Syme, *Vedius Pollio.* Cf. also Bowersock, *A&GW*, 45f.; *PIR²*, V.3(1987), N 84; J. Christes, *Sklaven und Freigelassene als Grammatiker und Philologen im antiken Rom*, (Wiesbaden 1979) 55f.; El. Rawson, *Intellectual Life in the Late Roman Republic*, (London 1985) 71f.; R.A.Kaster, C.Suetonius Tranquillus, *De grammaticis et rhetoribus*, (Oxford 1995) 170-172; Holtheide, 29. Especially on Nikias as tyrant of Kos also: Berve, *Tyr.*, 438f., 727; Sherwin-White, *Cos*, 141-145.

[17] See *BMC* Caria, pp. xcvii and 210ff.(nos. 165-169, 177, 192-193); Head, *HN*, 634. Cf. Burnett, *RPC*, 452.

[18] Ibid., 452f., nos. 2724-2731, with pl. 118. In September 1998 I was allowed a short study of the unpublished numismatic material kept at the Museum of Kos: I discovered there three new specimens of the Nikias series, one dated after Olympichos, one after Antiochos (both dates already known from other Nikias coins), and one on which the magistrate's name was unreadable. I could not detect any significant further elements of the iconography of Nikias on these coins.

characteristically large bronze coins bearing on the obverse the portrait of a man whose name appears as the legend of the same side (on the left of his head): ΝΙΚΙΑΣ. The reverse bears a portrait of Asklepios with a legend consisting of a (magistrate's) name in the nominative,[19] and the typical genitive ΚΩΙΩΝ. The specimens of these coins currently known are dated under eight different archons. So Nikias' important role on Kos must have lasted for at least as long a period.

His portrait deserves and has already received some analysis, especially in A.Burnett's lemma on Kos in the recent, monumental *Roman Provincial Coinage, I*. Burnett has drawn attention in particular to the influence of Octavian's Roman coin portraits (since 43 B.C.)[20] on that of Nikias; this is a first valuable chronological indication. Unfortunately, most of Nikias' coins are well worn so that the details of his face are only partly discernible.[21] What one can certainly see are the traits of a young man with rather curly hair, broad forehead, hooked nose, some sparse chin hair, and a serious expression conveyed by his eyes and the downward line of his lips. Despite the realistic details one cannot help feeling that this is an idealistic representation. On Nikias' hair there is a kind of headband tied just above the nape of his neck. B. Head[22] thought this was a diadem. Were this so, there would be important consequences on our view of Nikias' political role and projected identity. As Burnett has already remarked, however, "this certainly does not look like a diadem."[23] A tied diadem looks very different as its strips are usually wider and fall distinctly and copiously apart.[24] Furthermore, the rest of Nikias' band from the point of tying seems to have a somewhat twisted form[25] where smaller and bigger "knots" of the same material alternate, in other words it is not a simple

---

[19] See above, ch. A, n.59.

[20] On his first coin types see M.Crawford, *Roman Republican Coinage*, (Cambridge 1974) 499f. (no.490), 740.

[21] My remarks rely here not only on the photographs published in Burnett, *RPC* (see above) but also on a personal inspection of the relevant material in the British Museum.

[22] As above (n. 17) and *BMC* Caria, p.213. His description of Nikias' head as "diademed" has been later adopted by, i.a., Neppi Modona, 51; Sherwin-White, *Cos*, 142. It is perhaps significant that Herzog, *N&X*, did not comment on this iconographic trait.

[23] *RPC*, 452 (on no. 2724).

[24] One may cite as examples some of the temporally nearest numismatic portraits of Rome's client kings: ibid., no. 3508/pl. 140 (silver drachma of Deiotaros Philadelphos of Cappadocia, 37-6 B.C.); 3871/pl. 148 (bronze coin of Tarkondimotos of Cilicia, ca. 39-31 B.C.); 3533/pl. 141 (bronze coin of Antiochos IV of Commagene from Lycaonia, 38-72 A.D.). Both this Deiotaros and Tarkondimotos (cf. below) achieved royalty through M.Antonius.

[25] This is especially discernible on ibid., no.2731/pl.118.

ribbon (or similar band) fastened round the head. An instructive comparison may be made between Nikias' hairdress on the obverse and that of Asklepios on the reverse. Burnett identified Asklepios' headtype as "laureate" and was then content to remark that Nikias' headband is "much slighter," although he believed that it also represents some kind of wreath, the backties of which are visible.[26] However, the typological similarity between the two heads in their headdress is too close to be overlooked, despite differences in size:

(a) Asklepios' head does not bear a laurel wreath but a headband of twisted shape (as if it also consisted of "knots" of uneven size, some almost round some oblong) on his curly hair. The difference between this type and other local, apparently somewhat later representations of Asklepios with a laureate head[27] is obvious.

(b) Apart from the type of hairstyle and headband, there is a striking similarity in the way the back "ties" of the band are shown. We see in both cases a small loop, under which the end of the one strip is rounded up; in Nikias' portrait the latter develops into the slightly more elaborate form of a small spiral.

(c) The hair of both Asklepios and Nikias is divided into small curls, more unruly and rounded in Asklepios, somewhat oblonger in Nikias.

(d) Finally, the end cut of the neck in both portraits looks very similar (it has somewhat the form of an obtuse angle), also contributing to the general effect of an intentional assimilation of various elements in the two figures.

If the headband examined is neither a diadem nor some kind of wreath (at least as far as one can see on the photographs published and the British Museum coins themselves), what can it be? We should begin with the obvious similarity of the two portraits: Nikias seems to be wearing a band like that of Asklepios. The conclusion seems then inevitable that Nikias' headband must have a religious significance of some sort.

Some archaeological observations on certain similar types of band are useful here.[28] Antje Krug in her very valuable dissertation on band forms in Greek art has assembled under "type 11" representations of

---

[26] Ibid. (as n. 23 above). I thank Dr. Burnett for an additional exchange of letters on this point.

[27] Burnett, *RPC*, nos. 2732, 2734/pl. 118 (Kos, Augustan period).

[28] In this section I am greatly indebted to bibliographical suggestions and a useful discussion of my views with Prof. Erika Simon.

"knotted" bands, very probably thought to be of wool, which were used to decorate various cult objects (e.g. statues) or attributes of gods/sacred places (e.g. the Delphic *omphalos*).[29] Krug's conclusion on the significance of this type of band may be quoted: "Unter den verschiedenen im Kultus verwandten Binden trägt allein die Binde 11 einen primär sakralen Charakter; ihre Wirkung besteht in der Konsekration."[30] Of course, her classification has shown that another, thick type of band (her "Wulstbinde" no. 12) was characteristic of Asklepios and other gods of chthonic character.[31] The sacred significance of the former band forms in antiquity, however, is further strengthened by the case of the Roman *infula* (a variation of it being *i. tortilis*, the one "twisted"), a woolen band type used also to decorate temples and sacrificial animals or the attire of priests.[32]

What could the common element of sacredness between Asklepios and Nikias be? To clarify this we should first recall a basic trait of Asklepios. The god of medicine was actually, as the ancient tradition itself unequivocally relates, a semi-god, that is a *heros* born of a god, Apollo, and a human female, the typically unlucky Koronis (according to the Epidaurian version).[33] Pindar[34] calls him explicitly ἥρωα παντοδαπᾶν ἀλκτῆρα νούσων. To put it bluntly, there was no qualifying difference between, for example, Herakles' and Asklepios' art of divine extraction and level. Success and later recognition were another story.[35]

Could Nikias have possessed a similarly elevated status , something between human and divine? The answer is derived from the second set of evidence on his personality: inscriptions. A great number have been preserved on or from Koan territory (presently twenty three examples are known for certain, see below and Appendix 2) of relatively small monuments, usually in the form of simple slabs of various sorts of stone,

---

[29] A.Krug, *Binden in der griechischen Kunst (6.-1. Jahrh. v. Chr.)*, (Diss. Mainz 1968) 37-41, 122-126 (cf. Anhang I, III).

[30] Ibid., 126.

[31] Ibid., 41-47, 126-130.

[32] Cf. K.Latte, *RE* IX.2(1916), s.v. infula, 1543.

[33] The main elements of this and the rival Messenian version in *Paus.*, 2.26.3-8. Cf. concisely and more recently (with the older literature): W.Burkert, *Greek Religion: Archaic and Classical*, (Oxford 1985) 214f. (+434: n.s).

[34] *Pyth.* III.7.

[35] On the only relative rigidity of the limit between god and hero in Greek religion, see S.Eitrem, RE VIII.1(1912), s.v. Heros, 1138f. Cf. also recently E.Kearns, "Between God and Man: Status and Function of Heroes and their Sanctuaries," in: *Le Sanctuaire grec* (ed. A.Schachter), Genève 1992 (*Entretiens Hardt*, 37), 65-99. On the relevant status of Herakles: P.Lévêque and A.Verbauck-Piérard, "Héracles, héros ou dieu," in: C.Bonnet and C.Jourdain-Annequin (éds.), *Héraclès d'une rive à l'autre de la Méditerranée. Bilan et perspectives* (Table ronde, Rome 1989), Bruxelles 1992, 43-65.

bearing the uniform text:

Θεοῖς πατρῴοις ὑπὲρ (or περὶ) τᾶς Νικία τοῦ δάμου υἱοῦ,
φιλοπάτριδος, ἥρωος, εὐεργέτα δὲ τᾶς πόλιος σωτηρίας.[36]

The letter forms suggest a date in the second half of the first century
B.C.. Thus the identity of this Nikias with the homonymous person on
the Koan coins of late Republican date (see above) and the Koan "tyrant"
of the literary tradition (see below) has been certain from the
beginning.[37] The small size of these monuments, their modest appearance
and the obvious character of most of them as steles, bases, or altars
makes it clear that they must be private dedications to the ϑεοὶ πατρῷοι
for the well-being (σωτηρία) of Nikias, kept in private houses probably
in response to a common appeal or ordinance for their erection .

To continue the argument, we can examine (for further aspects see
below) two expressions of this Nikian titulature of public character (and
perhaps prescription). Nikias is here principally τοῦ δάμου υἱός, and also
ἥρως. Nikias' name is not followed by any usual patronymic: whether his
human father's name could be used here or not (more on this later), his
only parentage visible on these inscriptions is his filial relation to the
damos. Now, this phrase, "son of the people," appears here for the first
time as a public title on Kos (and in general). In later periods, as we shall
see, the same phrase has been added to the name of other similarly
illustrious Koans on the same kind of private votive inscriptions. Paton
remarked that the expression τοῦ δάμου υἱοῦ "immediately following the
name does not...mean quite the same as the honorary title δάμου υἱὸς
added after other titles"[38] in later cases. Furthermore, the use of the
definite article (τοῦ δάμου υἱοῦ) itself suggests the idea of a symbolic
paternal personification.[39]

The notion of a "son of the people" seems to have been much closer
to concrete political and religious entities of Koan life at that time than
one might suppose. For the *damos* was not only the body politic of Kos
but also a deity. We already knew of a cult of the Koan *Damos*,[40]
paralleled by similar phenomena in other Greek cities.[41] The relevant

---

[36] The only variation worthy of note is the omission of ἥρωος in one of these inscriptions
(see Appendix 2, no. 14 below).
[37] Already accepted e.g. in *PH*, p.125f.
[38] Ibid.
[39] Cf. in the example of Segre, *I.Cos*, ED 146 cited below: τῷ τε Διὶ καὶ τῷ Δάμῳ (A.7).
[40] The evidence known before Segre, *I.Cos* has been collected and discussed by Sherwin-
White, *Cos*, 332f.
[41] See the evidence collected and studied in Olga Alexandri-Tzahou, *LIMC* III.1(1986),
s.v. Demos, 375-382 (375f.). Add on the cult of the Demos and the Charites founded in

evidence, however, was dated approximately from the first century B.C. Thus Nikias' case had no clear relation to it (the question was legitimate whether Nikias had inaugurated the deification of the Damos himself). Segre, *I.Cos*, ED 146 (A.7, B.4/5) is now evidence for a cult of Zeus and the Damos in the early second century B.C. on Kos. This inscription is a decree of the Koans accepting a donation by Phanomachos son of Thessalos for that (probably so founded) cult and regulating various aspects of it.[42] Thus by Nikias' times the Koan Damos had been venerated as a god for at least a century and a half. Against this political/religious background it is not difficult to understand that Nikias was υἱὸς τοῦ Δάμου, i.e. not simply the "son of the people" in a metaphoric/honorific sense of familiarity between a local magnate and the people (as to be seen in later examples). He was the local statesman who was elevated to the position of a son of the Damos, the people deified. When this is perceived, the further designation ἥρως attributed to Nikias also gains its proper meaning. Nikias' heroic identity naturally resulted from his divine parentage as he was the publicly recognized son of a known Koan god. The usual reluctance of Greek communities to accept a living person as a *heros* was thus adroitly circumvented. In the light of these observations the numismatic and the epigraphic evidence on Nikias reveals for the first time a perfect match: Nikias is in both cases represented as a semi-divine nature, the child of the Koan Damos.

In examining Nikias' coins, this aspect is further supported by a rare detail deserving more attention than it has received. One of Nikias' issues dated under the archon Antiochos varies from all the rest (even from the others under the same archon) in that it should bear the extended legend on the obverse: NIKIAΣ. O ΔAMOΣ. Burnett has not included this variant type in *RPC*, although it has been cited by Herzog in his reconstruction of Nikias' career.[43] The rare coin in question should have been once in the *Museum Hedervarianum* (the collection of the count of Wiczay in Hungary) and has been described by the famous pioneer numismatist of the late eighteenth/early nineteenth century Domenico Sestini, in a treatise of 1828.[44] It should bear the no. 5182 in

---

Athens in 229 B.C.: C.Habicht, *Studien zur Geschichte Athens in hellenistischer Zeit*, (Göttingen 1982) 84-93; more generally on the cult of the Demos (that of Rome included) in Greek cities: id., "Samos weiht eine Statue des *Populus Romanus*," *MDAI(A)* 105(1990), 259- 268 (259-263).

[42] See Habicht, *I.Kos*, 85.

[43] Herzog, *N&X*, 208 (n.2). This detail has also been omitted by Sherwin-White, *Cos* in her discussion of Nikias (n. 16 above).

[44] *Descrizione delle medaglie antiche greche del Museo Hedervariano...per Domenico Sestini*, Parte Seconda, (Firenze 1828) p.240 (no.36). I have been able to study this and other, equally rare publications of Sestini in the library of the American Numismatic

the catalogue of that collection. Sestini describes its obverse thus: "ΝΙΚΙΑΣ. O ΔΑΜΟΣ. Caput Niciae filo tenui redimitum." There is no reason to doubt Sestini's testimony: he has frequently preserved valuable information on various monuments, and he seems to have been well aware of the uniqueness of this specimen among Nikias' coins. In one of his previous works,[45] he mentions in the entry devoted to Kos the coins of "Nicias Tyrannus. *Epigraphe.* ΝΙΚΙΑΣ," and notices they are of bronze. Thus it is highly unlikely that he would have confused something in his description of the Hedervar collection since the standard, simple legend on the obverse of these series was already familiar to him.

Thus the exceptional addition O ΔΑΜΟΣ to Nikias' name on his coin portrait shows clearly how the close relationship to the deified people was Nikias' basic method and source of political legitimation. It seems hazardous to attempt any further conclusions from the case in which this addition appears (nominative and not genitive, as one would reasonably expect). Was it a complete identification of Nikias himself as "the People" or simply a more discreet, side by side expression of the symbolic parentage—the relation of the possessor of power to its asserted source? We cannot say, but the relationship between the heroic portrait and the rare but pregnant addition to the legend seems probable.

The connection between Nikias' portrait and the *Damos* may also be suggested on iconographic grounds by later but relevant numismatic evidence. For *Demos* is represented on some imperial civic coin types in the Greek East[46] with features that are very similar to Nikias' portrait. The nearest parallels I was able to find date from the second century A.D., but an iconographic tradition seems possible. They are: *SNG* v.Aulock, nos. 2440-3, 2444 (the closest parallel), all from Aphrodisias;

Society (New York). On Sestini's work and life, see Er.Babelon, *Traité des monnaies grecques et romaines, I: Théorie et doctrine*, Tome premier, (Paris 1901) 194f.; B.Pace, "Per la storia dell'archeologia italiana in Levante. Viaggi dell'abate Domenico Sestini in Asia Minore (1779-1792)," *ASAA* 3(1916-1920), 1921, 243-252; G.Pugliese Carratelli, *Enciclopedia Italiana*, vol.31(1936), s.v. D.Sestini.

[45] *Classes generales seu moneta vetus urbium, populorum et regum ordine geographico et chronologico descripta*, (Florentiae 1821²) p. 91.

[46] The relevant evidence has been collected by Alexandri-Tzahou (n. 41 above), 376ff. Cf. now also H.Yilmaz, "Demos." Zur späten Überlieferung einer klassischen Personifikation," *MDAI(R)* 102 (1995), 211-218 who dates the first examples of the youthful *Demos* in plastic representations from Asia Minor to Neronian times and connects the invention of this type with the parallel iconographic development of senatus/σύγκλητος and *genius populi Romani* in the same area and Rome. The gaps in our knowledge render it unwise, however, to exclude the possibility of an older Greek prototype for the youthful version of *Demos* in art.

SNG Copenhagen, nos. 106-107, 109-114, again from Aphrodisias; H.v.Fritze, *Die antiken Münzen Mysiens* (1913), nos. 355-6, 358-9 (cf. pl.VI.5, 6), from Attaia in Mysia. On all of these coins there is the bust or head of a young man wearing a band on his head recalling that of Nikias and accompanied by the legend ΔΗΜΟΣ (or ΙΕΡΟΣ ΔΗΜΟΣ). It is noteworthy that the band the *Demos* wears in these cases (in many other examples his head is laureate) is often described in coin publications as a diadem, although it is again clear that this is at least not the "typical diadem" worn by kings.

To sum up: Nikias' iconographic type reveals a basic aspect of his official position on Kos as hero, son of the *Damos*. Therefore the similarities both with Asklepios' figure on the reverse of the same coins and with the traits of various later portraits of *Demos* on civic coinages are quite natural.

c. Nikias (II): The *tyrannos* of the literary and other sources. The ban on his public memory.

We now turn to those bits of literary tradition we have on Nikias during his Koan political career in order to see how they may relate to this new approach and evaluation of Nikias' iconographic and historical portrait. The basic source is Strabo[47] who mentions Nikias among illustrious Koan savants with the phrase: καὶ καθ' ἡμᾶς Νικίας ὁ καὶ τυραννήσας Κῴων..., to add a little later a brief entry on his main political opponent: ...ἦν δὲ καὶ Θεόμνηστος ὁ ψάλτης ἐν ὀνόματι, ὃς καὶ ἀντεπολιτεύσατο τῷ Νικίᾳ.

Strabo was a contemporary of M.Antonius and Octavian/Augustus so that his short chronological allusion (καθ' ἡμᾶς) fits all the other evidence about Nikias. The crucial facts he discloses are two: that Nikias had established a *tyrannis* on Kos (interestingly implied as an addition/consequence of his rest, important personality: ὁ καὶ...) and that he was opposed by an equally memorable (though otherwise apparently unattested)[48] artist, Theomnestos, the "renowned harper." The latter fact, that Nikias was engaged in a kind of political rivalry (ἀντεπολιτεύσατο), suggests the climate of a general confrontation, a typical Greek *stasis* with two leaders and parties opposed to each other.

That Nikias' memory was that of a tyrant (by whatever contemporary view of the real character and acceptance of his rule, see

---

[47] 14.2.19 (C 658). Cf. Herzog, *N&X*, 207f.

[48] Herzog, *N&X*, 214, n.4 has tentatively connected the inscription Θεομνήστου on a tile from the temple of Demeter in the deme of Isthmos with Nikias' opponent.

below) is corroborated by further sources. (a) Aelian preserves in his Ποικίλη Ἱστορία (I.29) the following anecdote:

Λέγουσι Κῴων παῖδες ἐν Κῷ τεκεῖν ἔν τινι ποίμνη Νικίου τοῦ τυράννου οἶν· τεκεῖν δὲ οὐκ ἄρνα ἀλλὰ λέοντα. Καὶ οὖν καὶ τὸ σημεῖον τοῦτο τῷ Νικίᾳ τὴν τυραννίδα τὴν μέλλουσαν αὐτῷ μαντεύσασθαι ἰδιώτῃ ἔτι ὄντι.

What is noteworthy is the local source from which Aelian was able to take this story. There was obviously a literary Koan tradition pertaining to Nikias. The content of the story also deserves some commentary. It is actually a τερατολογία, a marvelous story, the intent of which should be to make Nikias' political ascendance seem fated, that is god-willed. The birth of a lion is a typical omen of a prominent and dominant political role, though not necessarily of tyranny proper. We should not forget that for example in Herodotus there appears not only the negative association with tyrannical power but also that with the position of a highly influential democratic statesman (Pericles in Agariste's dream!).[49] We could also recall Aristophanes' opinion about Alcibiades, put into Aeschylus' mouth in the *Frogs* (1431-3): the city should either not have favored the growth of a lion or obey him. So the allusion in Nikias' case need not have been conceived as a negative one: it could also come from the circle of his adherents.

Perhaps we may go a little farther: the pastoral setting of the story is worth examining. A lion born from a ewe certainly elicits an element of surprise, thus implying a parallelism with Nikias' unexpected rise from the position of an ἰδιώτης (we should understand: "a simple private man") to that of a local ruler. The further reasonable inference is that also Nikias' familial background had no political tradition whatsoever. That the monstrous birth should have taken place "in a flock *of Nikias*"[50] does not necessarily mean that Nikias *owned* all those animals. He may have simply been their shepherd, an element in the organization of animal husbandry well known from ancient (and modern) Greece.[51] So we

---

[49] *Hdt.*, VI.131.2. The connection with tyrants is exemplified in ibid., V.92β.3 (the oracle on Kypselos' birth). Cf. also ibid., V.56.1 (the oracle alluding to Hipparchos' assassination). Cf. Sherwin-White, *Cos*, 142.

[50] The translation "in some flock from an ewe of Nikias" seems also possible as Νικίου τοῦ τυράννου may be connected either with ποίμνη or with οἶν, or with both.

[51] E.g. in Theocritus there is both the case of flocks belonging to the goatherd (*Id.* 5.1) and that of a goat- and (temporarily) oxherd taking care of another's flock (*Id.* IV.1-6). There is also a mention of a Cretan goatherd (Lykidas of Kydonia) working on Kos in *Id.* VII. Unfree shepherds whose work is leased by a sanctuary (Diktynnaion) are also known from Crete: *IC*, II.XI.3,9f. (late first cent. B.C.), cf. An. Chaniotis, *EBGR* 1992 (in

should refrain from any conclusion on Nikias' social status based on Aelian's passage: according to the latter's text Nikias' origin does not seem to have been either a family of any political prominence or even a necessarily opulent one.[52]

(b) The dead Nikias was also the dramatic subject of a fine epigram by Krinagoras of Mytilene (*AP* IX.81):[53]

Μὴ εἴπης θάνατον βιότου ὅρον· εἰσὶ καμοῦσιν
ὡς ζωοῖς ἀρχαὶ συμφορέων ἕτεραι.
Ἀθρεῖ Νικίεω Κώου μόρον· ἤδη ἔκειτο
εἰν Ἀίδη, νεκρὸς δ' ἦλθεν ὑπ' ἠέλιον·
ἀστοὶ γὰρ τύμβοιο μετοχλίσσαντες ὀχῆας
εἴρυσαν ἐς ποινὰς τλήμονα δισθανέα.

The word *tyrannos* is not pronounced here but in the fate of Nikias' corpse one may easily recognize a retrospective variant of the typical denial of burial to deceased tyrants.[54] This act is represented as a wrathful civic crowd's vengeance on Nikias: the crucial implication is clearly that the Koans were for some reason unable to punish him while he was alive. Obviously they (all or a part of them) could express their real feelings only some time after his death. Krinagoras also implies that faults of the dead statesman provoked this spirit of postmortem justice (ποινάς). We should notice further that the infamous end of the dead Nikias meant also the end of his grave (*tymbos*), the bolts of which had to be violated to pull out the corpse. The desecration and lynching of Nikias' body must have simultaneously meant the end of a civic, perhaps impressive monument, an expression of the city's own historical face.[55] Some coins and slabs might survive but not that central symbol of

---

KERNOS 9(1996), p.377 (no. 106). Cf. also in general the valuable study by St. Hodkinson, "Animal Husbandry in the Greek Polis," in: C.R.Whittaker (ed.), *Pastoral Economies in Classical Antiquity*, Cambridge Philological Society Suppl. 14(1988), 35-74 (esp. his remark, 55, that "some [free herdsmen] could be owners of their own flocks, but there is sufficient evidence for the employment of hired labour as an alternative to slave herdsmen to suggest that they could equally be servants of richer owners").

[52] *Contra:* Sherwin-White, *Cos*, 142.

[53] Best edited and commented upon in Gow-Page, *GA*, I.210f.(no.XXII= *AP* IX.81), II.230f. Krinagoras has also written an epigram on the doctor Praxagoras of Kos: ibid., I.228f.(no.LI= *APl.* 273).

[54] Cf. the case of the Kypselids: Nicolaus of Damascus (*FgrHist* 90), 60.1. It seems to have been some sort of principle in Greek cities that a tyrant's corpse should remain unburied: Theopompos (*FgrHist* 115), 352; *Liv.*, 24.21.3; *Plut., Pelop.*, 36 and *Mor.*, 262 C-D.

[55] Cf. the same spirit regarding a tyrant's gravestone and votive monuments as expressed in *OGIS* 218.120ff. Cf. below on a further parallelism of this "Ilian Law against Tyrants" with the aftermath of Nikias' epoch on Kos.

political memory and reference. On the whole, one cannot resist the impression that the Koans engaged in all this because they wished to reckon emphatically and ostensibly with a part of their recent history that under new conditions was at least embarrassing.

Krinagoras' own stance is no less interesting: his sympathy for Nikias, who was erroneously thought to have passed beyond human turbulence, is the final note of the whole poem (τλήμονα διϑανέα).[56] The cruel tide of fame and popularity for the local statesman of his times[57] as well as some possible personal connection[58] may explain the shocked interest of the Mytilenaean poet.

Last but not least, a further chronological indication for Nikias is provided here. Krinagoras was active diplomatically and politically between Mytilene and Rome under Caesar and Augustus, the last evidence of his diplomatic activity pointing to ca. 25 B.C. and his poetry to ca. 11 A.D.[59] So, in combination with Strabo's testimony (see above) and the lack of any hint of Augustus on Nikias' extant coins (issued under eight archons), the latter's rule on Kos has already been firmly established before Actium and the Koan overthrow in the early Augustan period.[60]

(c) A last puzzling piece of direct evidence on Nikias as tyrant is the small bust of a child from Kos (the exact provenance seems unknown) with the inscription : ΝΙΚΙΑΣ ΤΥΡΑΝΝΟΣ. The bust and the inscription are known only from Iakopich's brief entry and photograph in a general chronicle of finds from Kos and the smaller islands of the

---

[56] The ms. reading δυσϑανέα has been corrected by Stephanus into διϑανέα, which was preferred in the Gow-Page edition. The point should be exactly that Nikias suffered a "second death" exactly when his "second life" in civic memory seemed assured.

[57] Mytilene must have also experienced its own kaleidoscope of Roman favor and local favorite statesmen between the age of Theophanes under Pompey, and Potamon, Krinagoras himself and their friends under Caesar and Augustus. Cf. concisely Bowersock, A&GW, 4, 11, 36f., 86; now also Labarre, 92ff.

[58] Krinagoras has written an epigram expressing some sympathy about Philostratos, Cleopatra's favorite sophist : AP VII.645= Gow-Page, GA, I.210f.(no. XX); cf. ibid. vol. II. 227 for the possibility of his having been personally acquainted with Philostratos during Cleopatra's visit in Rome in 45 B.C. The poet has also twice made Cleopatra Selene, the daughter of Antonius and Cleopatra, the subject of his art: AP VII.633= Gow-Page, GA, I.208f.(no. XVIII), cf. II.225; AP IX.235= Gow-Page, GA, I.212f.(no. XXV). This late Ptolemaic link of Krinagoras (and Lesbos saved perhaps some memories of her older status as Ptolemaic dependency in the later third century B.C., cf. Bagnall, 161f.) might have also involved some acquaintance of his with Antonius' and Cleopatra's man on Kos that Nikias should have finally been.

[59] The relevant evidence assembled and discussed in Gow-Page, GA, II.210-213.

[60] Sherwin-White, Cos, 143f. offers the last systematic argumentation for these datings and the correction of an older view in PH, xl.

Dodecanese.[61] The inscription should actually be a *graffito*—it is distinctly engraved without much care for symmetry on the middle left folds of the *himation* worn by the child represented. That the word *tyrannos* accompanies the name of Nikias also points to this, I think, excluding the possibility of an original artistic engraving. Did Nikias appear here as a child? Was the bust perhaps part of a family monument? We cannot know. However, the denigration of the "Son of the Damos" as tyrant should belong either to a climate of opposition and counter-propaganda during his rule or to the phase of dramatic change in the political situation on Kos revealed by the violation of Nikias' tomb. In any case, the label *tyrannos* cannot be here but a clear ideological attack against Nikias, alive or not.

Finally, an item of indirect evidence that can be very probably connected with Nikias and the vicissitudes of his physical and memorial presence on Kos is (d) the well-known decree with the appended list of priests of Apollo from Halasarna.[62] More precisely, this whole document (written on three sides of a big stele) consists in the reiteration and final execution of the decision to erect a new inscription with a purged list of those priests. Herzog first studied and historically interpreted this decree (probably of the local deme of Halasarna) and "re-edited" list with the priests until this enactment as well as the subsequent ones (respectively forty eight and eighty five names).[63] His exact chronological pattern for the list, i.e. its *terminus a quo* (placed by him in 30 B.C.), was later revised by F.Hiller v. Gärtringen.[64] The latter recognized in the entry of the priest no. 106 a lower *terminus a quo* and connected it on external reasons with the beginning of Titus' reign, 79 A.D.[65] So he moved the era of the reform and all the priesthoods to three years later (from 27 B.C. on). This ingenious combination, although incapable of being proven, is the foundation of the more probable (and current) chronology of the list.[66] However, what matters in the present context is this

---

[61] G.Iakopich, "Musei, esplorazioni e scavi nelle isole minori," *Clara Rhodos* I(1928), 92ff.(95-6 with fig. 77). Cf. Sherwin-White, *Cos*, 142 (n.323). I have been unable to re-discover this piece on Kos in May and December 1997.

[62] Original and basic publication: *Herzog, Hal.*, no.4 (p.483ff.). The decree has been republished as *Syll.*[3] 793 and Sokolowski, *LSCG*, 174; a part of the list (from the priest no. 17 on, the first with a Roman name) also as *IGRR* IV.1101. Cf. also on the significance of this tabulation Chaniotis, *H&H*, 203 (cf. 189f. with n. 407).

[63] Three of these latter have been erased.

[64] *Syll.*[3] 793 (n.5). Cf. Hiller's triangular mark before the number of this inscription, ibid., and his notice in the preface of *Syll.*[3], p. xvii. Sherwin-White, *Cos*, 147f. has inadvertently ascribed this revision of Herzog's views to Dittenberger himself.

[65] More on this in the final chapter, p. 142ff.

[66] Hiller's chronological revision has been later accepted by Herzog himself, *N&X*, 215 (n.3). Cf. also Sherwin-White, *Cos*, 147f. (n.353).

"reformed list" itself and the way its need and eventual realization is described. For the erection of the new catalogue is expressly to be preceded by an action in which "all the inadmissibly and illegally engraved inscriptions will be destroyed by the servant of the deme."[67] Obviously, there were other lists or partial commemorations of other priesthoods that had long been officially rejected as unauthorized and unlawful, and were now eventually to disappear from the public eye. The temple proceeds not to a measure of simple conservation but of reformation in its own priestly tradition.

The priest of the reform year (no. 48) is discernible on the inscription because his name is the last entry in a uniform writing style, while different ones characterize the rest, which were clearly inscribed each following year. Although we cannot rely on an absolutely certain chronology of this reform and the preceding and following name entries, some prosopographical observations on certain priests predating that organizational turning point have been already plausibly reached by Herzog.[68] Thus the priest no. 19 is Γάιος Ἰούλιος Εὐαράτου υἰὸς Εὐάρατος who may well be the important Koan Euaratos at the court of king Herodes (ca. 8 B.C.), known from Josephus. His influence there is presented as rivaling that of Augustus' other notorious favorite, C.Julius Eurycles.[69] Thus Augustus' similar grant of Roman citizenship to this Euaratos seems probable. This prosopographical and chronological association is mutually strengthened by the apparent identity of the priest no. 25 Νικαγόρας Δαλιοκλέους with the homonymous Koan archon on the reverse of a series of imperial Koan coins with Augustus on the obverse[70] and the also homonymous priest of Augustus (alive) in the deme of Haleis under the monarchos Antanor.[71] The priests no. 17, Μᾶρκος Σθένιος Λευκίου υ(ἱ)ὸ(ς), and no. 21, Ἀπολλωνίδης Θεαρήτου φύ(σει) δὲ Ἀπολλωνίδου, reappear as *hierophylakes* in a votive inscrip-

---

[67] ...πάσας μὲν τὰς ἀ/συνχωρήτος ἐπιγραφὰς καὶ τὰς παρανό/μως ἐνκεχαραγμένας ἐκκολάψαι διὰ τοῦ/ δαμοσίου (ll.8-11).

[68] *Herzog, Hal.*, 487-489.

[69] *J., B.J.*, 1.26.5; *A.J.*, 16.10.2. Some doubt on identifying the Euaratos in Josephus with the Halasarnan priest in Sherwin-White, *Cos*, 250 (n.171). On C.Iulius Eurycles cf. G.W.Bowersock, Eurycles of Sparta, *JRS* 51(1961), 112-118(here: 115f.) and now G.Stainhauer's dissertation (Univ. of Athens, 1988), rich in new epigraphic material, yet still unpublished.

[70] Burnett, *RPC*, no. 2732. His patronymic is here abbreviated as ΔΑ.

[71] *PH* 344.1-4:...ἱερέως δὲ Αὐ/τοκράτορος Καίσαρος Θεοῦ υἱο[ῦ]/ Σεβαστοῦ Νεικαγόρα τοῦ Δαλιο/κλέους... The identity of the three Nikagoras has been accepted by Herzog, *Hal.*, 488; Fraser-Matthews, s.v. Νικαγόρας (42). Sherwin-White, *Cos*, 493 identified only the priest of Augustus with the homonymous Halasarnan priest.

tion for the welfare of Tiberius and Livia (before her death in 29 A.D.).[72]
So we would not seriously err if we place the second decade of priests in
the list roughly in the period of Augustus. Consequently, the beginning
of this revised list, that is not the year when the reform was finally
realized, but the one in which it was retroactively carried out, should
probably be connected with some change in official legitimacy in
Halasarna, and more generally on Kos. This change falls approximately
in the years when Augustus defeated Antonius or the principate began.

Herzog pointed to the testimony of the famous "Law against
Tyrants" from Ilion[73] where the erasure of the names of all enemies of
democracy from public record is foreseen, also from priestly lists: ...ὅτου
ἂν τι ὄνομα ᾖ τούτων ἐάν τε ἐν τοῖς/ ἱερ(ητ)εύσασιν...ἐκκόπτειν...
(ll.119-121). Herzog concluded that the list of Halasarna presents the
names of priests of Apollo after Nikias' postmortem condemnation, the
otherwise and approximately reached date of which falls in the same
period. His conclusion, by now generally accepted,[74] finds further
support in the erasure of M.Antonius', and possibly also his partisan's
names, from the above discussed text of the Lex Fonteia. Nikias' fall into
official disgrace on Kos seems to have resulted in similar measures
against his more prominent adherents.

What Herzog also noticed[75] but we should emphasize is the very
long delay (forty-eight years!) in the implementation of this purge in the
official temple records. Since the cause of the reform and its execution
must revert to the developments following Actium, the removal of the
"inadmissible and unlawful" names from official record postdated the
entire age of Augustus, having been ultimately enforced somewhere in
the reign of Tiberius. Nikias' rule must have had very strong roots on
Kos (as already suggested by the number of preserved private
dedications for his welfare, see above). Thus the process of "Enttyran-
nisierung" should have been a delicate and protracted one. Conversely,
the "tyrant's" memory must have retained some degree of actuality to
warrant this persistence in persecution. It is also certainly significant that
while we find some later descendant of the next great political figure of
Kos, C.Stertinius Xenophon, active and honored on the island (see
below), there is no respective trace of Nikias' family. The ban on his

---

[72] *Patriarca*, 11= *AnÉp* 1934, 89.
[73] *OGIS* 218 (third century B.C.). Cf now on the various stipulations of this document the
detailed study of C.Koch, "Die Wiederherstellung der Demokratie in Ilion. Zum Wandel
der Gesetzgebung gegen die Tyrannis in der griechisch-makedonischen Welt," *ZRG*
113(1996), 32-63.
[74] See the literature mentioned above (ns. 62, 66).
[75] Herzog, *Hal.*, 487.

public memory might have been difficult and its enforcement only gradual but it also seems to have been definitive. This point further supports the view that Nikias' political association can have been only with Antonius and not Augustus: for example, the latter's friend C.Iulius Eurycles in Laconia was able to leave behind an important family of imperial aristocrats despite his temporary personal disgrace.[76]

The assumption of a longer transitional period between Nikias' postmortem fall and the extinction of all public traces and ramifications of his rule may also be conveyed by a comparative analysis of the archons' names on the Koan coins of his period on the one hand and those on the Augustan coinage of the island as well as the list of Halasarnan priests on the other. One of Nikias' coins[77] is dated under the archon ΧΑΡΜΥΛΟΣ while one of the Koan coins with Augustus' head on the obverse under ΧΑΡΜΥΛΟΣ B.[78] Despite previous views, it seems impossible to identify these two archons or to interpret the legend of the second as meaning "Charmylos (archon) for the second time."[79] For the addition of a capital beta (B) after a name in the nominative is a regular way to abbreviate a homonymous patronymic in Greek inscriptions.[80] That this method was practiced on Kos, too, may be shown by the study of local examples.[81] In Patriarca, 11 (=AnÉp 1934, 89) we find a college of three hierophylakes: the names of the two of them include an express patronymic while the third (mentioned at the second place, that is between the other two) has the form: ΘΥΡΣΟΣ B. It is clear that Thyrsos was not here hierophylax for the second time but simply the "son of Thyrsos."[82] In the list of Halasarnan priests (see above) we also find many such examples.[83] Nos. 33 and 131 of the list are very instructive in

---

[76] His son, C.Iulius Laco (PIR², I 372 with the sources), was in full (though equally intermittent) imperial favor between Tiberius' and Claudius' reigns. Cf. the studies cited above (n. 69).

[77] Burnett, RPC, no. 2731.

[78] Ibid., no. 2734. Cf. no. 2735, with different reverse but most probably under the same archon (his name here abbreviated as ΧΑΡΜΥ).

[79] The identification pondered (but the correct view preferred) by Ot.Stein, RE XVII.1(1936), s.v. Nikias (14), 334. Burnett, RPC, 452 equally did not exclude it but also thought it would necessarily mean a second archonship of the same man (: ΧΑΡΜΥΛΟΣ B).

[80] B should be understood here, of course, as β', i.e. in the sense of a numeral adverb (δίς). Cf. the basic study by R. Körner, Die Abkürzung der Homonymität in griechischen Inschriften, Sitzungsberichte Akad. Berlin, Kl. für Sprachen..., 1961, no.2, 9ff. (with examples from various places and periods).

[81] Cf. already the experienced remark by Segre, I.Cos, EV 175 (comm.), and below on the usual way a second period of service in the same magistracy seems to have been expressed on Kos (as elsewhere).

[82] So understood already by Patriarca, ibid.

[83] The priests no. 1, 2, 5, 10, 28, 33, 35, 49, 58, 72, 76, 82, 91, 124, 131.

this respect. In the first case we have the entry: Ἀπολλώνιος β' τοῦ γ',[84] which must mean "Apollonios(I) son of Apollonios(II) son of Apollonios(III)." In the second entry we find: Πωλλίων β' Σεργιανὸς ἱερεὺς τὸ β', that is while the first beta serves as a sign of homonymity inside the name, the fact of a second priesthood (obviously something unusual, as the list itself suggests) is analytically stated.[85] Various other Koan examples of this significance of beta on inscriptions of the late republican/early imperial period could be adduced.[86] Moreover, the evidence of other Koan imperial coins is equally clear: on the three Koan coin types under Caligula[87] we find in the obverse legends respectively the archon names ΠΟ ΟΠΤΙΜΟΣ ΕΥΔΑΜΟΣ Β; ΠΟ ΟΠΤΙΜΟΣ; ΕΥΔΑΜΟΣ Β. It should be clear that here, too, the sign B does not mean the iterated magistracy but the homonymous patronymic (also in three name forms probably referring to the same person).

Thus Charmylos the magistrate under Nikias was not the same as the one under Augustus. Nevertheless, the mention of a homonymous patronymic to clarify the latter's identity strongly suggests some form of relation to his namesake in Nikian times. So I think it is quite possible that the two magistrates were father and son, the not too distant service of two members of the same family in this post being further an indication of a certain political continuity between the period of coinage with Nikias' and that with Augustus' portrait on Kos.

We may find some parallel evidence comparing certain earlier entries of the Halasarnan list of priests with the names of the magistrates on Nikias' coins.[88] One of the latter is Eirenaios.[89] In the list of Halasarna we find two priests with that name: no. 26, son of Euaratos, thus possibly connected with the priest no. 19, C.Iulius Euaratus (see above), and no. 42, son of Xenodamos. Both priests should belong roughly in Augustus'

---

[84] The numeral character is indicated on the stone, as usual, with a superimposed dash (the sign of abbreviation) on the respective letter.

[85] Cf. how the iterated *monarchia* of Xenophon is indicated in Segre, *TC*, 193, 194 through the form τὸ β', that is with the addition of the definite article.

[86] So, i.a., in *IG* XII.8.260; Segre, *I.Cos*, ED 230; Carratelli, *Rom.Cos*, p.819. This practice was apparently not established yet on Kos in the second cent. B.C.: cf. Segre, *I.Cos*, ED 235 A.

[87] Burnett, *RPC*, nos. 2740-2742.

[88] That for example the Koan *monarchia* and the priesthood of Apollo at Halasarna could be successive stages of a local career is shown by the entry no. 125 of the Halasarnan priest list: Λού. Οὐιψτάνιος Λου. υἱὸς Φιλόφρων ὃς μετὰ τὸ μο(ναρχῆσαι) Κώων ἱεράτευσε γεννηθεὶς ἐν Ἀλασάρνῃ (ca. 98 A.D.). Cf. Herzog, *Hal.*, 490.

[89] Burnett, *RPC*, no. 2726.

period.[90] Neither the name Eirenaios nor that of another magistrate under Nikias, Eukarpos, are common on Kos.[91] In the list of Halasarna we find no. 24, the priest Eukarpos son of Theudotos, again assignable to Augustus' age. Finally, another magistrate on Nikias' coins is Polychares, a still rarer name on Kos. Only two more certain examples of it are known from Kos,[92] one of them the father of an apparently remarkable local figure in the Augustan age, Diogenes, the *prostateuon* of the union of γρυτοπῶλαι/scrutarei appearing in a bilingual dedication of this association to Augustus.[93] Diogenes allows himself here to use the title *philokaisar*, at least an indication of some local recognition and political influence (more on this and similar titles below, p. 101ff.).

Admittedly, these cases seen separately do not amount to much. However, taken together they seem indeed to suggest some degree of continuity between the period of Nikias and that of Augustus on Kos. At least some people continued to be useful and influential, so that neither the animosity of the desecrating crowd nor the official condemnation of an age could have so rapid results on all levels. We shall return to this and related points in the final attempt of synthesis on Kos in the republican/Augustan period.

d. Nikias (III): Further analysis of Nikias' honorary inscriptions. Elements of a civic ideology.

We should now complete the analysis of the votive inscriptions for Nikias' σωτηρία the standard text of which has been already quoted above (p. 34). These small monuments present many important aspects, not the least of which is probably that they seem to have created a kind

---

[90] A connection of one of them, or both, with Eirenaios the dedicant of a probable earlier dedication for C.Iulius Artemidorus, Caesar's influential Knidian friend, on Kos (according to Höghammar's, p.160, no.50 quite plausible restoration of *PH* 134) seems also possible.

[91] Fraser-Matthews, s.vv. Εἰρηναῖος, Εὔκαρπος list respectively ten and six bearers of these names on Kos.

[92] Sherwin-White, *Cos* (Onomastikon), 515. There are two more possible cases, abbreviated as ΠΟΛΥΧΑ(ΡΗΣ?) on Koan coins (see Fraser-Matthews, s.v. Πολυχάρης, nos. 7, 9).

[93] Maiuri, *NS*, 466. Their trade was thought by him to concern women's cosmetics but it seems rather, as the relevant evidence accrues, to have consisted in dealing with frippery: cf. M.Hombert, "Tablette de bois: un prêt sur gage," in: A.E.Hanson (ed.), *Collectanea Papyrologica. Texts Published in Honor of H.C.Youtie*, (Bonn 1976) II, 621-6; more recently: J.Reynolds-R.Tannenbaum, *Jews and God-fearers at Aphrodisias*, (Cambridge 1987) 117.

of local political tradition: for their genre[94] was later continued—despite the ban on Nikias' memory!—in the cases of major and minor civic magnates (see below). The gods to whom all these modest plaques, altars and (exceptionally) bases of portraits/busts (see Appendices 2-4) are dedicated are the θεοὶ πατρῷοι ("paternal gods"). The relative anonymity (or collectivity) of these gods is interestingly matched by the total absence of any indication in the text about their dedicants. It is obvious (and recognized long ago)[95] that these were perfectly identifiable by the place where each such monument originally stood, that is, the respective private house. At the same time, the dedication refers to the person honored (Nikias) in an indirect form, that is not mentioning him in the accusative (even in the rarer cases where an image of the actually honored seems to have "crowned" the inscription), but only through the modest formula "for the sake of Nikias' preservation." So the formal structure of the votive text gives apparently the first place not to Nikias' personality but to the "paternal gods" and their protection of him. This "syntactic tact" is then wholly outbalanced by the array of Nikias' attributes, following his name and placed inside that prepositional phrase.

Who were actually these "paternal gods"? The cult adjective Πατρῷος is associated with various gods in the Greek world, for example, Apollo in Athens. Practicing the cult of Ἀπόλλων Πατρῷος was one of the conditions to be fulfilled by Athenian candidates for archonship according to Aristotle, *Ath. Pol.* 55.3. Apollo seems to have been thought of as the common tutelary god of all Athenians because of his son Ion, their common ancestor.[96] From Kos itself we have now a small votive inscription to Zeus Patroios,[97] while a relative of C.Stertinius Xenophon (see below) was the provincial high-priest of Asia Θεᾶς Ῥώμης καὶ Θεο[ῦ]/ Σεβαστοῦ Καίσαρος Διὸς Πατρῴιου.[98] A more

---

[94] The nearest thematic relatives of these dedications on Kos are similar ones offered to various combinations of deities (not named "paternal") "for the preservation et sim." of the *polis* or the emperor and meaningfully self-styled (εὐ)χαριστήριον or ἱλαστήριον: Segre, *I.Cos*, EV 6, 101, 127, 199 (by individuals/associations for the city); PH 81 (by the *damos* of Kos for Augustus, quoted below n. 114).

[95] PH, p. 126. Cf. Herzog, *KF*, p. 67; Sherwin-White, *Cos*, 142f.

[96] Pl., *Euthd.* 302 D. Cf. P.J.Rhodes, *A Commentary on the Aristotelian "Athenaion Politeia,"* (Oxford 1993²) 617f.; W.Leschhorn, *"Gründer der Stadt,"* (Stuttgart 1984) 113. Apollo has been venerated as πατρῷος at various other points of the Greek world, too: K.Wernicke, *RE* II.1(1895), s.v. Apollon, 63; on his cult as θεὸς πατρῷος κτίστης at Side recently: J.Nollé, *Side im Altertum. Geschichte und Zeugnisse*, I, (Bonn 1993) esp. 113, 262f. (no. 4).

[97] Segre, *I.Cos*, EV 329. The attribution of this epithet to Zeus at Kos is genealogically quite understandable; he was Hercules' father on a Dorian island.

[98] Ibid., EV 219.16-17.

relevant case seems to be a decree of the Koan deme of Isthmos mentioning a fine to the benefit of the "paternal gods to whom the sacrifice is offered" (θεῶν πατρῴων οἷς ἁ [θυσία συντε]/λεῖται.)[99] The decree accepts a private donation, probably for the support of cult on tribal basis in the *demos* (the three local tribes are expressly and jointly mentioned as the recipients of the gift), and meets various arrangements for the conduct of this cult. As far as one can see here (the text is only partly preserved), the cult actions foreseen are mainly sacrifices. Thus the conclusion is probable that the cult of the paternal, common tribal gods of Isthmos was the actual beneficiary of the donation. If so, we would have an example of the connection between a collective cult of θεοὶ πατρῷοι and the inter-tribal unity of a Koan deme. This partial example would then accord well with what seems to be the meaning of this cult on the level of the whole *polis*, too (see below).

On the other hand, the collective mention of θεοὶ πατρῷοι in dedications from other parts of the Greek world remains neither common nor instructive for our purpose. Especially rare and significant are the cases of a context pertaining to the welfare of a politically important person (or persons). This variant is known to me only from Kos (cases of Nikias and later local statesmen, see below), Myndos (for Trajan's father)[100] and Olbia (for Septimius Severus and his family).[101] The votive inscriptions from the two latter places present, however, some differences from the Koan examples (apart from the apparent lack of earlier examples at both places): in Myndos (three examples known so far) the dedication is made in common to the "paternal gods" and Apollon Archegetes while the (private) dedicant is expressly mentioned in each case. In Olbia the inscription is longer and concerns the dedication of a whole balneum by the city to the paternal gods.[102] So the group of the Koan dedications to the "paternal gods" with a political context is incomparably richer, includes the earliest examples (for Nikias but also for Xenophon, see below), and bears the mark of a distinct local tradition. The only help we get from the non-Koan examples of such

---

[99] Carratelli, *Isthmos*, VI.a.27f., cf. b.12 (p.163).

[100] L.Robert, "Études épigraphiques, III.Inscription trouvée a Kos," *BCH* 1936, 199-202= id., *OM* II.906-909.

[101] *IPE*, I².174.

[102] The indirect way of referring to the honorand(s) discussed above (cf. also below on similar cases of dedications "for (the welfare)" of Hellenistic monarchs) is here somewhat clumsily but characteristically (regarding the essentially equal perception of paternal gods and imperial family as recipients of the dedication) attenuated by the use of the conjunction καί between the formal dedication in dative and the following ὑπέρ-formula: Θεοῖς πατρῴοις καὶ ὑπὲρ τῆς [αὐτοκράτο/ρ]ος Λουκίου Σεπτιμίου Σευήρου...καὶ τοῦ σύμπαντος αὐτῶν οἴκ[ου ἀιδίου δι/α]μονῆς...

dedications to clarify the identity/character of the "paternal gods" is the wider attestation of a probable connection between some form of political patronage over a city by certain influential persons (in these later cases: *not* local citizens) and the dedication "for their well-being et sim." to the "paternal gods."[103]

Of course, the first thought that would come to mind on these gods' identity (on the basis of the usual broader significance of the adjective πατρῷος)[104] is that they included all the ancestral gods of Kos. L.Robert[105] has already preferred to identify the *patroioi theoi* of Myndos with the "dieux ancestraux de la ville." What seemed to complicate the similar question on Kos was the evidence of another Koan inscription[106] on which Artemis, Zeus *and* the θεοί πατρῷοι receive together a sanctuary and a cult through a private donation. P.M.Fraser concluded from this that the Koan "paternal gods" could not include *all* the gods of Kos; at least some of them had to be extra mentioned in this case.[107] The remark was clever but only half true: for Zeus was here mentioned as Hikesios and Artemis with a respective (not preserved) cult adjective. So in both these latter cases the cult of deities as πατρῷος/πατρῴα (like Zeus in the example cited above) were not concerned. This leaves the possibility open to include all cults of Kos traditionally bearing the attribute πατρῷος in a collective group of θεοί πατρῷοι.[108] It seems then that the essential point was not the inclusion or exclusion of some gods but the common significance of their cults expressed separately by the addition of πατρῷος to their names and jointly (apparently more often in such a political context) with the constitution of a group of θεοί πατρῷοι. Therefore the "paternal gods" on Kos (and probably in the similar dedications from other places, too) included all the ancestral, traditional gods of the community exactly as they represented the original, authentic religious tradition, generation after generation, and the consequent divine protection of the respective πατρίς, the *father*land. This last connection (πατρίς-πατρῷοι θεοί) had a glorious tradition for the Greeks at least

---

[103] Trajan's father, M.Ulpius Traianus (see concisely J.B.Campbell, *OCD*[3], 1570), was proconsul of Asia in 79/80 A.D. Olbia seems to have become part of Moesia Inferior under Septimius Severus: Latyschev at *IPE*, I[2].174 (comm.); C. Danoff, *Der Kleine Pauly* 4, s.v. Olbia(1), 273.

[104] Cf. *LSJ*, s.v. (I).

[105] o.c.(n. 100), 201= 908.

[106] *SEG* XIV.529, 1-3: [ἱερὸν ἔστω τόδε] τὸ τέ[μενος καὶ τὸ] vvvvv/ ἱερὸν Ἀρτέμιτο[ς........]ας καὶ Διὸς Ἱκ[ε]/σίου καὶ θεῶν πατρώιων...

[107] *BSAA* 40(1953), 39f. Cf. Sherwin-White, *Cos*, 330-332.

[108] Cf. for example Maiuri, *NS*, 475 where Apollo should appear three times with a different cult adjective each time; also Segre, *I.Cos*, EV 18c, 1-2 (juxtaposition of Zeus Philios and Theoi Soteres).

since the Persian Wars when the signal of the Greek attack at Salamis mentioned successively the liberation of fatherland, families and "the seats (sanctuaries) of the paternal gods."[109] We find later a similar connection in Thucydides.[110] So it would be reasonable to assume that in the Koan examples also the dedication to the "paternal gods" bore in itself the connection with the whole Koan community and its fate.

It is significant that this fatherland-connection recurs in one of Nikias' attributes: the statesman honored was φιλόπατρις, "lover of (his) fatherland." Although the concept of the beloved fatherland actually underlies some Homeric phrases,[111] the adjective φιλόπατρις—as far as I can see—seems not to antedate the Hellenistic period, where its use becomes more and more frequent in both literary and epigraphic texts.[112] One may think of two reasons for this later expanded use of the word: first, in the classical period the parallel word φιλόπολις ("lover of one's own city") was in use, that is, a term designating the "patriot" in the same sense as above—for practically the greater part of the Greek world, which lived in poleis. Second, the characterization of a citizen as "loving his fatherland" was probably superfluous in common usage, exactly as the title euergetes for a city's own citizens had actually no sense. Only since the Hellenistic period had the degree of the cities' dependence on their prominent citizens' practical contribution towards the upkeep of their community become a specially laudable virtue (with a corresponding honorific title), succeeding a previously implicit standard readiness to serve the common good.[113] Thus the attribution of this adjective to Nikias must be also explained by the need to describe his outstanding merit towards his fatherland.

To return now to the question of the paternal/ancestral gods, this emphasis on the fortune of the fatherland suggests a closer association between πατρῷοι θεοὶ and Nikias the φιλόπατρις. The dedication to the gods of the fatherland for the preservation of such a citizen very probably

---

[109] A., Pers., 401ff.(Broadhead) : ...ὦ παῖδες Ἑλλήνων ἴτε, ἐλευθεροῦτε πατρίδ', ἐλευθεροῦτε δὲ παῖδας, γυναῖκας, θεῶν τε πατρῴων ἕδη...

[110] VII.69.2 : ...ἄλλα τε λέγων (sc. Nikias shortly before the final Athenian failure to break out from the sea-blockade at Syracuse, in September 413 B.C.) ὅσα ἐν τῷ τοιούτῳ ἤδη τοῦ καιροῦ ὄντες ἄνθρωποι...εἴποιεν ἂν, καὶ ὑπὲρ ἀπάντων παραπλήσια ἔς τε γυναῖκας καὶ παῖδας καὶ θεοὺς πατρῴους προφερόμενα...Cf. A.W.Gomme-A.Andrewes-K.J.Dover, A Historical Commentary on Thucydides, IV, (Oxford 1970) ad loc.

[111] So e.g. Od., IX.34-5: Ὡς οὐδὲν γλύκιον ἧς πατρίδος οὐδὲ τοκήων γίγνεται...

[112] Cf. the representative examples assembled in LSJ, s.v. and L.Robert, Hellenica XIII(1965), 215. One of the earliest examples of its use as a personal attribute on Kos should be seen in Segre, I.Cos, ED 243 (first cent. B.C.) in which it follows the name of three persons in the extant fragment of a list. See also below.

[113] I may refer here to the well-known "dialogue" between the theses of P.Veyne, Le pain et le cirque, (Paris 1976) esp. 230ff. and Gauthier, C&B.

meant that his life and action were presented as the guarantee for the welfare of the fatherland itself. The gods could actually do nothing better for their city than preserve the person and work of its apparently most eminent citizen Nikias.[114] Obviously the same idea fits very well the rest of the cases of such religious-political dedications mentioned above. It also neatly fits the choice of the word σωτηρία to describe Nikias' preservation: for this term seems to have been much more often and meaningfully associated in the political vocabulary of the Hellenistic age with the fate of communities/cities than individuals.[115] However, the reference to an individual of decisive importance for a city was simply a natural variant of the main usage (cf. the well-known use of the attribute Σωτήρ for monarchs as "saviors" of cities etc.).

Nikias' attribute τοῦ Δάμου υἰὸς (cf. above) presents an aspect that may now be seen more clearly. His description as *philopatris* immediately follows the one as "the son of the Damos." This is a well-chosen sequence of terms, "people" and "fatherland" being very close to each other ideologically. Nikias' love for his fatherland is implicitly parallel with his quality as child of (and, we should understand, his filial devotion to) the People. It is here noteworthy that the term φιλοπατρία in its—as far as I can see—chronologically first literary example denotes exactly this filial love and devotion.[116] Love of the father Damos and the fatherland were perfectly combinable in word and essence.

Beyond this last connection the religious-political term "son of the Damos" assigned to Nikias deserves some additional comment. As noticed above, this is chronologically the first use of this name-title in our present Greek evidence. Obviously, it corresponded so well to the needs of political expression in the cities of the Greek East from that time on that later examples of it and the related terms υἰὸς πόλεως, υἰὸς βουλῆς, υἰὸς γερουσίας etc. at various places abound.[117] It is also very

---

[114] The text of *PH* 81 is similar and different at the same time: Ὁ δᾶμος ὑπὲρ (τ)ᾶς Αὐτοκράτορος/ Καίσαρος,/ Θεοῦ υἰοῦ, Σεβαστοῦ, σωτηρίας/ Θεοῖς ἱλαστήριον. Here the *damos* appears as collective dedicant and the gods (unspecified) as dedicatee. Thus both the personal connection with individual Koans and the reference to the *paternal* gods are absent.

[115] Collection of much relevant material and useful remarks in Anastasiadis (n. 158 below).

[116] Used by the chorus of Bdelykleon's behavior to Philokleon in *Ar., V.,* 1465. Cf. the annotated edition of the *Wasps* by D.M.MacDowell (Oxford 1971), ad loc.(p.321): "love for his father."

[117] See esp. the examples collected and the remarks by W.Liebenam, *Städteverwaltung im römischen Kaiserreiche*, (Leipzig 1900) 131f.; Dittenberger, *OGIS* 470, n.6; above all, L.Robert, in: J. des Gagniers (et al.), *Laodicée du Lycos. Le Nymphée*, (Québec/Paris 1969) 317-320. Cf. also below on the case of C.Iulius Pardalas and the Koan examples of such terms later than Nikias. The same concept could be geographically enlarged:

characteristic that despite some assimilating tendency in the honorific vocabulary of cities in Latin West and Greek East the above terms remained specifically Greek under the Empire, no exact Latin equivalents having ever been coined.[118] So it is in every respect important to throw the maximum light possible on the apparently first conception of this title on Kos.

What strikes one here (and has been just alluded to above) is that the symbolic filiation of Nikias as "son of the Damos" has completely replaced any mention of his real parentage. As we shall see, the name-title δάμου υἱός simply follows, in subordinate place, the real filiation in the later similar votive monuments for Xenophon and other Koan notables.[119] By that time the wider use of this and similar designations has undoubtedly detracted from its original force. A "son of the people" (et sim.) was no more loftily or rigorously conceived as the heroized son of a local deity. It is significant that in one of the earliest such examples after Nikias' period—the case of the Sardian magnate C.Iulius Pardalas, *archiereus* of Rome and Augustus in Asia in a year between 2 B.C. and 14 A.D.—real and symbolic filiation turn up in unconcerned symbiosis

Herodes Atticus was named υἱὸς Ἑλλάδος (*Syll.*[3] 854), we know an υἱὸς τῆς Λέσβου (*IGRR* III.87), an υἱὸς Μακεδόνων καὶ τῆς πατρίδος (A.Tataki, *Ancient Beroea. Prosopography and Society*, Athens 1988, no.1321) etc., on which all cf. again L.Robert, esp. *REA* 62(1960), 310f. (= id., *OM* II.826f.) and *Bull.* 1966, 186.

[118] This has been correctly noticed already by P.Veyne, *REL* 38(1960), 460 with regard to *Apul., Met.* IV.26.3 and υἱὸς τῆς πόλεως. Cf. now the careful analysis by Corbier, *Parenté*, esp. 842f., 853 (with the correct reservation of H.W.Pleket, *SEG* 39, p. 405 on equating the meaning of υἱὸς πόλεως with that of τρόφιμος πόλεως, and the corresponding Latin titles *alumnus municipii/coloniae/patriae*).

[119] The examples of such titles pertaining to C.Stertinius Xenophon, M.Aelius Sabinianus and M'.Spedius Rufinus Phaedrus will be discussed in subsequent chapters and appendices. There are some additional persons styled δάμου υἱός/θυγάτηρ on Koan inscriptions: Nikagoras, son of Eudamos, to whom we have a dedication, apparently by the deme of Halasarna, as φιλοπάτριδι, δάμου υἱῷ, ἥρωι, φιλοκαίσαρι (Herzog, *KF*, no. 212, p.135= Höghammar, no.82). The same person with the same titles should reappear in Maiuri, *NS*, 460= Segre, *I.Cos*, EV 226[2](more on him in the part on Xenophon's family below). The priest of Apollo no. 65 (ca. 38 A.D.) in the list of Halasarna (see above, n. 62) C.Hetereius P.f. Lautus is styled there additionally as δήμου υἱὸς ἥρως νέος (more on this below) φιλοσέβαστος. We find a mention of Λευκίου Κοσ[σι]νίου Λευκίου υἱοῦ Βάσσο[υ] Οὐ(α)λεριανοῦ, δάμου υἱοῦ, φιλοκαίσαρος in *PH* 130 (Segre, *I.Cos*, EV 206 is no improvement on this edition apart from verifying the letters ΟΥΛΕΡΙΑΝΟΥ on the stone, which I have also checked. There can be no question of reading here instead [τ]/οῦ Λεριανοῦ δάμου υἱοῦ and supposing that this person had been "adottato dal popolo di Lero." First, there is no room at the beginning of l. 3 for restoring a tau and, had there been here a reference to the people of Leros, this would have certainly taken the standard form τοῦ Λερίων δάμου (cf. G.Manganaro, *ASAA* 41/42(1963/64), 1965,298). There is also the priestess of Hera Claudia Polla, appearing as δήμου θυγατρὸς in an announcement of the deme of Hippiotai (G.Pugliese Carratelli, *PP* 13(1958), 418f.). At

as Παρδαλᾶ καὶ τοῦ δήμου τοῦ Σαρδι[αν]ῶν υἱοῦ[120] Is the contrast with Nikias' exclusively "unreal" filiation merely due to the latter's concern to be associated just with the deified People? Was there no reasonable room for humans beside the People if Nikias' filiation should have the proper effect or was the divine exclusivity of his projected parentage additionally motivated by his humble descent? The remarks on Aelian's story about Nikias (see above) should be borne in mind. As Nikias should also be, according to all indications mentioned above, a partisan of Antonius, one may also recall that the triumvir's favorites and staff in the Greek East often belonged to the lower classes. They were either descendants of ordinary families (like Hybreas of Mylasa, see below) or even freedmen (like Theophilos, Antonius' representative at Corinth,[121] or Demetrios who had a similar function on Cyprus).[122] The rise of a favorite freedman in a provincial city, even under the "stricter" Augustus, has been well illustrated by the splendid career and local honors for the latter's *libertus* C.Iulius Zoilus of Aphrodisias.[123] Curtius Nicias (according to Herzog's basic identification) could also be an example.[124]

---

least in this last example the connection of the title with a *local demos* (not the whole demos of Kos, expressed ibid. as *polis*) should be evident.

[120] *OGIS* 470 (= *IGRR* IV.1611= *I.Ephesos* 3825), 9-11: ...γνώμη Γαΐο[υ/ Ἰ]ουλίου, Παρδαλᾶ καὶ τοῦ δήμου τοῦ Σαρδι[α/ν]ῶν υἱοῦ, Παρδαλᾶ... On person and date cf. recently Campanile, no. 26 (p.48f.). L.Robert, Laodicée (n. 117), 318 collected and commented on further, later examples.

[121] *Plut., Ant.*, 67.7: ...γράψας (sc. Ἀντώνιος) πρὸς Θεόφιλον τὸν ἐν Κορίνθῳ διοικητὴν ὅπως ἀσφάλειαν ἐκπορίσῃ καὶ ἀποκρύψῃ τοὺς ἄνδρας ἄχρι ἂν ἱλάσασθαι Καίσαρα δυνηθῶσιν. Οὗτος ἦν Θεόφιλος Ἱππάρχου πατὴρ τοῦ πλεῖστον παρὰ Ἀντωνίῳ δυνηθέντος, πρώτου δὲ πρὸς Καίσαρα τῶν ἀπελευθέρων μεταβαλομένου καὶ κατοικήσαντος ὕστερον ἐν Κορίνθῳ.
Cf. on this, the next and similar cases among the republican principes' men in the East most recently (on the occasion of C.Iulius' Zoilus' career, see next note): R.R.R.Smith, *The Monument of C.Julius Zoilos* [Aphrodisias I], (Mainz 1993) 9f.

[122] *D.C.* 48.40.6: ...ὕστερον δὲ ὑπὸ Δημητρίου ἑάλω (sc. Λαβιῆνος)· οὗτος γὰρ ἐξελεύθερός τε τοῦ Καίσαρος τοῦ προτέρου ὤν, καὶ τότε τῇ Κύπρῳ πρὸς τοῦ Ἀντωνίου προστεταγμένος, ἀνεζήτησέ τε αὐτὸν μαθὼν ὅτι κρύπτοιτο, καὶ συνέλαβε.

[123] See esp. Reynolds, 156-164 and now the monograph of Smith (n. 121), which successfully covers all the evidence on Zoilos. The Aphrodisians dedicated a monument to him on which he was represented as shaking hands with the Demos and crowned by the Polis of Aphrodisias (fig.5). The spirit of this representation (cf. Smith, ibid. esp. 39 on the implication of an equality of status by the handshake) is remarkably similar to Nikias' imagery discussed above.

[124] *PH*, p.126 had already remarked: "We may be sure that there were good reasons for not mentioning the name of Nicias' father." Herzog, *KF*, p.64 has hesitantly completed this line of thought: "Wir hätten dann in ihm einen kühnen νόθος zu sehen, der sich getragen von der Volksgunst zu einer gewaltsam erlangten und vielleicht ebenso gewaltsam verlorenen Herrschaft emporgeschwungen hätte. Zur Entscheidung dieser Frage haben wir zu wenig sicheres Material." Herzog, *N&X* did not return to this point after his identification of the *grammaticus* Curtius Nicias with the homonymous tyrant of

After all, the notion of a "popular filiation" (not yet a formal name or title) appears in classical Greek history in connection with lower classes of free-born, slaves, or ex-slaves. One may adduce here first the brilliant rivalry between the slave Paphlagon and the base-born sausage-seller Agorakritos for the guardianship (ἐπιτροπεύειν) of the aged Demos in Aristophanes' *Knights*, where the image of quasi-filial devotion repeatedly appears in Agorakritos' action: so for example when the latter asserts (769-70) κἄγωγ᾽, ὦ Δῆμ᾽, εἰ μή σε φιλῶ καὶ μὴ στέργω, κατατμηθεὶς ἑψοίμην..., or when he addresses Demos as "father" (πάτερ, 724) or "papa" (παππίδιον, 1215). The simulation of a filial role towards the Demos is clearly implied for the lower-class but benevolent demagogue contending for the control of the people.[125]

A more pronounced father-son relationship between the Athenian people and a freedman exists in the case of Agoratos, the ex-slave whose liberation and spurious enfranchisement in Athens Lysias presents in the speech against him. According to Lysias[126] Agoratos described the Athenian *demos* as his adoptive father (ποιητὸν πατέρα) although he proved very unthankful towards both his natural and adoptive fathers. Agoratos' version of how this new parentage occurred was that he was given not only freedom but also citizenship by the *demos* for his collaboration in the assassination of Phrynichos, the leader of the Four Hundred. Obviously, such a brave act—whether actually performed by him or not—would entitle him to regard the Athenian people in theory and sentiment as his adoptive father. Thus there appears again a man of low origin and (purportedly) high merit towards the *demos*, who is at the same time beneficiary and benefactor of the people in an imaginary

---

Kos. His opinion that a *nothos* would have been unable to present a publicly acceptable patronymic on Kos (or elsewhere) has been rendered improbable by Sherwin-White, *Cos*, 333 with n. 388. On the other hand, what we know of Curtius Nicias the grammarian cannot exclude his libertine status (see below).

[125] Cf. also ibid., 211f., 426, 741, 773, 790f., and the relevant remarks of B.S.Strauss, *Fathers and Sons in Athens. Ideology and Society in the Era of the Peloponnesian War*, (Princeton 1993) esp.155-7, and L.Strauss, *Socrates and Aristophanes*, (New York 1966) 103 (the sausage-seller "acts as if, having been exposed as an infant, he has now recognized his father and been recognized by his father, who repents his mistake"), 317(in contrast with that relation Paphlagon, i.e."Kleon claims to be the father of the *demos* (1037-9), but never to be its child"). The image of the demagogue as *epitropos* of the people recurs in *Peace*, 685-7. The simile seems to have been also more generally applied to the relation of any popular leader, actual or potential, to the *demos*: cf. Plato's (?) *Fifth Letter*, 322 B (the author would have given his advice to the demos καθάπερ πατρί).

[126] XIII.91, cf. 70, 72. The authenticity of 91 has been sometimes doubted (so Blass and Gernet in the Budé edition), without sufficient reasons, I think (so Hude in the OCT edition). Cf. also the still useful commentary in the old edition by H. Frohberger, *Ausgewählte Reden des Lysias...*, I², (Leipzig 1880) p.166f.

filial-parental relation.

Was Nikias a similar, later example of a man adroitly concealing his obscure origins under a solemn patronymic remunerating his services to the Koan *damos*? It is remarkable in this respect that: (a) he preferred to appear in those inscriptions without his Roman name-form, although for example Theophanes of Mytilene did not refrain from doing so as a Pompeian client about a generation before.[127] All later important Koans honored on the same type of small votive monuments as Nikias appear there with their full Roman names (see below).[128] (b) The decree for the final erection of the revised Halasarnan priest-list (see above) lays emphasis on the authorized tabulation of the priests, including the latter's patronymics (πατριαστεί, 1.13).[129] (c) Curtius Nicias in Cicero seems not to be simply a man of letters but also a shrewd news-agent and businessman who differed once with a Vidius on the repayment of a debt.[130] If Syme[131] was correct in his replacement of Vidius with Vedius— thus integrating this element into the ingeniously reconstructed life of P.Vedius Pollio, the later, notorious protégé of Augustus who was of libertine origin and habits—we get perhaps a glimpse of the real social milieu of parvenus in which Nikias' gourmet and idle nature (according to Cicero's[132] allusions) would fit perfectly. This view of Nikias' formal social status remains a distinct possibility with our present evidence.

Nikias was also a "benefactor of the city" (εὐεργέτας τᾶς πόλιος) and a "hero" (ἥρως).[133] We are left to guess on the kinds of benefaction he offered the city (see below) but, obviously, his heroic elevation (whatever his social origin actually) should mirror the greatness of his *euergesiai*. One should add here that to be recognized as a civic hero *in lifetime* was not yet a usual honor for a Greek, and, as far as we know,

---

[127] *Syll.*³ 755; L.Robert, *CRAI* 1969, 52 (= id., *OM* V.571).

[128] Herzog, *N&X*, 209 (n.1) noticed this trait of Nikias' official nomenclature on Kos but tried to get over it too easily: "...Daß Nikias von seinem nicht sehr klangvollen römischen Bürgernamen Curtius als Tyrann keinen Gebrauch mehr machte, ist leicht verständlich, da er eben als echter Sohn seiner Vaterstadt gelten wollte." Theophanes of Mytilene certainly had the same wish!

[129] However, this seems to have been a traditional minimum requirement in the demotic lists of Halasarna: *Syll.*³ 1023.29ff. On the more extensive, basic requirements of Koan citizenship cf. Sherwin-White, *Cos*, 153f.

[130] Cic., *Ad fam.*, IX.10.1 (cf. Suet., *De gramm.* XIV).

[131] *Vedius Pollio*, 25.

[132] *Ad fam.*, IX.10.2; *ad Att.*, XII.26.2 (...nosti Niciae nostri imbecillitatem, mollitiam, consuetudinem victus). Cf. Herzog, *N&X*, 199-201 (his translation of *mollitia* in the latter passage just as "Ansprüche macht" is a certain understatement).

[133] There is only one inscription where he is not given this title: see Appendix 2, no. 14.

had never before occurred on Kos.[134] Deification of living kings/dynasts (and then the emperors) and formal heroization/heroic honors for important living politicians, generals etc. was known from the beginning of the Hellenistic age.[135] However, such a public recognition, under scrutiny, shows that only outstanding merit of the Greek honorand, and this only rarely, could gain him the name and/or the honors of a hero in his own city during his lifetime.[136] The same is true, *a fortiori*, for the outright "godlike honors" (ἰσόθεοι τιμαί) decreed by cities for great benefactors.[137] As far as I can see,[138] there are only two certain examples of this last category from the late Hellenistic period: (a) the Pergamene honors including a priest, a sanctuary etc. for Diodoros Pasparos,[139] who brought about the political rehabilitation of his initially pro-Mithridatic city versus Rome in the early sixties, and (b) the similar treatment of

---

[134] Charmylos the "hero of the Charmyleioi" (see ch. A above) should have been granted this status posthumously—and not by the whole city but by his own clan. Cf. also the somewhat earlier phase (ca. late fourth century B.C.) of the same development represented by the cult of Herakles Diomedonteios founded by a certain Diomedon on Kos. Here the cult epithet of the traditional and generally recognized hero distinctly suggested a parallel elevation of the founder's role (Herzog, *HG*, no. 10= Sokolowski, *LSCG* 177= Segre, *I.Cos*, ED 149.2; cf. ibid. 33-36 the probable mention of a libation or a sacrifice to some other deities, Herakles *and* Diomedon. Cf. Sherwin-White, *Cos*, 364f.; F.Graf, "Bemerkungen zur bürgerlichen Religiosität im Hellenismus," in: M.Wörrle & P.Zanker (eds.), *Stadtbild und Bürgerbild im Hellenismus*,(München 1995) 112.

[135] Apart from the standard accounts by M.P.Nilsson, *Geschichte der griechischen Religion*, II, (München 1974³), 135ff. (esp. 142-4) and K.Latte, *Römische Religionsgeschichte*, (München 1960) esp. 312-6, always basic on these developments (with further literature): C.Habicht, *Gottmenschentum und griechische Städte*, (München 1970²) esp. 204f., 266-8; L.Robert, *REG* 94(1981), 358-360; Price, *R&P*, 23ff. (esp. 47-52); Gauthier, *C&B*, 60-66.

[136] This seems e.g. to have been the case of Diogenes, the last commander of a Macedonian garrison in Athens (229 B.C.): Gauthier, *C&B*, 64f.

[137] Cult honors of various sorts and grades for Roman generals and governors in the East (games bearing their names, paeans, priesthoods for their cult, perhaps even temples) proliferated from Flamininus until the early imperial age (see below). At least some of these honors, as in the case of Flamininus himself (so e.g. in Chalkis in 191 B.C.: Plut., *Flam.*, 16; cf. H.Gundel, *RE* XXIV(1963), s.v. T.Quinctius (45) Flamininus, 1076), must have been granted during the honorand's life. Cf. Price, *R&P*, 46f.; A.Lintott, *Imperium Romanum. Politics and Administration*, (London, 1993) 180f.(+229), who is correct in stressing the importance of *Cic., ad Qu.fr.* I.1.26 and V.21.7 on the promagistrates' cult in Asia being also associated with the erection of temples. However, the absence of separate archaeological remains rather suggests that this would usually take the form of the governors' association in the cult of a traditional god or Roma (as for example in the case of P.Servilius Isauricus in Ephesos): cf. esp. Tuchelt, 105-112 where all the relevant sources are collected and scrutinized.

[138] Cf. recently C.Habicht, "Ist ein 'Honoratiorenregime' das Kennzeichen der Stadt im späteren Hellenismus?," in: *Stadtbild und Bürgerbild* (n. 134), 90.

[139] *IGRR* IV.292.35ff., 293a.I.43-45, II.16-18, 38(ἰσοθέων ἠξιωμένος τιμῶν). Cf. also ibid. 294 and on Diodoros' whole personality and date of activities and honors C.P.Jones, "Diodoros Pasparos and the Nikephoria of Pergamon," *Chiron* 4(1974), 183-205. Cf. Bernhardt, *I&E*, 160f.

C.Iulius Artemidorus of Knidos by his homecity.[140] He was the son and political heir in Augustan times of C.Iulius Theopompus, thanks to whom the city eventually regained the status of a *civitas libera*, from the initial patron of both father and son, Caesar (cf. above).[141]

Later deifications of private, grand benefactors were understandably checked by the growing institution of the Roman emperor cult[142] but even the granting of lower, heroic honors like the bestowal of the title of hero itself or the institution of special, honorific *agones* was rather the exception for living citizen benefactors.[143] Apart from the Koan material (where the case of Nikias set a sort of example, see below), the only certain case of early imperial date I was able to find is that of the honors conferred by Gytheion[144] under Tiberius to C.Iulius Laco, the son of the notorious Spartan favorite of Augustus C.Iulius Eurycles.[145] Two days of θυμελικοὶ ἀγῶνες (theatrical competitions) were founded here: the first "to honor his (the deceased Eurycles') memory" (εἰς μνήμην, l.19) with the reasoning εὐεργέτου τοῦ ἔθνους καὶ τῆς πόλεως ἡμῶν ἐν πολλοῖς γενομένου (l. 20); the second "to his (the living Laco's) honor" (εἰς τιμήν, ibid.) as the city regards him κηδεμόνος τῆς τοῦ ἔθνους καὶ τῆς πόλεως ἡμῶν φυλακῆς καὶ σωτηρί[α]ς ὄντος (ll.21-2). It is noteworthy that these

---

[140] See *I.Knidos*, 59.11-19 (the last words, τιμαῖς ἰσοθέοις, summarize the previous honors: Artemidoros' golden statue is made *synnaos* of Artemis Hyakinthotrophos and Epiphanes, whose lifelong priesthood the benefactor has; he is also accorded an altar, sacrifices and a quinquennial athletic festival, the Artemidoreia). Cf.Gauthier, *C&P*, 62 with n. 190.

[141] Caesar as patron of Artemidoros, too: *Plut., Caes.*, 65. Cn. Pompeius Theophanes was venerated as Zeus Eleutherios on Mytilene only after his death: *Tac., Ann.*, 6.18.2 (defuncto Theophani); *Syll.*³ 753; coins: D.Salzmann, *MDAI(R)* 92(1985), 258-260. Cf. ibid., 251ff.; unduly hesitant: Price, *R&P*, 48.

[142] Cf. Price, *R&P*, 50f. (correctly interpreting the phrase θεοῖσι καὶ τοῖς ἰσσοθέοισι in the important document of the Augustan period *IGRR* IV.1302= *I.Kyme* 19.15 as referring to "traditional gods" and emperors); Habicht (n. 138).

[143] Even the similar, once liberal practice for living Roman governors (see n. 136) seems to have been restricted; there seems to be only one certain case—C.Vibius Postumus honored by the Samians during the third year of his proconsulate in Asia (ca. 15 A.D.): Ὁ δῆμος Γαΐῳ Οὐιβίῳ Ποστόμ[ωι] τὸ τρὶς ἀνθυπάτωι, ἥρωι εὐεργέτηι (*IGRR* IV.963). The phrase τὸ τρὶς (not τῷ τρὶς!) has dating value and clearly indicates that Postumus was then alive: cf. e.g. *IGRR* III.91 (...δὶς ἀρχιερέα καὶ τὸ β΄πρῶτον ἄρχοντα); Marek, *PBNG*, Pomp. 4 (p.137): Cn.Claudius Severus is honored as δὶς ὕπατον, the otherwise known year of this second consulate, 173 A.D., coinciding with the date after the provincial era mentioned at the end of the document (cf. ibid., Pomp. 3). Lafaye, *IGRR* IV.963 also dated the honor during Postumus' life. Confronted with Robert's authoritative general rule (see n. 147 below) later opinions hesitated: Fraser, *RFM*, 167 (n.451): "might not be posthumous"; Tuchelt, 106; Price, *R&P*, 51, n.132: "perhaps posthumous." On the contrary, the case of the cult accorded to C.Marcius Censorinus (*PIR*² M 222) in Mylasa (*I.Mylasa*, 341,410) ca. 3 A.D. should rather postdate his death, being simply the natural expression of the feelings mirrored in *Vell.Pat.*, II.102.1.

[144] *AnÉp* 1929.100= *SEG* XI.923= Oliver, *GC*,15.I.18ff.

[145] See ns. 69 and 76 above.

days of honorific performances will be added to a series of six other such days referred to as τὰς τῶν θεῶν καὶ ἡγεμόνων ἡμέρας (l. 18) and devoted in turn to Augustus, Tiberius, Livia, Germanicus, Drusus and T.Quinctius Flamininus. A real hierarchy of cult honor is implied, in which even the living member of an important local dynasty of *euergetai* does find a final place after the imperial gods and *hegemones*, and his own father, the deceased hero.[146]

The name of a hero does seem to be accorded more freely to living persons in the later empire. This does not entitle us to suppose, however, that there were similar habits for the end of the first century B.C. or the beginning of the first century A.D., where in most of the known cases only dead benefactors received it.[147] Thus Nikias' case is finally, and naturally, brought much nearer the figures of his roughly contemporary, deified "model citizens" who were obviously instrumental in their cities' status and privileges being regained or secured under Roman control in such a decisive way that they were considered to deserve civic honors

---

[146] Price, *R&P*, 50 with n. 122 also perceives these honors as heroic.

[147] Some later examples where ἥρως should characterize living persons: *IGRR* I.979= *IC* I.xviii.55 (Lyttos, Flavian or post-Flavian), where the combination ἥρωα καὶ κοσμόπολιν for the honorand seems to prove that both words were understood as titles, so the first does not necessarily indicate a deceased person. Peek, *GVI*, 655 (Trachonitis, second/third cent. A.D.): ἥρως is here (l.7) the apparently surviving relative of the deceased, who erected the latter's funeral monument and is described as καὐτὸς ἐὼν βασιλῆος ἀμύμονος ἐσλὸς ὀπάων (l.8). *I.Stratonikeia* II.1, 1018 (ca. fourth cent A.D.), where the governor and local benefactor Eutheios is described, in Homeric diction (cf. *Od.* I.371), as θεοῖς ἐναλίγκιος ἥρως. M.Guarducci, "*Heros* nell'età imperiale romana," *Atti del III. Congresso Nazionale di Studi Romani*, IV(1935), 328-332 argued for a much more expanded use of ἥρως to denote a living honorand in Greek documents of the whole imperial period. L.Robert, *Hellenica* X(1955), 19 (n.1), has rightly objected to this "inflationist view" of living *heroes* under the Empire, and especially clarified the point that, in many cases where the word *heros* is connected with "serving" magistrates of Greek cities in the imperial period, it should be understood as denoting posthumous magistracies of the respective persons in accordance with an endowment they had made while still alive (so correcting e.g. F.W.Hasluck, *Cyzicus*, (Cambridge 1910) esp.239f.). Cf. also Graf, *NK*, 127-135 (on the occasion of the Chian *heroes* Phesinos and Megon). It would be equally unsafe to formulate a strict rule (so L.Robert, *Hellenica* 13(1965), 207, cf. also *Bull.* 1977, 489; followed e.g. by P.Herrmann, *MDAI(I)* 44(1994), 208 with n.17), however, bringing the use of ἥρως in exclusive connection with dead persons even in the early Empire. The Koan material (its importance partly noticed by Fraser, *RFM*, 166f., n.451, who pointed to exceptions of Robert's rule, and rather underrated as a "Sonderfall" by Graf, ibid.,130, n.71; see also below) should warn us, I think, against such a generalization. It would be better to treat each case as a special problem and admit uncertainties, especially in references to distinguished citizens, as for example in an inscription from Adramyttion published by E.Schwertheim, *EA* 19(1992), 126 (first cent. B.C.) and some Koan examples to be mentioned right below.

that transcended the human sphere.[148]

Neither the public name nor the honors of a hero were something ordinary—as the evidence of Kos itself may finally show. For we find here one more certain, later case of a living benefactor receiving the name of a hero: the Claudian/Neronian magnate of Kos C.Stertinius Xenophon in some Koan inscriptions. However, neither Xenophon nor his still later Koan "peers" M.Aelius Sabinianus and M'.Spedius Rufinus (on all this see below) appears with this honorific name on the same kind of small votive monuments to the *patroioi theoi* as those on which we see Nikias' concise *Bürgerspiegel*. It is also significant that the other cases where ἥρως/ἡρωίς is used in honorific/dedicative Koan inscriptions after Nikias' age consist in three applications of these terms for honorands of whom we cannot be actually certain whether they were alive or not, and a fourth for a young dead person. All four persons concerned were of high social status: the three first[149] belonged to the very distinguished local family of Ti. Claudius Alcidamus, tracing their ancestry back to Herakles and Asklepios and related to Xenophon's family (see below), while the fourth died as priest of Apollo at Halasarna and was also a member of a family important on imperial Kos, the Hetereii.[150] At any rate, even these additional examples of Koan imperial *heroes* can only lend more weight to the attribution of a heroic identity to

---

[148] Apart from Diodoros Pasparos and C.Iulius Artemidorus whose honors were expressly equated to those of the gods (see above), a distinct but so far unnoticed aureole of heroization seems to have attached to Antonius' Magnesian favorite, the citharist Anaxenor, honored by his city through the erection of his statue in the theatre with an inscription citing Homer (cf. *Od.*, I.371 and the inscription of Stratonikeia cited in the previous n.): Anaxenor was θεοῖς ἐναλίγκιος αὐδῆ ("similar with the gods in voice"), *Str.* 14.1.41(648) and *Syll.*³ 766 (cf. *Plut., Ant.*, 24). Anaxenor's case was more like Nikias, similar to the ones of Hybreas and Euthydemos of Mylasa, also of the Antonian/Augustan age, who received a posthumous heroic cult as *euergetai* of their city (see L.Robert, *AJA* 39(1935), 335; *Hellenica* VIII, 95f.; his information included in A.Akarca, *Les monnaies grecques de Mylasa*, (Paris 1959) 28f., n.2). On Hybreas see also below.

[149] Herzog, *KF*, 212 (p.135). *PH*, 106. Maiuri, *NS*, 461.

[150] Herzog, *Hal.*, no.4, priest no.65 (p.484): Γάιος Ἐτερήιος Ποπλίου υἱὸς Λαῦτος δήμου υἱὸς ἥρως νέος φιλοσέβαστος (ca. 38 A. D.). On the meaning of ἥρως νέος cf. esp. the same title in the legend Λεσβῶναξ ἥρως νέος accompanying on Mytilenaean coins of ca. the same period the portrait of a young man, very probably the early deceased son of the famous magnate of Lesbos in Caesarian/Augustan times Potamon son of Lesbonax: see recently R.W.Parker, *ZPE* 85(1991), 125f.(citing all relevant sources), and further on the meaning of this special title Graf, *NK*, 134f. with n.s). On the status of the Koan Hetereii cf. esp. Segre, *I.Cos*, EV 177 (Γάιος Ἐτηρεῖος Γαίου υἱὸς στραταγήσας θεοῖς, "I sec. d. C."); ibid., ED 228(= Carratelli, *Rom.Cos*, p. 818).36 (Ἐτερηία Γα(ίου) θυ(γάτηρ) Πρόκιλλα, the only woman among the newly accepted into the *presbytika palaistra* of Kos in Flavian times (on the date cf. below).

a living individual on late republican/early imperial Kos,[151] and thus enhance retrospectively the value of the honor once accorded to Nikias. To be publicly accepted as a living hero was obviously nothing debased in those periods.

The formula referring to Nikias in the dedications to the *patroioi theoi* (ὑπὲρ/περὶ τᾶς Νικία...σωτηρίας) deserves also further examination of its possible models and character.[152] This indirect form of honoring a man or woman in power should have as ultimate sources of inspiration: (a) various votive texts of private individuals who chose to indicate in this way who was entitled to the divine attention and care corresponding to their offering. Thus by the use of the ὑπὲρ-formula they stated either their sharing these potential benefits with some relative(s) or they completely conceded them to this/these last. In an Attic dedication from the fifth century B.C.,[153] for example, Smikythe dedicates after a dream a statue to Athena [εὐξ]αμένη δ[εκάτην/ καὶ] ὑπὲρ πα[ίδων/ κ]αὶ ἑαυτῆ[ς]. The second alternative is found for example already in fourth century B.C. dedications from Olbia, in the one ὑπὲρ τοῦ πατρὸς by Mestor the son of Hipposthenes to Apollo.[154] This usage went on in later periods (so for example in various dedications to Asklepios from Athens, Paros and Kos, and to the Egyptian Gods on Delos).[155] In these latter cases the dedicant credited some beloved person's spiritual account, we could say.

---

[151] On these cases of heroization on Kos cf. also Sherwin-White, *Cos*, 366f. (where the Nikagoras, son of Eudamos of Herzog, *KF*, 212 is steadily misprinted as "Nicanor").

[152] A good treatment of this dedicative ὑπὲρ-formula in Greek texts (inscriptions and papyri) has been offered on the occasion of such Ptolemaic dedications by Fraser, *PA*, I.226f., II.374-376 (n.s 297-8). However, I see no reason to accept his rigid distinction (375) of the meaning of ὑπὲρ+bare genitive of person and the more expanded forms like ὑπὲρ τῆς ὑγιείας, τῆς σωτηρίας etc. Cf. also M.Guarducci, *Epigrafia greca*, II, (Roma 1969) 125, 147, who tried (I think, in vain) to establish a difference in essence between such cases classified as "dediche votive" and "dediche onorarie" (approximately the groups (a) and (b) here): only the importance of the persons "recommended" to the gods' favor distinguishes the second category (not at all devoid of a religious content) from the first. Cf. now also the important study by K.Dijkstra, *Life and Loyalty. A Study in the Socio-Religious Culture of Syria and Mesopotamia in the Graeco-Roman Period Based on Epigraphical Evidence* [Religions in the Graeco-Roman World, 128], (Leiden 1995) esp.287-295 (conclusions), who collects and examines primarily the Aramaic but also the Greek and Latin forms of such dedications ("for the life/safety of...") from the Roman imperial period and the area of the Nabataeans, Hatra, Palmyra and other places in Syria/Phoenicia. A very interesting aspect of his results is the distinct probability that the wide diffusion of these formulas in the Hellenistic East since much earlier times might be partly due to a longstanding Near Eastern (already Assyrian) tradition of such dedicative concepts and patterns.

[153] *IG* I³ 857 (≈I² 524). 3-5, ca. 470-450 B.C.

[154] *Syll.*³ 215 (cf. 211, 213).

[155] Athens: *IG* II² 4351, 4365, 4367, 4372, 4374, 4400, 4403 etc. On Paros and Delos cf. the cases cited by Fraser (n. 152), II.375. Kos: Höghammar, no. 70.

(b) Equally old, and obviously stemming from the same concept, was the public custom of expressing the sacrifices offered to some god(s) for the sake of a community, a state etc. by the same formula. An early example is the Athenian decree on the colony at Brea where we find the mention ...καλλ]ιερέσαι hυπὲρ τες ἀποικίας.[156] Further, we often find the more or less standard mention of sacrifices ὑπὲρ τοῦ δήμου/τῆς πόλεως/τῆς βουλῆς in Athenian texts (literary and epigraphic) of the classical period.[157] An interesting development in the Hellenistic period was the specific formulation of the purpose of such sacrifices of the prytaneis as ἐφ' ὑγιείᾳ καὶ σωτηρίᾳ τῆς βουλῆς καὶ τοῦ δήμου,[158] to which during the Macedonian control of Athens under Gonatas and Demetrios II the royal family could be added, so for example καὶ ὑπὲρ τοῦ βασιλέως Ἀντιγόνου καὶ Φίλας τῆς βασιλίσσης καὶ τῶν ἐκγόνων αὐτῶν.[159]

This last example of a "royal version" of the discussed formula is not at all isolated. There are many such examples of sacrifices/other votive offerings for members of all the major Hellenistic royal houses or their dignitaries either in the simpler form, consisting in ὑπέρ+genitive of the name/s, or the expanded ones, comprising a mention of the kings' etc. preservation ± health. So officers and soldiers of the Attalid garrison on Aegina make a dedication to Zeus and Athena ὑπὲρ βασιλέως Ἀττάλου (Attalos I),[160] while a gymnasiarch of Andros under Eumenes II or Attalos II had offered—among contributions to the performance of the royal cult in the city—sacrifices ὑπέρ τε τῆς τοῦ βασιλέως ὑγιείας καὶ σωτηρίας.[161] The indirect but definite, special association of monarchs with the cult of other gods through this formula facilitated its use becoming widespread.[162] In contrast there seems to be scanty evidence of

---

[156] *Syll.*[3] 67= Meiggs-Lewis[2] 49.5.

[157] See e.g. the various citations in P.J.Rhodes, *The Athenian Boule*, (Oxford 1972) 130ff.; *Syll.*[3] 144.25, 473.11-12 etc.

[158] See the useful study by V.I.Anastasiadis, "Οἱ ἐπὶ σωτηρίᾳ θυσίες στὰ ἀθηναϊκὰ ψηφίσματα τῆς ἑλληνιστικῆς ἐποχῆς," *ΕΛΛΗΝΙΚΑ* 41(1990) 225-233 where many such examples are collected and analyzed.

[159] *SEG* 33.155, 23-5. On Kos we have the similar case of Segre, *I.Cos*, ED 5.15ff. where the beneficiaries of the divine attention sought through sacrifices to various deities will be both the *damos* and the royal family of Cappadocia under Ariarathes IV: ...ὑπὲρ τε τὰς ὁμονοίας]/ καὶ σωτ[ηρίας] τοῦ τε δάμου κ[αὶ β]ασ[ιλέως Ἀριαράθου καὶ]/ τᾶς ὑγι[είας τ]ᾶς βασιλίσσας Ἀντιοχίδ[ος καὶ τῶν τέκνων]/ αὐτῶν (cf. on the date, ca. 180 B.C., G.Pugliese Carratelli, *PP* 27(1972), 184f.).

[160] *AE* 1913, 91= Moretti, *ISE*, I.36, 2f.

[161] *IG* XII.Suppl. 250.11.

[162] Such public offerings honoring Roman emperors are later frequent and appear also on Kos: so for Augustus (*PH*, 81) and Tiberius (Patriarca 11= *AnÉp* 1934, 89).However, the difference with Nikias' case is not chronological: the votive texts for the imperial

similar usage in honoring private grand benefactors of Greek cities such as Archippe of Kyme. This last example[163] (ca. 150-100 B.C.) is probably characteristic in that Kyme chose a sacrifice to the gods ὑπὲρ τῆς Ἀρχίππης σωτηρίας καὶ ὑγιείας (ll.18/9, 32) on the occasion of her partial recovery from a serious illness and so as a special thanksgiving offering (χαριστήρια, ll.15/6, 30).[164] On Kos itself there seems to be, apart from the votive offerings to the *patroioi theoi*, only one other case of a public dedication ὑπὲρ τᾶς σωτηρίας of a local benefactor, which should be, however, later than Nikias and occurred on the level of the *damos* of Halasarna.[165]

Thus the mainly monarchical background of the form given to these dedications "for the sake of" Nikias, as well as the distinct undertone of a sentimental relationship between dedicant and beneficiary of the dedication should have clearly emerged. Tactful but effective connection with the traditional gods was combined with a sense of affection for those who really mattered in these dedications, the powerful in the political realm.[166]

Of equal importance is the form these dedications take (cf. above)— they are usually small slabs that could be built into some wall etc. or steles to be put into a stand or, less frequently, bases for a small portrait et sim. These strongly recall—as has already been seen—[167] similar monuments with the simple text Ἀρσινόης Φιλαδέλφου that have been found at various places under Ptolemaic control/in alliance with the Ptolemies in the Aegean and in Egypt. L.Robert[168] has convincingly

---

beneficiaries are presented generally "to the gods" (Ͽεοῖς) and are characteristically called ἱλαστήριον ("propitiating offer").

[163] *SEG* 33.1038.

[164] Cf. also the older (ca. 320 B.C.) case where Nesos offered sacrifices (σωτήρια ἔ[Ͽ]υσε) because of the safe return (?) of the local benefactor Thersippos: *OGIS* 4.43.

[165] Herzog, *Hal.*, 7 (p.494)= Höghammar, 81: for Philion, adopted son of Aglaos and real son of Nikon, also known from his friendly relationship to Herodes Antipas (*PH* 75) and recently from his mention in an important but fragmentary testament (Segre, *I.Cos*, ED 200.21, "I sec. a.C.").

[166] One may recall here similar expressions from modern Greece, where, for example, many unsophisticated families used to place the kings' or leading (and favored) politicians' portraits right under an icon of Christ et sim., or where wishes for the well-being of such persons were incorporated into the evening prayers of small children or, as for kings, officially included, as the so-called *polychronion*, into the liturgy.

[167] Sherwin-White, *Cos*, 143.

[168] "Sur un décret d'Ilion et sur un papyrus concernant des cultes royaux," *Essays in Honor of C.B.Welles* [American Studies in Papyrology, I], (New Haven 1966) 175-210 (202-208), where all the relevant evidence was assembled. Some examples published later are included in the "corpusculum" of all such Cypriote cases given by Ino Michaelidou-Nicolaou, *RDAC* 1993, 226f. Add also: *SEG* 40.739(Minoa/Amorgos), 763(Eretria); 44.895 (Kaunos).

analyzed why these monuments should be interpreted as parts of altars in private houses for the cult of the great Ptolemaic queen whose involvement and influence on the Aegean policy of her brother and husband seems even to have outlived her death. Thus in addition to a monarchic source, there is probably, and more specifically, a Ptolemaic source of inspiration for Nikias' honors in private milieu, something not surprising for a partisan of Antonius and Cleopatra.[169] What was a straightforward, direct dedication to a deified queen was possibly adapted through the votive ὑπέρ-formula, which seems again to have been used for the Ptolemies more than for any other Hellenistic dynasty.[170] In its more modest form it satisfied better the needs of both religious tradition and ideological innovation on Kos.

There is perhaps something more to be said on the likelihood of that Ptolemaic "micro-monumental" model regarding prescription and freewill behind these acts. It is obvious that the standard text of both dedications (for Arsinoë and Nikias) presupposes a certain central coordination by some royal/civic officials. Nevertheless, why only for Arsinoë and then first for Nikias? Exactly that later Koan benefactors were honored in the same form (with the changes naturally resulting from the partly different conditions of their times, see below) betrays the success of this form of political expression. Frequency and method of engraving count, too: to date there are twenty three known dedications of this sort for Nikias' well-being; these amount to about half of those for Xenophon and the same as those preserved for Sabinianus (see Appendices 2-4). If one also takes into account the ban on Nikias' memory (see above), what remains is certainly the indisputable testament to his popularity. To emphasize a previous remark, if this type of dedication recalled simply a cruel tyrant's reign of terror (and there is no other case of a Greek tyrant where such a private vehicle of propaganda occurred, let alone succeeded) it seems improbable that anyone would have chosen to continue it in the following generations. Furthermore, each one of these texts seems to represent a different, personal script;[171] at least some of them were very probably engraved by the men into whose households they were integrated, or by some literate relative. This reinforces the personal character suggested above for the relation between citizen and "model citizen." Whatever public impetus there was

---

[169] Cf. above, n. 58 on Krinagoras and Nikias.

[170] Cf. Fraser, *PA*, I.226: "...largely, though not entirely, confined to Ptolemaic Egypt."

[171] Cf. e.g. the remark of Herzog, *KF*, on no.18 (p. 63): "Schrift flüchtig." The same seems to hold true on some of the later similar inscriptions for Xenophon, so e.g. Maiuri, *NS*, 476 ("scrittura irregolare") or Segre, *I.Cos*, EV 298 (cf. Appendix 3 below, no. 36).

(perhaps through a decree,[172] see below on Xenophon's titles) to honor Nikias in this way, what matters is that a considerable number of Koans were found willing to respond to it with their own hands. It is more probable, I think, to see here genuine (though certainly not unanimous) popularity than some sort of constraint. Nikias must have had a substantial, devoted following during his lifetime, and even after his death these small monuments bear no marks of the wrath exhibited at his tomb.[173]

It is remarkable that no place was found for some allusion to Rome in this apparently self-sufficient triangle of Koan patriotism (*patroioi theoi*-Nikias-dedicating citizens). Neither Nikias' Roman name-form (*tria nomina*, cf. above) nor any title referring to his relation to Rome and the triumviral princes of the Republic appears. If we did not know the historical context, one could have supposed that the Romans had not yet crossed the Adriatic and Kos was still enjoying the relatively undisturbed period of peace in the heyday of Hellenistic *chez nous* policies. As for the avoidance of the Roman name-form there could be personal reasons: Nikias' social origin, for example (see above). The Kos of Nikias' age might not yet be Zoilos' Aphrodisias. Nevertheless, the contrast does remain not only with some later magnates of Kos like Xenophon[174] rejoicing in their display of titles-references to their various Roman connections-functions (see below) but also, for example, with Tarcondimotus, Antonius' contemporary and favorite client-king of the mountainous area of Amanon, who proudly appears on his coinage as φιλαντώνιος.[175] Other kings and dynasts in the Orient had already put on the badge of φιλορώμαιος long before the Augustan age. The first example seems to be Ariobarzanes I of Cappadocia, Sulla's choice and life-long dependent on Roman favor and support.[176] The title is ascribed

---

[172] Sherwin-White, *Cos*, 143 thought of "an official ordinance...emanating directly or indirectly from Nicias" himself.

[173] Cf. already *PH*, p.126: "...it is somewhat remarkable that so many stones with his name intact have come down to us."

[174] That still later M.Aelius Sabinianus and M'.Spedius Rufinus were also not decorated with such insignia of Roman clientship (see below) is perhaps remarkable.

[175] Burnett, *RPC*, 3871 (ΒΑΣΙΛΕΩΣ ΤΑΡΚΟΝΔΙΜΟΤΟΥ ΦΙΛΑΝΤΩΝΙΟΥ). Cf. W.Hoben, *Untersuchungen zur Stellung kleinasiatischer Dynasten in den Machtkämpfen der ausgehenden römischen Republik*, (Mainz [diss.] 1969) 207.

[176] So e.g. mentioned in *OGIS* 354, 355; P.Herrmann, *MDAI(A)* 75(1960), 98ff.(no. 5). Cf. the good discussion of this and similar Roman titles of client kings by Braund, 105-107 (+116f.: n.s); on the Bosporan kings also: Nawotka (cf. also below on Xenophon's titles). One may add that: (a) the title φιλορώμαιος is borne by a woman (or one of her ancestors?) honored by the δῆμος and οἱ πραγματευόμενοι Ῥωμαῖοι in an inscription from Halikarnassos from the first half of the first century B.C.: *SEG* 34.1067; (b) for Strabo, 14.2.5 the epithet is already a standard royal attribute.

in the first century A.D. to various Koans, most notably Xenophon, as we shall see later on. So Nikias' apparent lack of such Roman "plumes" may tell something more. Despite his own dependence on good relations with Antonius (quite possibly also other Roman generals in the East before him), Nikias was mainly concerned with establishing himself inside the political traditions of Kos. It was perhaps too early for a civic potentate there to display his foreign political connections in a rather offensive way. The city itself might not yet consent to the intrusion of such a new sense of political values.[177] Nikias' features on his coins might be influenced by the young Octavian's portrait (see above) but, to be accepted, all the rest had to look as Koan as possible. There is some natural similarity, too, as we shall see later, between Nikias' position and policy and those of some of his coeval colleagues, the variously talented middlemen between Roman power and Greek cities under Antonius' overlordship.

---

[177] Cf. the roughly contemporary (late first century B.C.) persistence of an outward pattern of autonomy in the behavior of Athens as recently shown by R.M.Kallet-Marx and R.S.Stroud, *Chiron* 27(1997), 190f.

C. Notes on C.Stertinius Xenophon's Roman career, family, titulature and official integration into Koan civic life and society.

a. Xenophon's Roman military posts and decorations.

C.Stertinius Xenophon, the notorious personal physician to the emperor Claudius and his chief link between Rome and Kos in the important Claudian phase of Koan history, counted among the assets of his Roman career, service in some military offices with the subsequent decorations. Two previously known honorary inscriptions for him[1] and two new ones (from Segre's posthumous Koan volume)[2] make this minimum military *cursus honorum* clear. In short, Xenophon was *tribunus militum* and *praefectus fabrum*; he received the awards of *corona aurea* and *hasta (pura)* during the emperor's British triumph.

To have the emperor's doctor fully involved in military activity, is unusual, but Claudius is known for his innovations in the Roman system of equestrian careers that allowed a nominal occupation of a military office. Suetonius credits him specifically with the creation of an "imaginariae militiae genus, quod vocatur supra numerum, quo absentes et titulo tenus fungerentur."[3] Claudius assured in this way the necessary acquisition of some elementary military titles for many educationally and administratively talented aspirants who later advanced into the equestrian civil service.[4] Indeed, there are in Claudius' and later periods examples of people in whose succession of offices one or both of Xenophon's above-mentioned posts appear, but they remain isolated from the purely civil

---

[1] *PH*, 345 (=*Syll.*[3] 804).5-10: ...χει/λιαρχήσαντα, καὶ ἔπαρχον/ γεγονότα τῶν ἀρχιτεκτό/νων, καὶ τιμαθέντα ἐν τῷ [τῶν]/ Βρεττανῶν θριάμβῳ στεφάν[ῳ]/ χρυσέῳ καὶ δόρατι... *Maiuri, NS*, 475.1-4: ...τιμαθέντα ἐν τῷ τῶ/ν] (Β)ρεττανῶν θριάμβῳ στεφάνῳ χρυσέῳ [καὶ/δ]όρατι ὑπὸ τοῦ αὐτοκράτορος Κλαυδίου Καίσα/ρος θεοῦ, ἔπαρχον γενόμενον ἐπὶ Ῥώμας τῶν/ τεχνειτᾶν...

[2] Segre, *I.Cos*, EV 219.10-13: χειλιαρχήσαντα, καὶ ἔπαρχον γενόμενο[ν]/ τῶν ἀρχιτεκτόνων, καὶ τειμηθέντα ἐν τ[ῶι]/ κατὰ Βρεταννῶν θριάμβωι στεφάνωι χρυσέ[ωι]/ καὶ δόρατι... EV241.6-7: ...χιλι[αρχή]/σαντα λεγιῶνος ὀγδόας[---, on which see further below.

[3] *Suet., Cl.*, 25.1. Cf. next n.

[4] See esp. the discussion of his measures on the equestrian military careers by Devijver, *C&MÉ* (esp.76f.); Demougin, *OÉ*, 293-8 (esp. 297f.); Levick, 86f.(+213), who rightly cannot recognize any anti-senatorial attitude in these measures.

character of the rest.[5] That scholars in the past tended to interpret these phases of Xenophon's career as a kind of sinecure, tantamount to his joining the emperor's retinue during the British expedition is understandable.[6] Furthermore, specialists in equestrian careers[7] thought that the addition of the words ἐπὶ Ῥώμας after the mention of Xenophon's *praefectura fabrum* in one of the cited inscriptions necessitated the separation of his prefecture from the context of the British expedition (into which it naturally seemed to belong). They imposed a later date for it, i.e. between 44 and 47 A.D.: because a *praefectus fabrum* was traditionally attached to a consul or proconsul to assist him in his duties (cf. below). Thus such an assignment was technically possible with another consul or the emperor himself, Claudius having been consul not only in 43 A.D. (the year of the expedition) but also in 47 A.D.[8] So Xenophon's assistance could be dated after 43 A.D. and restricted to Rome, where it seemed to lack any specifically military or paramilitary character. Xenophon appeared to be a nominally upgraded and vainly decorated, idle follower of Claudius to Britain, whose sole service was likely to have been no more than his ongoing care for the emperor's good health. The distinctions after the war would then have completed a pure mockery of military service and reward. Claudius is known for example to have boldly given the award of the *hasta pura* to his freedman and eunuch Posides after the same expedition.[9]

A crucial detail here is that prior to the publication of Segre, *I.Cos* Xenophon's military tribunate was simply a "titular" case, lacking any specification,—that is the name of a legion attached—thus strengthening the impression of a post without real content, a true application of Suetonius' "imaginaria militia."[10] An inscription in Segre's posthumous publication however,[11] has now adduced the missing connection:

---

[5] Cf. the examples collected and analyzed by Dobson, 72-78 (esp. 77f., with n. 57); Demougin, *OÉ*, 297f. (with further bibl.).

[6] So Herzog, *N&X*, 226; Pflaum, *CPÉ*, I.16 (p.43f.); F.Millar, *JRS* 53(1963), 196f. and *ERW*, 86; Dobson, 73; Saddington, 538f.; Demougin, *Pr.*, 487 (p.397); Levick, 86f.

[7] Pflaum and Demougin, while Millar, Dobson and Saddington (all in previous n.) saw no problem in the temporal connection of tribunate and prefecture. Devijver, *PME*, S 79 (p.759) hesitated but pointed to the parallel of Balbillus (see below).

[8] See concisely D.Kienast, *Römische Kaisertabelle*, (Darmstadt 1990) 91.

[9] *Suet., Cl.*, 28.

[10] Cf. esp. Millar's (n.6: *JRS*) remarks on the case of C.Iulius Spartiaticus (*Corinth* VIII.2, 68) and Demougin, *Pr.*, 496 (p.409) on Xenophon's uncle Ti.Claudius Philinus (see below). Devijver, *PME*, S 79 (p.759) noticed apparently in the same sense on Xenophon himself: "tribunus militum, legionis alicuius (?), expeditione Britannica..."

[11] EV 241 quoted above (n.2). I have checked the reading on the stone. There is no question of restoring some additional ordinal numeral after ὀγδόας on historical grounds:

Xenophon has been *tribunus militum* λεγιῶνος ὀγδόας, that is of the *legio VIII Augusta*. This legion, stationed after 9 A.D. and up to ca. 45 A.D. in Pannonia,[12] had to be one of those remaining on the eve of the British expedition under the orders of the governor of Pannonia A.Plautius who was the commander of Claudius' expedition against Britain. We know that he took with him the *legio IX Hispana/ Macedonica*, also stationed in Pannonia at that time.[13] The participation of the *VIII Augusta* in the same expedition has been a problem for specialists: Ritterling thought that the detachment of some of its *vexillationes* to the British front was probable, although there was no conclusive evidence.[14] The new detail of Xenophon's career seems to offer the missing link here. It seems reasonable to accept that Claudius' doctor was given a post in one of the legions, parts of which Plautius led to Britain, and this specific engagement earned Xenophon his decorations during the final triumph in Rome. It is further noteworthy that this new piece of evidence brings Xenophon's career very close to that of Ti.Claudius Balbillus[15] whose parallel service as *tribunus militum* of the *legio XX Valeria Victrix* during the British expedition never posed a problem. It was naturally interpreted as an initiation into his subsequent civil career in posts of the central imperial administration (*ad legationes et responsa*) and in Egypt. Balbillus' tribunate is mentioned in his cursus honorum just before[16] his own *praefectura fabrum divi Claudii*—another point of similarity with Xenophon's career which we shall presently come to consider. To sum up: Xenophon's tribunate (as was true of Balbillus') did not exist in some bureaucratic vacuum. It was not simply a title without a real connection with place and time. Thus his decorations fit better into what gradually emerges as a distinct (and distinguished) chapter of his Roman career.

There is no reason to disconnect Xenophon's *praefectura fabrum* from the British campaign either. The above-mentioned addition "in Rome" after the title of his post does not necessarily mean that Xenophon's respective duties had nothing to do with the *expeditio Britannica* where his tribunate may now be safely placed. This is already

---

the eighteenth legion was never reconstituted after Varus' disaster and there was no twenty-eighth (see concisely and recently J.B.Campbell, *OCD*³, s.v.legion, 842).

[12] Ibid., 841.

[13] On Plautius: M.Hofmann, *RE* XXI.1(1951), s.v. Plautius (39), 27f. On the *legio IX Hispana/Macedonica*: Campbell (n.11), 841.

[14] E.Ritterling, *RE* XII.2(1925), s.v. Legio (VIII Augusta), 1647.

[15] Pflaum, *CPÉ*, I.15 (p.34ff.); Devijver, *PME*, C 124; Demougin, *Pr.*, 538 (p.447ff.).

[16] The inscribed cursus (*AnÉp* 1924, 78) follows, as often, the inverse chronological order.

implied by the juxtaposition of his tribunate and this prefecture in his inscriptions as it is also the case with Balbillus' similar career. Actually, specialists differ about the contemporaneity of the two posts in both careers. Some have attempted to date each post in a separate year; others have preferred to regard both posts as parallel assignments associated with the needs of the war in Britain.[17]

I think that this latter view can only be corroborated, and Xenophon's duties in these posts somewhat clarified, if we consider what a *tribunus militum* and a *praefectus fabrum* were probably expected to do. A *praefectus fabrum*, as far as our sources go, seems never to have had clearly defined duties in the Roman army and administration.[18] It is probable, as both the Latin term itself and its Greek translation (ἔπαρχος ἀρχιτεκτόνων/τεκτόνων/τεχνιτῶν/χειροτεχνῶν)[19] imply, that his job had initially to do with forms of "technical" support for the army's operations.[20] Perhaps its flexibility in practice caused both a lack of clarity and its high success in the Late Republic when people like Mamurra,[21] the notorious *praefectus fabrum* of Caesar, were considered some sort of general aides-de-camp to the mighty commanders preparing the principate in civil war and prefiguring it in organization. This is a crucial point: a *praefectus fabrum* was then and later personally attached to a consul or proconsul/propraetor whose confidence he obviously deserved and enjoyed. The exact extent of his real duties was at the discretion of his chief.[22] Atticus, for example, seems to have accepted

---

[17] On Xenophon see above with n. 7. On the similar difference of views on the date of Balbillus' *praefectura fabrum* see Pflaum, *CPÉ*, I.15 (p.35) and Demougin, *Pr.*, 538 (p.448) who placed it in 42 A.D. (Claudius was consul in that year, too), while Dobson, 72 and Saddington, 538 did not see any problem in the contemporaneity of the two posts (43 A.D.) in Balbillus' case either. Devijver, *PME*, C 124 (p.243) and Millar, *ERW*, 86 preferred the latter view.

[18] Cf.the still useful, concise sketch by E.Kornemann, *RE* VI.2(1909), s.v. Fabri (praefectus fabrum), 1920-4 and the later, basic studies of Dobson (here esp. 62, 76-8) and Saddington (both of which contain the greatest part of the epigraphic evidence for the early Empire and further literature). On the decisive Late Republican phase of the institution, see also the recent and useful study by K.E.Welch, "The Office of Praefectus Fabrum in the Late Republic," *Chiron* 25(1995), 131-145 (with further bibl.), whose main results are not affected, I think, by E.Badian's equally valuable corrections and suggestions on various points in her argument: "Notes on a Recent List of Praefecti Fabrum under the Republic," ibid. 27(1997), 1-19.

[19] Mason, 138 (cf. the quotations s.vv.).

[20] *Vegetius, Epit. rei militaris*, II.11(Lang). Cf. esp. Saddington, 536; Dobson, 62f. seem rather too sceptical on the value of Vegetius' passage in regard to the original connection of name and post. However, the connection has now clearly emerged from the Late Republican examples studied by Welch (n. 18).

[21] Recently and concisely on him: C.E.Stevens-S.Hornblower, *OCD*³, s.v.

[22] Cf. Dobson, 64: "...the real lesson to be learnt from our scanty information on the prefect's duties is that these were in effect decided by the individual who chose him."

many such positions without following the respective commander to the province (and the ways of enrichment), *honore contentus.*[23] In the imperial period the post remained in the administration of both Rome and the provinces, but gradually and frequently became simply a lower assignment for an equestrian *cursus honorum* without being a distinct step toward promotion.[24] Often, as mentioned above, it was the only military-like element of an otherwise civil ("procuratorial") or municipal career, as for example in the recent example of Ti.Claudius Apollonius from Perge.[25] In these latter cases especially, where no other connection with the imperial administration is visible, the probability increases that *praefectus fabrum* was a mere title, as it had sometimes been under the Republic (e.g. Atticus). In addition, as there were *praefecti fabrum* both in the central and the provincial administration, it was obviously important to distinguish the former from the latter by the addition "in Rome."[26] Thus this label probably expressed the level of Roman command by which the respective *praefectus fabrum* was supposed to offer his services.[27] This meant further that the *praefectus fabrum* "in Rome" was often personally attached to the emperor, whether the latter happened to be a consul at that time or because of his extensive proconsular *imperium*.

The emperor could assign some administrative duties to a *praefectus fabrum* "in Rome," and these were not necessarily directly connected with the army. This direct connection was probable if his future career was to be military. If not, the prefecture seems to have been either a preparatory step for a civil administrative career or, in a purely municipal framework of service, simply a title.[28] Initially, this might lead one to suppose that the character of Xenophon's *praefectura* corresponded to his purely civil career (he was also ἐπὶ τῶν ἀποκριμάτων= *ab responsis* of Claudius, see below). However, the important difference is that his prefecture appears combined with the tribunate as in Balbillus' case, and both functions clearly seem to have caused his final decorations after the success in Britain. The synthesis of prefecture, tribunate, and decorations

---

[23] *Nep., Att.,* 6. Cf. Dobson (previous n.) and F.Millar, *G&R* 35(1988), 43.

[24] Cf. the development as delineated by Dobson, 76-78.

[25] S.Sahin, "Studien zu den Inschriften von Perge, II. Der Gesandte Apollonios und seine Familie," *EA* 25(1995), 1-23 (here no.1.10-11, p.2; cf. p. 19). Cf. Dobson, 67f.

[26] Cf. Dobson, 65f.; Saddington, 536f.

[27] Such a distinction, not a primarily geographical one, may be also implied by the variant Greek term ἔπαρχον ἀρχιτεκτόνων δήμου Ῥωμαίων (*IG* II² 3546, late first cent. A.D.).

[28] This may have been the case with Apollonios of Perge (n. 25) who followed a purely municipal career and was precisely ἔπαρχος ἐν Ῥώμη τεχνειτῶν.

seems to strengthen the impression of some actual assignment having been performed.

How military was the tribunate itself? There are a considerable number of cases where its function is administrative rather than military (cf. above). Some observers have aptly spoken of "desk-borne" tribunes whose main responsibility was to ensure the "material well-being" of the legionaries.[29] Here is an example of the growing need not only to accommodate educated people at an initial stage of an equestrian (and subsequently civil) career but also to cope with the various para-military tasks needed to sustain the Roman army. When Plinius recommends a man to a provincial governor for such a post, for example, his praise of the candidate's juristic knowledge and loyalty to friends is not at all unusual. The governor certainly needed qualified men to handle discipline problems or questions about the soldiers' legal transactions.[30]

So we may perceive that the dilemma in Xenophon's case—where both the tribunate and the prefecture seem to have co-existed—is not necessarily that between a real military assignment and a titular sinecure. The Roman army also needed persons to perform para-military tasks that may have been equally important,[31] especially under certain circumstances. If Xenophon's combined military service and distinctions seem to be more substantial than previously assumed, the nature of these assignments can be verified only after a careful consideration of the tasks Claudius had to face because of his daring British plan.

Claudius' British expedition might appear in some respects to be a virtual parody of an imperial march. The emperor, safely placed in the rearguard until the final blow, ironically contrasts with the exuberant, almost childish victor he became.[32] Nevertheless, although Claudius stayed on the island for only sixteen days, he was away from Rome for

---

[29] Levick, 86: "...a desk-borne job of little military or political importance." Devijver, *C&MÉ*, 76: "Les tribuns équestres étaient responsables du bien-être matériel des légionnaires..."

[30] *Pl., Ep.*, 7.22. Cf. the case of Q.Decius Saturninus (*ILS* 6286, Augustan period) whose cursus includes the following sequence of posts: "...trib. mil., praef. fabr. i. d. et sortiend. iudicibus in Asia," with the remarks of Dobson, 65 and Saddington, 537.

[31] Cf. Saddington, 541, discussing the essence of the duties of a *praefectus fabrum*: "...The prefects of the proconsul of Asia are found to be carrying out judicial and administrative functions. But in the Roman context "military" can be understood in a wide sense."

[32] The foundations for such a picture exist already in the ancient tradition: *Suet., Cl.,* 17 and *D.C.,*60.21, 23(cf. esp. the "haste," ἠπείχθη, of the return and the multiple imperatorial salutations in 60.21.5). Cf. the sober judgement of C.Wells, *The Roman Empire*, (Cambridge, Mass. 1992²) 111: "All had been stage-managed to give Claudius his triumph with a minimum of risk and effort on his part." Cf. n. 35.

six months,[33] while his army (under A.Plautius, see above) went through various hardships before the final victory mainly due to good planning and careful preparation for a predictably unusual war among marshes and torrents.[34] Cassius Dio mentions in his basic report on Plautius' campaign that, when the general stopped his advance (the Britons were collecting their forces for a counter-attack after the death of Togodumnus) and waited for Claudius to go on, he did so in accordance with the expedition plan..[35] He adds: παρασκευή γε ἐπὶ τῇ στρατείᾳ πολλὴ τῶν τε ἄλλων καὶ ἐλεφάντων προσυνείλεκτο. In other words, the whole expedition had precipitated extensive Roman preparations (armaments etc.) that included even the formation of an elephant division. In all phases of the campaign, the crossing of rivers and the construction of improvised bridges would have also been essential.[36] Who would have been charged with all this? Certainly not a single man, and not just after the beginning of the war in Britain. A carefully planned logistical and (in the wider sense) strategic work in Rome and in the provinces opposite to Britain must have preceded what then developed as a series of successful Roman solutions to the various difficulties encountered during the expedition. It seems reasonable to recognize here the work, among others, of the *praefecti fabrum* connected with the expedition. We should note at this point that the relatively certain large number (three)[37] of them has already caught scholarly attention and elicited the comment: "quite a number of prefects for Claudius on a short campaign, but he may have been prodigal with appointments, as he was with decorations."[38] But why substitute monarchical whims for obvious needs? Thus Xenophon can very well have had important work to do as Claudius' *praefectus fabrum* "in Rome," as well as on some sites of the actual campaign.

His tribunate in the eighth legion under A.Plautius' command may have similarly been nothing but a sinecure, however unwarlike. A

---

[33] *D.C.*, 60.23.1; *Suet., Cl.*, 17.2.

[34] Claudius could proudly claim later that his victory had been reached "[sine] ulla iactur[a]" (*ILS* 216).

[35] *D.C.*, 60.21.1-2. However, cf. *Levick's*, 142 justified disbelief in the Dionian picture of Plautius' stopping the operations out of *fear* about advancing further and, only then, sending Claudius the directive to leave Rome. The emperor was likely already on his way to the front.

[36] *D.C.*, 60.20.2-6, 21.4. Cf. on the Roman methods of bridge building in war G.Webster, *The Roman Imperial Army*, (London 1979³) 234f.

[37] Xenophon, Balbillus and Glitius Barbarus (*CIL* V.6969, cf. *PIR*²⋅ G 182), who had reached the post after a purely military career. Cf. Dobson, 73f.; on two further possibilities (M.Stlaccius C.f. Coranus, *ILS* 2730, and Ti.Claudius Dinippus, *Corinth* VIII.ii.86-90): Saddington, 543 (n.31).

[38] Dobson (previous n.).

significant case in point is the initial resistance Plautius' encountered in persuading his troops to follow him to Britain, "outside the world" (ἔξω τῆς οἰκουμένης) as they appear to have exclaimed in Cassius Dio.[39] Dio further reports that the soldiers' reluctance forced Claudius to send Narcissus, his libertine right-hand-man in administration (he had the post of *ab epistulis*), to address the troops and persuade them.[40] Narcissus would have then spoken to the soldiers from the commander's (i.e. Plautius') tribunal, but they fiercely opposed the idea of a freedman taking, even temporarily, the position of their general and grudgingly consented to follow Plautius to Britain. The relevance of this story lies in Claudius' use of one of his high administrative aids in Rome as liaison with the "front" where he assisted with its various needs. Even if Plautius was beyond any suspicion, as it seems he was,[41] another *amicus principis* with desk-experience on the commander's side would certainly do no harm. We know that Xenophon later assumed the office of *ad responsa Graeca* in Rome—exactly the same subsequent advancement as in Balbillus' case. One may suppose that Claudius felt safer knowing that some of his closest friends and assistants were "planted" in inferior but important positions in the campaigning army, where they were able not only to consult and help where administrative tasks had to be performed but also kept direct contact with the emperor at all times.

A legitimate objection is, of course, that Claudius' doctor should have remained near him. But in this case, where the emperor had to leave Italy, the proper preparation and conduct of all operations as well as his being kept informed about them, were certainly important to him. He risked more in this expedition than any other time during his reign. Xenophon, as his physician, would have also been the best choice to prepare Claudius' travel under conditions that would not adversely affect the latter's health. After their meeting (probably at some point of Claudius' advance to Britain) he certainly stayed with the emperor for the final phase of the expedition and returned to Rome with him. During their separation Claudius may have been treated in Rome and on the way to Britain by Xenophon's colleagues or assistants, for the latter was styled later *archiatros*, "doctor in chief," of the emperor (cf. below, p. 95

---

[39] *D.C.*, 60.19.2.

[40] Ibid., 2-3. I agree with Levick, 141 in her preference to date Narcissus' dispatch before the actual trouble with the troops began, but not in her general underestimate of this incident.

[41] Cf. M.Hofmann (n. 13) and recently T.Wiedemann, *CAH*[2], X.235f.

on this title).[42] Thus his temporary detachment somewhere else for a special purpose may have been more understandable.

The emperor properly rewarded Xenophon's success during the expedition. Paramilitary services had proved their usefulness, and it was perhaps for missions like this (and Narcissus') that even Posides proved worthy of his own *hasta pura* (see above). Xenophon's subsequent advancement to the post *ad responsa Graeca* clearly proved that the emperor's doctor was capable of offering not only medical services; he could also be entrusted with playing a key role in formulating Claudius' Greek policy. Britain proved to be the supreme administrative and personal test for Claudius. His doctor-in-chief deserved to head more departments and contribute more to the formation of imperial policy. [43]

It is further noteworthy that Xenophon's family seems to have followed his example (with his help, no doubt). Three of his relatives appear also to have had a military tribunate, although none of them presents the same combination of prefecture and tribunate that indicates some form of real service. Two of them, his maternal uncle Ti.Claudius Philinus and his otherwise unspecified relative C.Iulius Dionysii f. Antipater (see below) present the bare title of *tribunus militum*,[44] while

---

[42] According to *Pl., NH*, 29.5.7-8 Xenophon had a brother of the same profession in Claudius' service (cf. below on Xenophon's family). On further Greek doctors of the emperors in the period between Tiberius and Nero cf. the evidence collected by M.Sapelli, *BCAR* 91(1986), publ. 1987, 82 (+88: n.s) and more recently the synthesis by G.Marasco, "I medici di corte nella società imperiale," *Chiron* 28(1998), 267-285 (with further bibl.).

[43] *PH* 345 (= *Syll.*[3] 804).4-5: ... ἐπὶ τῶν Ἑλληνικῶν ἀποκριμάτων. Maiuri, *NS*, 475.4-5: ...γενόμενον δὲ καὶ ἐπὶ τῶν ἀποκριμάτων. Both texts in which this office of Xenophon appears date from Nero's reign while other honorary inscriptions for him of Claudian date (Segre, *I.Cos*, EV 219, 241; cf. on the temporal classification of all these honorary texts below) fail to mention it. Nevertheless, it seems safer (cf. below on Xenophon's role in the correspondence between Claudius and the Koans) to keep the Claudian date of this post since it is certainly the case with *archiatros*, both being most naturally and probably further distinctions given after the British expedition. Xenophon's responsibility for the Greek *apokrimata* of the emperor should be primarily understood as giving the proper, written answers to the various embassies to the emperor from the Greek world (cf. esp. *Syll.*[3] 804, n.3 and Herzog, *N&X*, 228, n.1); the more specifically juristic sense of the term (*apokrimata=rescripta*, cf. Mason, 126) appeared rather later. Xenophon as head of the bureau *ad responsa Graeca* need not have been simply a subdivision of Narcissus' office (*ab epistulis* of Claudius) as a certain rivalry between the two men, the first a friend and the second an enemy of Agrippina, cannot be excluded (cf. already Herzog, l.c.). On Claudius' general policy to enrich the governing elite of the empire with worthy provincials as illustrated by his famous oration to the senate in 48 A.D. cf. also K.Buraselis, "A Contribution to the Study of Imperial Oratory: Remarks on the Tabula Claudiana," *Acts of the Third Panhellenic Symposion of Latin Studies*, (Thessaloniki 1989) 191-213 [in Greek with an English summary].

[44] Philinus: *Syll.*[3] 806= Segre, *TC*, 146; cf. Demougin, *Pr.*, 496. Antipater: Segre, *I.Cos*, EV 219.

the third, his brother Ti.Claudius Cleonymus, had a specific assignment as *tribunus militum* of the *legio XXII Primigenia* "in Germany."[45] While senior relatives' titles do look like sinecures, the specific mention of the local context in the tribunate of Xenophon's brother probably indicates actual service. His legion, stationed at Mogontiacum (Mainz), must have defended the imperial border against the attacks of the Chatti, incidents that fall in Claudius' reign.[46] The services of Xenophon's brother at this post need not have been very different from Xenophon's own in Britain. However, Cleonymus' further services to the empire developed on the local level of Kos where he was twice *monarchos*.[47]Those who gained Claudius' trust in the imperial service were more reliable and would act more successfully as liaisons in civic administration: Cleonymus served repeatedly as envoy of Kos to the emperors, a role Xenophon played with apparent constancy while in Rome. He was at least twice *monarchos* on his native island after Claudius' assassination and his own retreat to a Koan *otium cum dignitatibus* (see on both points below). Men like Xenophon knew how to adapt their talent even to basic needs of Roman wars, and profit from it.

b. Xenophon's familial network. The Claudii Iuliani.

Xenophon, an Asclepiad (see below), apparently belonged to a very old Koan family. Herzog has studied in detail the stemma of his relations.[48] This, and more generally, the network of his Koan

---

[45] *PH*, 94= *Syll.*[3] 805. Re-edited by Segre, *I.Cos*, EV 233 who preferred the following form of the passage in question (ll. 4-7): ...χειλιαρχήσαντα ἐν Γερμανίᾳ λεγιῶνος ΚΒ Πριμιγενίας δίς, μοναρχήσαντα..., that is connected the adverb δίς with Cleonymus' tribunate and not his *monarchia*. Segre based this change on the "segni di interpunzione" on the stone, one of which comes after the adverb. However, as he also observed and my personal inspection of the stone on Kos (Knights Castle) showed, these punctuation marks (dashes) come not only after the end of a phrase (l. 4, after Ξενοφῶντος; l. 10, after Σεβασ/τούς) but also inside it, that is, after the abbreviations ΚΥΡ(είνᾳ), l.2, and ΚΒ ("Legion *twenty-second* Primigenia"), l. 6. In these two latter cases there is also a superimposed, longer dash (above the letters) to denote, as usual, the abbreviation. So the additional dash after the letters should rather have here a superfluous, decorative character. This also seems to be the case with the dash after δίς. The stonecutter also used signs in the form of acute angles (<) to fill the remaining space at the end of ll. 3 and 7. His care for symmetry and a neat impression of the script is obvious. Therefore I see no reason to suppose a strange *second* tribunate of Cleonymus in the Twenty-second Legion. I stand by the opinion that Cleonymus became twice *monarchos* of Kos, as did his brother (see below). Cf. also Segre, *I.Cos*, EV 26, 51 (bis).

[46] Cf. H.Bengtson, *Grundriß der römischen Geschichte*, (München 1982[3]) 301f.

[47] See n. 45.

[48] Herzog, *KF*, 190-199 (with the older literature); id., *N&X*, 218 (n. 3), 224f. (n. 1), 227, 246 with n.s. Cf. Patriarca, p. 21f.

connections may be now considerably enriched by Segre's recently published epigraphic evidence and the conclusions it draws. The main results of the following observations will be summarized in a tabular form at the end of this section.

We know little about Xenophon's parents. It is certain that he was named after his maternal grandfather as we deduce from the filiation included in his mother's name.[49] There is an older doctor Xenophon, a disciple of the Koan Praxagoras in the fourth/third century B.C.[50] In spite of some legitimate doubts on the disciple's own place of origin (he is, only once, specified as *Alexandrinus*),[51] the fact that Claudius himself called his doctor an Asclepiad,[52] as Praxagoras and his disciple must have been too, makes it highly probable that the latter was reputedly an homonymous ancestor of our Xenophon.

Despite this distinguished ancestry, however, his family does not seem to have reached a particularly elevated status in the society of imperial Kos, where there were certainly more Asclepiads, before Xenophon's career under the emperors. The only probable distinction antedating this phase, and at the same time apparently the beginning of his Roman advancement, was his correctly inferred participation in the Koan embassy to Tiberius and the senate (23 A.D.) that managed to have the *asylia* of the Asklepieion confirmed by Rome.[53] This view rests on Herzog's observation[54] that Xenophon as a Roman citizen assumed the gentilicium and praenomen of C.Stertinius Maximus, one of the consuls of that year, who would have presided over the deliberations of the senate on the Koan petition.[55] He would have come into personal contact with the young Greek with both his diplomatic and medical skills. There can be no doubt that Maximus provided his Koan friend with Roman

---

[49] Κλαυδίαν Ξενοφῶντος θυγατέρα Ἡδεῖαν in Maiuri, *NS*, 459 (with the correction of ἠδεῖαν into Ἡδεῖαν already by G. De Sanctis, *RFIC* 54(1926), 61f.).

[50] The relevant evidence collected and discussed in the basic article by F.Kudlien, Xenophon (13), *RE* IX.A 2(1967), 2089-2092.

[51] In a late antique catalogue of Greek doctors: M.Wellmann, "Zur Geschichte der Medicin im Alterthum," *Hermes* 35 (1900), 349ff. (370). However, he could have been also remembered as an "Alexandrian" because of his long sojourn in that city. We should consider that there seem to have existed in both Rhodes and Alexandria citizens bearing no *demotikon* but just the *ethnikon* (Ῥόδιος, Ἀλεξανδρεύς), probably of recent naturalization: cf. the observations of Fraser, *PA*, I.47-49.

[52] *Tac., Ann.*, 12.61: ...adventu Aesculapii artem medendi inlatam maximeque inter posteros eius celebrem fuisse...Xenophontem...eadem familia ortum...

[53] *Tac., Ann.*, 4.14 (cf. above, p.16).

[54] Herzog, *N&X*, 221f.

[55] He should have also been instrumental in supporting a similar request from the Samians (*Tac.*, n.53) at the senate: *IGRR* IV. 1724; P.Herrmann, *MDAI(A)* 75(1960), 90ff. (no.5).

citizenship.[56] Nevertheless, Xenophon remained the only Stertinius of his family: the rest of his closer relatives were promoted to Roman citizenship, some Roman posts/titles (see above) *and* important local functions through Xenophon's connection with Claudius.[57] Thus they were all (Ti.) Claudii: his mother (see above); his brother Τιβέριος Κλαύδιος Κλεώνυμος and his wife Κλαυδία Φοίβη;[58] his maternal uncle Τιβέριος Κλαύδιος Ξενοφῶντος υἱὸς Φιλῖνος[59] and the latter's son, Xenophon's first cousin, Τιβέριος Κλαύδιος Τιβερίου υἱὸς Ξενοφῶν.[60] Philinos, who was probably provided with a titular Roman military tribunate, might have some connection with homonymous illustrious Koans of earlier periods (see on both points above). Nothing further is known about Xenophon's cousin. Xenophon's brother offered some services to the Roman army and, later it seems, was twice *monarchos* (see above); he was also many times ambassador of Kos to "the emperors."[61]

The rest of our knowledge of Xenophon's relatives is mainly limited to:

(a) a homonymous descendant (ἀπό[γονος]) of his, honored as benefactor in a later (second century A.D.), fragmentary decree of the demos of Antimachitai, Aigelieis and Archiadai on Kos.[62] The portion of this text that Herzog has published shows that one of his benefactions was the distribution of money (and food ?),[63] apparently to the *demotai*, on the celebrated birthday of Xenophon the *heros* (on this public quality

---

[56] Herzog, *KF*, 191, n.1 (after R.Briau, *RA* 43(1882), 211f.) and *N&X*, 222, n. 1 connects Xenophon's acquisition of Roman citizenship with Caesar's old, general grant to doctors residing in Rome (*Suet., Caes.*, 42.1). However, even if this practice had remained valid until Tiberius' time, which is doubtful, the consul's patronage must have been the decisive factor in Xenophon's achieving his new Roman status.

[57] Even if we place the beginning of Xenophon's medical activity in Rome under Tiberius (so Herzog, *N&X*, 224 with n.1 on the basis of *Pl., NH*, 29.5.7; cf. Devijver, *PME*, S 79 and Demougin, *Pr.*, 487), which is possible but not necessary, we should note that his higher position with the emperors seems to have begun only with Claudius.

[58] *PH*, 94= *Syll.*³ 805≈ Segre, *I.Cos*, EV 233 (cf. above).

[59] *Syll.*³ 806=Segre, *TC*, 146; *PH*, 46.6-7. Cf. *PIR*² C 959.

[60] Patriarca, 18= *AnÉp* 1934, 92.

[61] (n. 58).7-10: ...καὶ πρεσβεύσαντα πολλάκις ὑπὲρ τῆς πατρίδος πρὸς τοὺς Σεβαστούς. The plural ("emperors") suggests that he had already served under some predecessor(s) of Claudius -so Demougin, *Pr.*, 495- or possibly that he continued similar services under Nero.

[62] Herzog, *N&X*, 246, n.2. The name of the deme has been partly restored, obviously on the basis of *PH*, 393, 394. Cf. Sherwin-White, *Cos*, 60f.

[63] The fragmentary text mentions [? ποιησάμενον καθ' ἑκάστην αὐτοῦ] γενέσιον διανο[μὰς---ἀξίως---τοῦ ἥρω]ος καὶ ἀργυρικὴ[ν---. The last word especially reveals the similarity with such cases as e.g. B.Laum, *Stiftungen in der griechischen und römischen Antike*, (Berlin 1914), II, no. 100 where we find ἀργυρικὰς διαδόσεις (ll. 22-23).

of Xenophon see below). Thus the memory of the great Koan lived on, almost like that of a modern local saint—his descendants having played a decisive role in memorializing him (not to their social disadvantage, of course). It is further probable that the localization of these posthumous honors and celebrations for Xenophon has some significance. Perhaps not only the residence of this later Xenophon but also his ancestor's grave, and birthplace are to be situated in that part of Kos.[64] For such distributions or memorial banquets etc. near the grave and on the birthday of the deceased donor/relative of the actual donor are well-known in Greek commemorative foundations.[65]

(b) There is also Γάιος Στερτίνιος Ἡγούμενός, priest of Apollo at Halasarna under Domitian (ca. 89 A.D.).[66] His name is followed on the priest list by Asklepios' symbol (staff with serpent), obviously alluding to his profession (cf. below on the representation of a serpent on Xenophon's and Sabinianus' inscriptions). So praenomen, gentilicium, and medical quality strongly suggest an otherwise unattested later member of Xenophon's *familia* here, too.

What has already occurred to Herzog[67] and remains valid is that mention of Xenophon's offspring is relatively rare in Koan evidence. Plinius implies that Xenophon and his brother (he means probably Cleonymos) left to a *common* heir their vast property amounting to 30,000,000 sestertii.[68] So it seems there were not many natural descendants. On the other hand, Xenophon's fame and political capital

---

[64] It is also noteworthy that one of Segre's new texts (EV 238) is the inscription on the base of a statue erected by the people (?) of Kos for a Ξενοφῶ[ν/τα---]ίχμου υ[ἱ/όν---]. Segre dated this to the first century A.D. and preferred to restore [Μενα]ίχμου which is possible but rather improbable in comparison with [Ἀριστα]ίχμου. The former name has not been found on Kos so far, the latter twelve times (Fraser-Matthews, s.v. nos. 6-17). A late testimony (probably third century A.D.) of this name is an Αὐρήλιος Ἡράκλειτος τοῦ Ἀρισταίχνου (= Ἀρισταίχμου) in a gymnasiarchic inscription found in the area of Antimachia (PH, 392). Could this late combination of the names Herakleitos (Xenophon's father) and Aristaichmos, otherwise unattested on Kos, as well as the locality of this latter find also provide some indication for a closer connection between C.Stertinius Xenophon and Antimachia? Future research may determine this.

[65] Cf. Laum (n. 63), I.74f., 99 (rarely mentioned, the place of these distributions was usually "die Bildsäule des Stifters oder seiner Verwandten"). A similar distribution connected with a commemorative *agon* should also be the case in Segre, *I.Cos*, ED 263.

[66] Herzog, *Hal.*, no. 4, priest no. 116 (p. 485 II).

[67] Herzog, *KF*, 199.

[68] Pl., *NH*, 29.5.8. Herzog, *N&X*, 224f., n. 1 has already shown that it is not necessary to assume the existence of a brother of our Xenophon named *Q. Stertinius* on the basis of this passage as transmitted in a part of the manuscripts. Herzog was also probably correct in identifying this brother with Cleonymos but not in denying him a medical identity (Plinius' *par et fratri eius merces* cannot be understood, I think, in the more general sense of "Gratifikation").

could leave one to think that some distant relatives may have continued his public role on Kos. We shall return to this after examining two more new inscriptions on Xenophon's family, honoring respectively his wife (Segre, *I.Cos*, EV 205) and one of his ancestors (ibid., 237).

In the first of these inscriptions the council (*boula*) and the people of Kos honor Βαιβίαν Γαΐου θυγατέ/ρα Ῥουφίναν, τὰν γυ/ναῖκα Γαΐου Στερτινί/ου Ξενοφῶντος. Her name looks Roman, perhaps more so than most of the family's female names. Xenophon's mother was Hedeia, his sister-in-law Phoibe (a living connection with local mythology).[69] Other possible female relatives had equally traditional names (see below). Not only the cognomen but the whole Roman name of Rufina (the filiation properly expressed and placed; a gentilicium that cannot be apparently connected with any important political *patronus* of a Koan family in the past) strongly suggests an origin outside the island. The question is, of course, whether Xenophon "imported" his lady from his circle of Roman connections or married a woman from the community of Roman families that had resided on Kos since the Republican period.[70] Baebii appear in the Aegean under the Republic;[71] it remains to be seen when their first traces on Kos can be dated. As far as I can see, there are currently only four other cases of Baebii known on Kos: (a) Βαιβία Σεβῆρα Ματρῶνα in *PH*, 135, which for prosopographical (see below) and palaeographical reasons should belong to the late second/third century A.D. (b) Baebia Maxima in a Latin inscription (Herzog, *KF*, 165) postdating 161 A.D. (c) A *monarchos* Βαίβιος Δημήτριος in a manumission from Kalymna (Segre, *TC*, 197). Segre dates the whole dossier of manumissions inscribed on Apollo's temple in Kalymna to the period from Tiberius to the end of Claudius,[72] but the latter time limit is certainly too early for some of these inscriptions (see below, p. 114). Thus even in this third case we cannot be sure whether the *monarchos* Baebius Demetrius is at least roughly contemporary with (he is certainly not considerably older than) Xenophon's wife. (d) The fourth testimony is Segre, *I.Cos*, ED 66

---

[69] Cf. Herzog, *N&X*, 227. Phoibe, Koios' wife, should have born her daughter Leto on Kos: *Herod., Mim.* II.98; *Tac., Ann.*, 12.61.1 (cf. Sherwin-White, *Cos*, 300f.).

[70] The best, concise picture of the history of the Roman community on Kos is still that by Sherwin-White, *Cos*, 250-255. Cf. also below, p. 146ff.

[71] There is a M.Baebius in a catalogue of *must(ae)* at Samothrace: *IG* XII.8, 207.15 (ca. middle of the first century B.C., cf. Hatzfeld, 59f., n.2). On further, imperial examples of Baebii from the Aegean area, some of which could go back to Italian emigrants of the Republican period: A.J.S.Spawforth, "Roman Corinth: The Formation of a Colonial Elite," in: *Rizakis, R.Onomastics*, 172; S.Zoumbaki, "Die Verbreitung der römischen Namen in Eleia," ibid., 201.

[72] Segre, *TC*, p. 172.

and contains a mention of [B]αιβίου Σ[---, followed after a line by another of some Τιβερίου Κλ[αυδίου --- (s. further on this inscription below). Here too, by the present evidence, the beginning of social ascent for Baebii on Kos seems to have occurred during the reign of Claudius, at least approximately. On balance, we should then not exclude the possibility that Rufina was one of Xenophon's acquisitions during his imperial service outside Kos.[73]

Xenophon's ancestry is also enriched with a new person in Segre, *I.Cos*, EV 237 (the basis of a statue):]ΛΙ [Ο]Σ Ἡρακλε[ί]/[του, π]ρόγονος τοῦ/ [εὐ]εργέτα Ξενο/φῶντος.[74] The inscription is dated (ibid.) to the first century A.D. Who may be that [π]ρόγονος ? If we look for suitable combinations of names on Kos,[75] the only attested possibility seems to be Φιλιάς Ἡρακλείτου, a female name known from a catalogue in the deme of Isthmos (ca. beginning of the second century B.C.).[76] Of course, this is just a possibility[77] suggested by the conservatism of Greek, and especially Koan, onomastics (cf. Xenophon's own name). What is certain is that we have here for the first time a mention of a *paternal* ancestor or ancestress of Xenophon, somewhat remote (to be termed just πρόγονος) but nonetheless worthy of some public representation because of his/her place in Xenophon's family tree.

Finally, there is a concrete example where we do have full names and an express statement of relationship to Xenophon: the important couple of Γάιος Ἰούλιος Διονυσίου υἱὸς Φαβίᾳ Ἀντίπατρος and Ἰουλία Πολυδεύκους θυγάτηρ Νικαγορίς in Segre, *I.Cos*, EV 219. This is one of the new honorary inscriptions for Xenophon, erected by this couple and their children for their "relative (τὸν συ[γ]/γενῆ) as an expression of their thanks and favor" (ll. 19-20). At first sight there seems to be no possible

---

[73] We may notice that one of Xenophon's "colleagues" in that period was C.Baebius Atticus, procurator of Claudius in Noricum: *PIR*[2] B 11; cf. G.Winkler, *RE* Suppl. XIV(1974), s.v. Baebius (21), 70f. There is also a C.Baebius P.f., *IIvir quinq(uennalis)* in Dium under Tiberius (ibid.).

[74] Segre commented on the form of the text: "Delle prime lettere è conservato soltanto il basso." His reading is supported by the published photograph: the traces of Λ, I and Σ at the beginning and the space of just one letter between I and Σ seem verified.

[75] In Sherwin-White, *Cos*, Onomastikon, s.v. Ἡράκλειτος (p. 455ff.) and Fraser-Matthews, s. eadem v. (p. 204 II).

[76] Carratelli, *Isthmos*, IX c 12, 27, 42 (p.172f.).

[77] The gap at the beginning of Segre, *I.Cos*, EV 237 would thus be satisfactorily restored: There seems to have been space there for three to four letters but the first line may have been a little indented as in other examples (e.g. Maiuri, *NS*, 468, 469). In view of the following discussion of Xenophon's extended family, it is perhaps noteworthy that the name Philias appears in the onomastic lists of Isthmos in familial connection with all three names Herakleitos, Nikagoras and Alkidamos (on the latter two: Carratelli, *Isthmos*, IX a 72 (p. 169); XXVI B, viii.19f., 27f. (p.200)).

connection to substantiate this claim of relationship. No Antipatros and no Dionysios are known from Kos (among the five and fourteen respective bearers of these names there)[78] that would have appeared in conjunction with one of the names known from Xenophon's family. As for Nikagoris, both her name and that of her father, Polydeukes, are unattested on Kos (hers also in the whole area of the islands).[79] Antipatros styles himself (apart from the titles φιλόκαισαρ and φιλοσέβαστος, on which see below) as χιλίαρχος καὶ ἀποδεδειγ-μένος τῆς Ἀσίας ἀρχιερεὺς θεᾶς Ῥώμης καὶ θεο[ῦ] Σεβαστοῦ Καίσαρος Διὸς Πατρῴιου (ll. 15-6). So he had also acquired an apparently titular tribunate, as had Xenophon's uncle, and had then been designated [80] high priest of Rome and Augustus in the province of Asia—an illustrious, much desired position for ambitious aristocrats of the cities of Asia.[81] Perhaps the boost Xenophon was able to give to his "relative" by this candidacy (probably also in getting the tribunate) was the prime motive for Antipatros' grateful reaction on Kos.

Are we to suppose that Antipatros resided or was born on Kos? Nothing seems to impose such a conclusion. There is no other Iulius Antipater/Dionysius known from Kos and, as far as I can see (see the final chapter), Kos was not a part of the *provincia Asia* in this time. Besides, this is the only honorary text for Xenophon in which no elements of the Doric dialect can be found,[82] a probable indication of non-Koan (quite possibly Ionian) origin. So one has the impression that Antipatros was, at least, a resident of a city in Asia Minor whose connection with Kos was limited to an expression of gratitude towards his powerful "relative" in the latter's homecity. We may also notice that Antipatros was a Iulius (he correctly mentions the tribus of the Iulii, Fabia):[83] insofar he seems to belong to a family established in provincial Roman society before Xenophon's closer relatives.

Where could the link of that more distant relationship lie? Perhaps the rare name Nikagoris could provide a clue. Like many female names

---

[78] Fraser-Matthews, s.vv. (pp. 47 I, 137 III).

[79] Ibid., s.v. Πολυδεύκης (p. 377 II), no entry Νικαγορίς.

[80] Cf. Mason, s.v. ἀποδείκνυμι (p. 24).

[81] Cf. Campanile, esp. 162-171. This Antipatros is now to add to her list of high priests of Asia.

[82] So we have the forms δήμου υἱόν (l. 3), εὐεργέτην (l. 4), Ἀσκληπιοῦ (l. 7) etc. Cf. the examples of Greek dedicatory inscriptions regularly expressed in the home dialect of the dedicant, that is not in the (possibly different) one spoken at the place of the dedication, in the still useful study by C.D.Buck, "The Interstate Use of the Greek Dialects," *CPh* 8(1913), 135ff.

[83] Cf. J.W.Kubitschek, *Imperium Romanum tributim descriptum*, (Prague 1889 = Rome 1972) 270.

this one, too, could be simply the female coordinate of a common male name in the family: cf. e.g. the pairs Ptolemaios-Ptolemais, Antiochos-Antiochis in the Hellenistic royal houses and abundant examples from the onomastic material of Kos itself.[84] So Nikagoris, an unicum in the onomastics of the Aegean islands, could simply come from a family where Nikagoras was a frequently given male name, perhaps the name of her own grandfather. Now, what we gain by this observation is that Nikagoras is not only a frequently found name on Kos but also one that may appear in connection with other name-links—finally leading to a possible line of relationship with Xenophon.

Before proceeding, however, we should examine another Koan family whose exact relation to Xenophon has also been a problem: the distinguished Koan family of Ti.Claudii Iuliani. It is obvious that this family owed its Roman citizenship to either Claudius or Nero, with the former more probable (because of his special relationship with Kos). It is equally probable that Xenophon was personally responsible for the family's gaining the *civitas*. A fragmentary inscription in the British Museum (*PH*, 46) seems strongly to suggest this and, even more, the family's relation to Xenophon. We have here the preserved left part of what looks like a list of Koan *euergetai*[85] and, subsequently, a list of competitors in some sort of games. Xenophon's name and usual titles (see below) may be restored with certainty first in the list of these benefactors. On the second place of the same list we find Τιβε.[Κλαύδιος, Ξενοφῶντος υἱὸς]/ Φιλεῖνος, that is Xenophon's maternal uncle. On the third place Paton has quite plausibly restored the name of a well-known man in Koan prosopography: Τιβε. Κλαύδι[ος.....Τιβερίου Κλαυδίου]/ Νικαγόρα υἱός, Ἀλκίδαμο[ς Ἰουλιανός... A mention of another Ἀ]/λκιδάμω... appears next and finally, before the list of competitors begins, a "son of Charmylos" and a Φιλοφρίω[ν]. The impression is that very distinguished Koans were mentioned here (see above on the various Charmyloi), and that Ti.Claudius Alcidamus Iulianus, son of Ti.Claudius Nicagoras[86] coming directly after Xenophon's uncle should be not only

---

[84] So Anthagoris, daughter of Anthagoras (*PH*, 10 d 58); Zopyris, daughter of Zopyros (*PH*, 389.2); Theudoris, daughter of Theudoros (Carratelli, *Isthmos*, IX a 13, p. 165); Aristagore, daughter of Aristagoras (Carratelli, *PP* 24(1969), 128f., no.3); Hekataia, daughter of Hekatodoros (*PH* 398.3-4); Kallistrate, daughter of Kallistratos (Carratelli, *Isthmos*, IX a 105, p.171); Onasikleia, daughter of Onasikles (ibid., IX a 75, p. 169); Sopatra, daughter of Sopatros (ib., XXVI B, iii 73, p. 193); Nikation, daughter of Nikandros (ibid., IX a 35, p. 167).

[85] Just before the list we find the fragmentary mentions: τὸ δεύτερον οἶδε [--- λ]όγον κατ' εὐεργεσ[ίαν (ll.2-3).

[86] The form of his name is ascertained by the testimonies of the father and the son in Koan inscriptions (see below).

roughly contemporary with him but probably also somehow related to his family. Herzog[87] saw this and correctly pointed to the common use of the name ἥρως for Xenophon, Ti.Claudius Nicagoras Iulianus[88] and his son Ti.Claudius Alcidamus in Koan epigraphy, indicating a certain similarity of status and political recognition (see below).

A certain and basic familial link between Xenophon and the Claudii Iuliani could have then been already deduced from the proud genealogy of a descendant of the latter in Maiuri, *NS*, 461. Here on the base of an honorary statue the inscription mentions its erection, according to a decision of council and people, for Κλαυδίαν Ῥουφεῖναν Ἰουλιανὴν[89] θυγατέρα Κλαυδίου Νικαγόρα Ἰουλιανοῦ ἀπόγονον Ἀσκληπιαδῶν καὶ Ἡρακλειδῶν. Her brother, homonymous with their father (Claudius Nicagoras Iulianus) had covered the costs of the monument. It should be clear that this lady—despite the omission of the praenomen Tiberius in her own, (already on palaeographical grounds)[90] later phase of the family—belonged to the same Claudii Iuliani,[91] and traced her family's ancestry back to the Asclepiads and Heraclids.[92]

That this claim of a heroic pedigree now recurs, with true genealog-

---

[87] Herzog, *KF*, 197, esp. n. 3: "...Trotz ihrer (: the family's of these Nikagoras and Alkidamos) Verbindung mit Xenophons Familie in PH 46 ist ein verwandschaftlicher Zusammenhang aus unserem Material nicht zu konstatieren. Vielleicht verschwägerten sie sich mit einander," cf. 135. Cf. Segre, *TC*, p. 192.

[88] Herzog (ibid., no. 212) identified him with Nikagoras, son of Eudamos; cf. below.

[89] Ἰούλιαν ἣν in Maiuri (ibid.) is an obvious inadvertence.

[90] Notice esp. the forms of omega in Maiuri's facsimile and cf. below, p. 115f. on their approximate date.

[91] It is also significant that she is styled here ἡρωίδα (l. 7), the heroic designation having also adorned some of the male members of the same family (see above).

[92] This Claudia Rufina, without the *agnomen* Iuliana but with the same claim to Asclepiad and probably Heraclid (restored!) descent, seems now to reappear (rather in her mature years) in another honorary inscription from Herzog's notebooks published by G.Pugliese Carratelli, "ΑΠΟΓΟΝΟΙ ΑΣΚΛΗΠΙΟΥ ΚΑΙ ΗΡΑΚΛΕΟΥΣ," in: *Storia, poesia e pensiero nel mondo antico. Studi in onore di M.Gigante*, (Napoli 1994) 543-547. The same text seems also to provide evidence for another brother of Claudia Rufina, and dedicant of the monument, whose name appears in Herzog/Carratelli's edition as [Τιβερίου Κλαυδίου / Νικ]αγ[ό]ρα υἱοῦ Ἀλκι]/δ[άμου]. However, the extent of restoration renders the whole name (the use of the praenomen included!) uncertain.

The claim of heroic descent is a frequent and historically eloquent trait in the behavior of the Greek elites—especially in the imperial period. Other examples and analyses (with further literature): J.Touloumakos, Συμβολὴ στὴν ἔρευνα τῆς ἱστορικῆς συνειδήσεως τῶν Ἑλλήνων στὴν ἐποχὴ τῆς ῥωμαϊκῆς κυριαρχίας, (Athens 1972) 62; W.Ameling, *Herodes Atticus, I.Biographie*, (Hildelsheim 1983) 3f.; Chaniotis, *H&H*, 225f.; Nigdelis, 105f.; Ch. Kritzas, "Δύο ἐπιγράμματα ἀπὸ τὸ Πετρὶ Νεμέας," in: Πρακτικὰ Διεθνοῦς Συνεδρίου γιὰ τὴν Ἀρχαία Θεσσαλία στὴ μνήμη τοῦ Δ.Ρ.Θεοχάρη, (Athens 1992) 402; Quaß, *Hon.*, 71-73.

ical precision, in Segre, *I.Cos*, EV 224 further supports the belief.[93] Despite the fragmentary state of the text, the preserved right end of the stone helps render Segre's restorations certainly correct. We have here again an honorary statue decreed by the council and the people,[94] for

Τιβέ/ριον Κλαύδ]ιον Τιβερίο[υ Κλαυδίου υἱὸν Ἀλκίδαμον Ἰου[λιανόν,/ ἀπόγον]ον Ἀσκληπιο[ῦ μὲν/ ἀπὸ γ]ενειᾶν ΛΕ Ἡ[ρακλέ/ους ἀπὸ] Ν̄, καὶ συγγεν[ῆ ὄν/τα πολλ]ῶν ἀνδρῶν τ[ετιμα/μένων ἀρ]ετᾶς ἕνεκα [καὶ/ εὐνοίας τᾶς] ἐς αὐτὸν (sc. τὸν δᾶμον)....

So this man, one of Claudia Rufina Iuliana's forefathers (see below), boasted of an exact descent from Asklepios and Herakles (by thirty five and fifty generations respectively) as well as of a relationship to many other persons of public renown.

It is clear that at least a part of this glorious ancestry coincided with Xenophon's, who also claimed to be an Asclepiad. Thus a remote but nonetheless important relationship of Xenophon's family with the Claudii Iuliani can be substantiated. We should also notice that Xenophon and the Claudii Iuliani are the only known cases of descent traced back expressly to Asklepios on Roman Kos.[95]

Further links can be recognized: (a) Claudia Rufina Iuliana bore the same cognomen as Xenophon's wife (Baebia Rufina). Of course, this is a widespread Roman female cognomen. Nevertheless, I can find only these two examples on Kos. (b) One of the last known scions of the Claudii Iuliani, Ti.Claudius Tullus etc. (see below on his long full name) was the husband of the Baebia Severa Matrona mentioned above as one of the few examples of Baebii on Kos. Perhaps the two families were interrelated through several generations—a tendency to endogamy has been noticed already in Hellenistic Kos (cf. Stavrianopoulou).

An examination of the beginnings of the Claudii Iuliani as a separate family may also establish some links with Xenophon. As already suggested above, and now made more probable through the preceding exposition, the Claudii Iuliani should have acquired their Roman citizenship under Claudius. However, this explains only their gentilicium (and praenomen, when they bear it); their familial agnomen, Iuliani, remains a problem. Salomies' recent, penetrating study of Roman adoptive and amplified name-forms under the Empire has shown,

---

[93] Carratelli, *Isthmos*, 151 had already made the "genealogical part" of this inscription known. Cf. Sherwin-White, *Cos*, 49, n. 104.

[94] The honorand has undertaken the costs: [δ]ι' αὐτοῦ at the end is a misprint for [δ]ι' αὐτοῦ.

[95] The claim of a descent from Herakles also in Segre, *I.Cos*, EV 214b.

through many examples, that the names in -ianus, usually associated with an indication of the original gens by Roman adoptions in Republican times, have later simply referred to a relation of some sort with another gens.[96] This is also verified by the most polyonymous member of the Claudii Iuliani already alluded to above (and to be examined below). So it would be reasonable to look here, too, for some Iulii who might be in some way related to the Claudii Iuliani, this relationship somehow adding to the latter's prestige. Since Nikagoras and Alkidamos seem to be the only Greek male names alternating in the family (after their acquisition of the *civitas*, see below), we may think further that these must have been old family names, possibly also present in the nomenclature of the Iulii. Thus there is precedent to consider here Iulia Nikagoris daughter of Polydeukes whose man claimed a link of his/their family to Xenophon. Could these Iulii, obviously having found access to Roman citizenship before the Claudii Iuliani, be the relative "summarized" in *Iuliani*? This would fit perfectly and enrich both families' independently established or suggested connections with Xenophon and his own "smaller family." Based on present evidence we cannot go further.[97]

The Claudii Iuliani have played a longer role in Koan municipal life under the Empire, succeeding in this their distant, (very probably since Claudian times) "reconnected" relative Xenophon. So this broader circle of Xenophon's relations makes the rarity of his direct descendants' appearance on Kos more understandable. The earliest members of the Claudii Iuliani attested so far are the already mentioned Ti. Claudius Nicagoras and his son Ti.Claudius Alcidamus Iulianus. Apart from the already discussed list *PH* 46, they appear also in: (a) *PH* 106, the inscription of an honorary monument decreed by the council and the people for Alkidamos styled ἥρωα, [ἱε]ρε[έ]α [τ]ὸν ἐφηβ--- (1. 4). (b) Segre, *I.Cos*, EV 116, a similar monument for the father, styled as [σωτῆρα κα]ὶ εὐεργέτην (1. 5), which has been decreed by the *gerousia* of Kos and erected by Alkidamos. This inscription is also important because it shows that at this point Nikagoras was a Iulianus,[98] a detail

---

[96] Salomies, esp. 61, 84-87. Cf. also his earlier study and collection of relevant material from the Greek East in *Arctos* 18(1984), 97-104.

[97] We may notice the later Ti.Claudius Antipater Iulianus, *prytanis* of 104 in Ephesos (Vibius Salutaris' donation: *I.Ephesos*, 27). Could there be some connection of his both with C.Iulius Dionysii f. Antipater the Asiarch and the Claudii Iuliani of Kos?

[98] L. 3f.: [Τιβέριον] Κλαύδιον/ [Νικαγόραν Ἰο]υλιανόν. Cf. ll. 6ff.: [ἀνέθηκε τὸν ἀ]νδριάντα/ [τοῦ γλυκυτ]άτου πατρὸς /[Τιβέριος Κλ]αύδιος/ [Νικαγόρα υἱὸ]ς Ἀλκίδα/[μος Ἰουλι]ανός.

otherwise restored or omitted (as e.g. in the previous mention of his name in the filiation-formula of his son). (c) ibid., ED 66 (cf. above) where the existing small fragment of the stone presents the traces in ll. 3-4: Τιβερίου Κλ[αυδίου ---]/ Νεικαγόρα [---. So we cannot be sure whether we had here a mention of father or son. The whole inscription seems to be some form of a decree (ἐπιψηφισα[μένου or -ων in l. 2) and important Koans seem to be involved: apart from a Baebius (cf. above) at the beginning there is also possibly a mention of Φλα]ουίου Κλωδ[ιανοῦ in ll.4/5, a little after the name of Nikagoras. There was a *monarchos* Flavius Clodianus known from the Kalymnian manumissions and an inscription from the deme of the Hippiotai.[99] It would be tempting to recognize here a further mention of him, so that the document would most probably postdate the Iulio-Claudian period and thus refer to the son rather than the father. We cannot be sure and may keep simply a general impression of the kind of people father or son was somehow associated with in public documents. (d) ibid., EV 224 where the son appears as Asclepiad and Heraclid (see above). (e) Segre, *TC*, 181, a manumission dated ἐπὶ μο(νάρχου) Ἀλκιδάμου Ἰουλιανοῦ, the name of the son being here abbreviated, as usual in these formulas.[100]

The next generation of the family is then most probably represented by the gymnasiarch Τιβέριος Κλαύδιος Ἀλκιδάμου υἰὸς Ἀλκίδαμος known from the list of persons that found entrance into the *presbytika palaistra* in his term of office.[101] One of these new members, Ἕλενος Ἑλένου τοῦ Διονυσίου,[102] was probably the son of Helenos son of Dionysios who was priest of Apollo at Halasarna ca. 41 A.D.[103] He and another priest of Apollo at Halasarna (ca. 76 A.D.)[104] appear as members of a board of temple magistrates (ναπόαι) there implementing for the local deme the erection of a statue of Titus.[105] So a date of the gymnasiarch somewhere in the Flavian period fits the data well.[106] The gymnasiarch's name form

---

[99] Segre, *TC*, 167-172; Carratelli, *PP* 13(1958), 418f. His gentilicium is mentioned only in the first of these testimonies (see next n).

[100] Cf. Xenophon's own case in Segre, *TC*, 193, 194 (simply Ξενοφῶντος); ib., 167 (Φλαουίου Κλωδιανοῦ), 197 (Βαιβίου Δημητρίου), 202 (Αἰλίου Σαβεινιανοῦ). The combination of gentilicium and cognomen was apparently equally distinctive as that of cognomen and agnomen.

[101] Carratelli, *Rom.Cos*, 818f.= Segre, *I.Cos*, ED 228.

[102] Ibid., l. 25.

[103] Herzog, *Hal.*, no. 4, priest no. 68.

[104] L.Antonius L.f. Bassus, ibid., priest no. 103.

[105] Carratelli, *Rom.Cos*, 819.

[106] Carratelli, ibid., 818 dated the list to the first century A.D. "dopo il regno di Claudio" and already thought that the gymnasiarch could be the son of Ti. Claudius Alcidamus Iulianus of *PH* 106 and 46. Sherwin-White, *Cos*, 253 preferred a date under Claudius without argument.

does not include the component Iulianus. His exact name does appear partly, but safely, restored in Segre, *I.Cos*, EV 228:[107] he makes there a dedication, typical for his office, to Athana Alseia [ὑπὲρ τᾶς τῶν νέ]ων καὶ ἐφήβων κοσμίου φιλ[οπονίας] (1.2). It is noteworthy that in his name the filiation no longer includes the praenomen and gentilicium, that is, we have Ἀλκιδάμου and not Τιβερίου Κλαυδίου Ἀλκιδάμου. The identity of the cognomen by both father and son obviously inspired a simplification, which may have extended to a possible brother of the gymnasiarch appearing in Maiuri, *NS* 592 as Τιβερίου Κλαυδίου Ἀλκιδάμου υἱοῦ Ξενοκράτου. This tendency towards simplification will continue and develop further in the next generations.

So a descendant (grandson?) of the gymnasiarch was the "Spanish nobleman" of the family, lavishly styled as Τιβέριος Κλαύδιος Ἀλκιδάμου Τύλλος Ἰουλιανός Σπεδιανός Ἀλλιανός in *PH* 135. We may say that various strata of Roman intrusion and integration into the society of Kos are recognizable in this name. We should also recall that the name of this man was given here with genealogical precision and allusiveness by his wife Baebia Severa Matrona (see above), who was probably very keen on stressing all the ramifications of her provincial *Romanitas*. So the new relations of the family, more probably acquired between ca. the Flavian and the late Antonine period[108] included the Spedii and the Allii. The former reached on Kos a certain prominence to which we shall return later. In regard to the Allii, they most probably belonged to the old *gentes* of *negotiatores* who took up their residence at various points of the Aegean in the Republican period. They are characteristically, as already noticed in the past, one of those gentes who are represented both on Delos in Republican times and later, among other places, on Kos.[109] There seem to be three or now possibly four cases of

---

[107] L. 1: [Τιβέριος Κλαύδιο]ς Ἀλκιδάμο[υ υἱὸς Ἀλκίδα[μος Ἰουλιανός]. The inscription was originally published by Maiuri, *NS*, 447 and later studied by Höghammar, no. 38 (incorporating the corrections by G.De Sanctis, *RFIC* 54(1926), 61) before Segre's publication. She tried to date it in the latter half of the first century B.C. However, my personal inspection of the stone on Kos has shown that the letter forms (advanced apication) clearly point to a date in the first/second century A.D. Her restoration at the beginning of the genitive of a participle, [Παιδονομοῦντο]ς, will also not do: we clearly need there the name of the dedicant in the nominative. So Segre's restoration and date ("I sec. d.C.") are certainly to be preferred.

[108] The lettering of the inscription, especially the forms of Υ and Ω given by Paton (ibid.), fits a date in the late second/early third century A.D. Cf. below, p. 115f.

[109] Carratelli, *Rom.Cos*, 819; Sherwin-White, *Cos*, 252, n.182. Cf. Hatzfeld, esp. 384 and, more recently, on other Allii of relatively early date in the general Aegean area, the examples studied by F.Papazoglou, *Chiron* 18(1988), 237, no.3(Styberra/Macedonia, 50/1 A.D.) and C.Antonetti, in Rizakis, *R.Onomastics* 153f. (Trichonion/Aetolia, second century B.C. ?).

Allii known on Kos. Their first certain mention does not antedate the Flavian period, but they appear twice in connection with the life of the local gymnasia and also twice with typically Greek cognomina; so a longer integration into Koan society seems to have preceded that *terminus ante quem* of their inscriptional emergence. We have in all: the new admission into the *presbytika palaistra*, under Ti.Claudius Alcidami f. Alcidamus (see above), Σέξ(τος) Ἄλλιος Βάσσος;[110] he should be either identical or a relative (son?) of a now very probably testified *epimeletes* of the *gerousia*, appearing in a dedication to Vitellius.[111] There are then a [Σ]έξτος Ἄλλ[ι]ος Ἐπίκτητος πρεσβύτερος παιδοτρίβης[112] and an Ἀλλία Εὐτυχία on a tombstone.[113] Perhaps even more important than these testimonies of Allii on Kos is the case of a member of the more renowned Spedii (see below), a hereditary priest whose full name was M.Spedius Beryllus *Allianus Iulianus*.[114] It is a clear sign that the Allii had also reached a higher level of social recognition on Roman Kos by the early third century A.D. (see also below, p. 116ff. on this person and his date). So by Tullus' time the Claudii Iuliani seem to represent accurately the actual nexus of some of the most honorable Roman families on Kos.

While one tendency in the later generations of the family was a kind of "onomastic baroque," another branch developed a natural, and quite Greek, trend to simplicity. This applies to the branch of the family to which the aforementioned Claudia Rufina Iuliana (Maiuri, *NS*, 461) belonged. Her own name and those of her father and brother (both named Κλαύδιος Νικαγόρας Ἰουλιανός) do not include a praenomen. They consist only in the combination gentilicium+cognomen+agnomen. The lettering of this inscription also fits well a later date, and so the father could be a descendant of the gymnasiarch of the Flavian period (perhaps a great grandson?).[115]

It is somewhat more difficult to trace the Claudii Iuliani back to the period when they lacked a Roman identity. Herzog was inclined to accept the identification of their apparent Roman patriarch, Ti.Claudius

---

[110] Carratelli, *Rom.Cos*, 818= Segre, *I.Cos*, ED 228, 20.

[111] Segre, *I.Cos*, EV 255, 6-7. Segre has given here the text ...ἐπιμ. Σέξ(του)/ [...]ου Βάσσου but he has also cited in his short commentary the namesake in the list of the *presbytika palaistra* (see above). We may restore: ...Σέξ(του)/[Ἀλλί]ου Βάσσου.

[112] Herzog, *KF*, 112.

[113] Maiuri, *NS*, 651.

[114] *PH*, 103.

[115] Notice esp. the degree of the apication and the form of the "tripartite" omega (cf. below, p. 116) in Maiuri's facsimile. Cf. n. 92 above.

Nicagoras Iulianus (see above), with Nikagoras son of Eudamos to whom a dedicative inscription from Halasarna refers as φιλοπάτριδι, δάμου υἰῷ, ἥρωι, φιλοκαίσαρι.[116] Even if this man was dead by the time of this honor, the combination of the terms "hero" and "son of the people" is still important (cf. below on Xenophon's titles) and points to an eminent social position. The use of one of these terms (hero, see above) in the public nomenclature of Ti.Claudius Alcidamus Iulianus, the son of the same Ti.Claudius Nicagoras, could also be a further link.

It seems preferable, however, to place one generation between Nikagoras, son of Eudamos and the first Roman Nikagoras, making the second a grandson of the first, because of some further prosopographical observations. There is first the honorary inscription on the base of the statue erected by the Koan people for the distinguished local priestess, Minnis, daughter of Praylos. Segre, *I.Cos*, EV 226[117] recognized that in l. 2, after Minnis' patronymic, some further description of her identity should stay, and proposed: ἀνέϑηκεν Μιννίδα Πραΰλου [τοῦ---. Now, in ll.3-4 we find the obvious sequence of these further prosopographical data on Minnis in the form: τοῦ Εὐδάμου φιλοπάτριδος δά[μου υἰοῦ]/ φιλοκαίσαρος, ἱέρ(ε)ιαν. The beginning of this is so strongly reminiscent of the name and titles of Nikagoras son of Eudamos in the inscription cited above that I propose here the restoration, fitting the space available and the estimated average number of letters in each line: ἀνέϑηκεν Μιννίδα Πραΰλου [γυναῖκα δὲ Νικαγόρα]/ τοῦ Εὐδάμου φιλοπάτριδος δά[μου υἰοῦ ἥρωος]/ φιλοκαίσαρος...[118] What this text further discloses on Minnis makes this restoration of names and identities even more probable. For Minnis is mentioned as priestess of a whole range of local gods, including not only the traditional local triad of Asklepios, Hygieia, and Epiona but also Rhea, the Twelve Gods, Zeus Polieus, Athena Polias and, last but not least, [τοῦ Σεβαστοῦ]/ Καίσαρος (ll. 6/7). A little later on in the text we find mentioned that Minnis was [τε]/τιμαμέναν δὲ καὶ ὑπὸ τοῦ Σε[βαστοῦ Καίσαρος τε]/[[τιμαμέναν]] τιμαῖς μαρ[μαρίναις... (ll. 9-11). Minnis' extensive concentration of cult functions and imperial honors matches very well the status of Nikagoras son of Eudamos with his own impressive collection of public titles, and strengthens the view that they were consorts. However, although Segre (ibid.) dated this

---

[116] Herzog, *KF*, no. 212, p. 135.

[117] An improved edition of Maiuri, *NS*, 460.

[118] I am glad to see now that this restoration (and family connection) already occurred to Herzog and was mentioned in his notebooks: see Carratelli (n. 92), 545. Similar descriptions of a woman's identity by the names of both her father and her husband are noted in the honorary inscriptions of Kos: *PH*, 115; Höghammar, 4.

inscription to the period of Claudius, the two latter passages together can actually prove an Augustan date.[119] Minnis' husband should then also belong, approximately, to Augustus' time. This is further supported by the entry of a namesake (Νικαγόρας Εὐδάμου) in the Halasarnan priest-list ca. 9 A.D.,[120] also significant in this connection because of the local affinity with the inscription mentioning Nikagoras son of Eudamos as *heros* (see above). So we would unjustifiably condense the development of the family if we accepted that Claudius granted Roman citizenship in very advanced age to this same man, who was already so important under Augustus.

There is a further prosopographical note that may support this conclusion. In Segre, *I.Cos*, EV 72 we find another priestess honored by the people whose name is partly preserved: ---]κίδα Ἀλκιδάμου [θυγατέρα ?]/ κεχρηματικυῖαν[121] [---/...]ν Λυσιμάχου, ἱἐρ[ειαν/ διὰ] βίου Τιβερίου Κλα[υδίου Καίσαρος]. That this lady was also invested with an imperial priesthood (this time for Claudius) and that the name of her father was Alkidamos make some connection with the early, "pre-Roman" history of the Koan Claudii Iuliani look probable. An Alkidamos might so be inserted between the Augustan Nikagoras and his Claudian namesake through whom the family acquired Roman citizenship.

We should add that there are probably more links with the imperial cult in these earlier phases of the family's history than hitherto assumed. Another Nikagoras, son of Daliokles, priest of Apollo at Halasarna ca. 3 B.C.[122] is probably identical with both Nikagoras son of Daliokles who appears as priest Αὐτοκράτορος Καίσαρος Θεοῦ υἱο[ῦ] Σεβαστοῦ in a

---

[119] In both cases a considerably longer restoration, one that would only accommodate the official nomenclature of Tiberius or Claudius (cf. for example Maiuri, *NS*, 462.8 -11 or Segre, *I.Cos*, EV 219.6-7, also right below) may be excluded on the basis of the roughly estimated average of letters in the rest of the lines. On the other hand, cf. Patriarca, 10= Höghammar, 69.7-8 and Segre, *I.Cos*, EV 219.17 on Augustus' description simply as Σεβαστὸς Καῖσαρ on Kos. Of course, it would still be possible, textually, to add to the restored words in both gaps θεοῦ (cf. e.g. the last case cited), and so assume that the date of Minnis' honors was post-Augustan. The accumulation of priesthoods in the person of Minnis, however, makes it highly improbable that she would simply retain her role in Augustus' cult under one of the subsequent emperors.

[120] Herzog, *Hal.*, no. 4, priest no. 36.

[121] She was probably adopted into the house of Alkidamos, her physical father being a Lysimachos: cf. on this use of ἐχρημάτισα/κεχρημάτικα to denote a previous identity e.g. *SEG* 28.1255 and the cases in K.Buraselis, ΘΕΙΑ ΔΩΡΕΑ, (Athens 1989) 142-4. As for her name, a distinctly Koan possibility would be to restore Ναννα]κίδα, cf. Fraser-Matthews, s.v. (p. 323 I).

[122] Herzog, *Hal.*, no.4, priest no. 25.

decree at the deme of Haleis[123] and the magistrate ΝΙΚΑΓΟΡΑΣ ΔΑ(ΛΙΟΚΛΕΟΥΣ) known from the Koan coins of the Augustan age.[124] He might be a somewhat older relative of Nikagoras son of Eudamos. Eudamos/Eudemos was then also the name of a priest of C.Iulius Caesar under Augustus at Kos, Eudemos son of Epikrates, known from a fragmentary Koan decree found at Olympia.[125] He could very well be the father of the same Nikagoras Eudamou above.

To sum up, Xenophon's larger network of Koan relations seems to have closely and continually connected itself especially with the imperial cult (and the rest of the cults of the island, sometimes in accumulative fashion as in the case of Minnis Praylou). This accords well both with the family's involvement in the forefront of local politics for generations and with one of Xenophon's own habits of inserting himself in an unprovocative but efficient way into the provincial Roman microcosmos of Kos, especially after his apparent retirement there following the death of Claudius. We deal with this subject next.

---

[123] *PH*, 344.1-3. The beginning of the decree (issued by the citizen and other residents of Haleis and Pele) presents a double date after the *monarchos* and this priest of Augustus, a parallel local date after the acting *damarchos* coming at the end. Thus it should be a pan-Koan, not a demotic, priesthood of the imperial cult that we encounter here (*contra* Paton, ibid.).

[124] Burnett, *RPC*, 2732 (p. 453). Herzog, *Hal.*, 488 already identified the three homonymous persons. He also expressed the interesting thought that the names of the local magistrates on the Koan coins with Augustus' head could be those of his Koan priests (and not the traditional responsible magistrates). In the only testimony of a double date, however, the decree from Haleis mentioned, the traditional date after the *monarchos* comes first, the date after the priest of Augustus second, thus having a supplementary character.

[125] *IvOl* 53. See further below, p. 134.

Stemma of Xenophon's larger family including the Claudii Iuliani

c. The imperial doctor on Kos. Titulature and official integration into Koan civic life and society.

Unlike Nikias, Xenophon never suffered a local form of *damnatio memoriae* on Kos. Thus various aspects of his personality and imperial as well as local career are celebrated not only in the most numerous surviving collection of private small dedications to the "paternal gods" (listed in Appendix 3), of the type launched under Nikias, but also in a large number of longer honorary inscriptions. Furthermore, he is found twice offering himself an epitome of his official positions and titles in dedications he presented to his final imperial patron, Nero. The proper historical interpretation of this material is very important because— among other things—it may help understand better Xenophon's relations to his city of origin. It may also indicate the mode in which he managed to insert his imported power and authority into that local socio-political framework.

Let us begin with the two dedicative inscriptions by Xenophon himself. The one is *PH* 92 in which he appears as the dedicant of a monument Ἀσκλαπιῶ Καίσαρι Ἀγαθῶ Θεῶ (ll. 5-7). Asklepios is here (cf. *PH* 130 and below) identified with the emperor who is also *Agathos Theos*. This latter identification is very interesting, because it combines an alignment with local religious tradition, in which Agathos Theos seems to have been a popular deity appearing in connection with Agatha Tycha, the Damos and other gods.[126] Trends of the imperial cult in other areas are equally significant. Nero appears as Ἀγαθὸς Δαίμων on Alexandrian coins and Egyptian documents.[127] Thus Herzog has already reached the right conclusion that the emperor to whom Xenophon dedicated the monument of *PH* 92 was Claudius' successor.[128] The dedicant styles himself here as εὐεργέτας τᾶς πατρίδος καὶ ἱερεὺς διὰ βίου (obviously of Asklepios Nero). Xenophon's other dedication stood on the basis of the cult statues in a small temple by the staircase of the middle terrace of the Asklepieion:

---

[126] Collection and discussion of the evidence in Sherwin-White, *Cos*, 361f. On the connection of Agathos Daimon and Agathe Tyche in the Hellenistic world, see also esp. Fraser, *PA*, I.210 (+ II.358, n.s).

[127] E.Christiansen, *The Roman Coins of Alexandria*, (Aarhus 1988) I.38ff. (passim); Burnett, *RPC*, 5210, 5219, 5230, 5240, 5249, 5260. *P.Oxy.* 1021= *Sel.Pap.*, II.235. *OGIS* 666= *IGRR* I-II.1110. Cf. R.Ganschinietz, *RE* Suppl. III (1918), s.v. Agathodaimon, 47.

[128] Herzog, *KF*, 196. Cf. id., *N&X*, 242.

Ἀσκλαπιῶι Καίσαρι Σεβαστῶι καὶ Ὑγίαι/ καὶ Ἠπιόνη ὁ ἱερεὺς
αὐτῶν διὰ βίου/ Γάιος Στερτίνιος Ἡρακλείτου/ υἱὸς Κορνηλία
Ξενοφῶν φιλο/ρώμαιος [[φιλονέρων]] φιλό/καισαρ φιλοσέβαστος
φιλό/πατρις δάμου υἱὸς εὐσεβὴς / εὐεργέτας τᾶς πατρίδος ἥρως/
ἀνέθηκεν.[129]

There is no alternative for Xenophon's erased title on l. 5.[130] Thus this
inscription, too, belongs into Xenophon's post-Claudian period on Kos
(cf. on both points below).

In both texts, Xenophon has silenced his Roman career. In the
shorter self-presentation he is simply the benefactor of his homecity and
priest of Asklepios Caesar Agathos Theos. In the longer one a closely
similar priesthood and his quality as *euergetes* appear again respectively
as the introduction and the end of a larger group of titles to be examined
below. The imperial doctor exhibits tact in describing himself on Kos as
the generous citizen and faithful worshipper of both the imperial and the
local gods. It does not seem to be by chance that two further brief
presentations of his personality highlight the same features. These are
Segre, *I.Cos*, EV 95, an inscription on a marble block (probably the base
of a statue) where he is simply ὁ εὐεργέτα[ς], and a coin type of the
imperial age from Kos where his bare, youthful portrait and name are
accompanied by the attributive legend [I]ΕΡΕΥ[Σ] on the obverse
while the serpent-staff appears on the reverse.[131] Segre's dating of that
mention of "the benefactor" in Xenophon's early career for the reason
that "manca tutta la titolatura normale" is not convincing. Conciseness
can have been useful in all periods in accordance with the nature of the
respective monument, and perhaps we should not underestimate the force
of the definite article: Xenophon was not "(a) benefactor" but "the
benefactor." On the otherhand, the coins need not belong to Xenophon's
time.[132] We cannot say more on the basis of the description and
photographs published. He could have been remembered later and
celebrated on Koan coinage as "priest"—this obviously being another
basic quality of his in the official local edition of his historical portrait. A
variation of that titular pair appears on the short dedication of an *exhedra*

---

[129] Originally published by Herzog, *AA* 1903, p. 193. Republished by Patriarca, 19=
AnÉp 1934, 93.
[130] Φιλοκλαύδιος would be too long for the space available. We also have an erasure of
φιλονέρωνα in *PH* 345.11. Cf. Herzog, *KF*, p.198≈ Segre, *TC*, 111.11-12 (...φιλονέρω/νος,
φιλοκλαυδίου..., neither title erased here).
[131] *BMC Caria* 215. Cf. ibid. 212-214: the bare head of ΞΕΝΟΦΩΝ (obv.)/ Hygieia
feeding serpent, ΚΩΙΩΝ (rev.).
[132] Cf. for example the posthumous appearance of Theophanes on the coins of Mytilene:
D.Salzmann, *MDAI(R)* 92(1985), 254-6, 258-60.

to Xenophon by the people (or the city) of Kos at the Asklepieion[133] where *heros* takes the place of the priestly function. His basic quality as "the benefactor of his homecity" remains the only other aspect of his personality included (see below on this combination).

An equally short but more secular (and pragmatic) view of Xenophon appears on the base of a hermaic stele apparently crowned with his portrait. The dedicant is here a freedman of Xenophon honoring τὸ[ν/ ἀρχίατρον] τῶν Σεβαστῶν καὶ εὐεργέ/[ταν τὰς πα]τρίδος (Segre, *I.Cos*, EV 245). We may also think of restoring here τὸ[ν/ ἀρχιερέα] τῶν Σεβαστῶν. Such a form of the *archiereus*-title, however, has not been preserved for Xenophon thus far, while there is a similar mention of his imperial doctorship (on both points see below), so that Segre's restoration is equally possible.

Xenophon's medical acumen and its recognition in imperial service is mentioned in four of the five longer preserved honorary inscriptions for him.[134] In the first of these, Xenophon appears as *archiatros* of the *Theoi Sebastoi*, in the rest simply as *archiatros*. Only in the honorary inscription of the altar dedicated by the Kalymnians and Kalymnian residents to Apollo for Xenophon's health and preservation is any mention of his medical service omitted.[135] Thus his medical service at the emperor's court was regularly (and rightly) deemed to be the basis for his entire Roman career (see above). The term *archiatros* itself deserves some comment. It does not seem to have been, at least in the early empire, a strictly defined imperial post but rather a high-court title, loosely applied to distinguished doctors of emperors, a direct legacy of Hellenistic etiquette.[136] It is noteworthy that Claudius refers to his doctor

---

[133] *PH* 93: [---] τὰν ἐξέδραν Γαίω Στερτινίω Ἡρακλείτου/ [---υἱῶ Κ]ορνηλία Ξενοφῶντι ἥρωι τῶ τᾶς πατρίδος εὐερ/γέτα εὐχαρ[ιστίας] χάριν.

[134] *PH* 345 (a dedication of a public or religious body on Kos); Maiuri, *NS*, 475 (dedicant unknown); Segre, *I.Cos*, EV 219 (from the monument erected for him by C.Iulius Antipater, see above); ibid., 241 (dedicants: council and people of Kos, cf. above).

[135] Segre, *TC*, 111. A possible explanation for this omission might lie in the close modeling of this Neronian inscription after the standard, older text of the dedications to the "paternal gods" for Xenophon (see below) in which this aspect is also absent. The same model seems to have influenced the relevant part of Maiuri, *NS*, 459 (: Xenophon's "picture" inside the honorary inscription for his mother). However, on five of those small monuments (see Appendix 3) we find an iconographical allusion to Xenophon's profession: the representation of a snake or a staff with serpent, in relief or engraved, points to the Asclepiad honorand's craft. Cf. also the symbol of staff with serpent following some of the entries in the Halasarnan priest list (Herzog, *Hal.*, no. 4, priests nos. 85, 105,113, 116) and Benedum, 240.

[136] On Hellenistic and imperial *archiatr(o)i*, see now concisely V.Nutton, *Der Neue Pauly* 1(1996), s.v. Archiatros, 990f. (with bibl.). Also the cases collected in Sapelli (n. 42 above), cf. *SEG* 36.929 (comm.)., and now Marasco (n. 42 above), 280ff. (final

in the second of his three still unpublished letters to the Koans (see, p. 138ff. below) simply as τοῦ ἰατροῦ μου. The same plain term for Xenophon's chief occupation and source of influence on the emperors is found on the base of another honorary monument for him on Kos: ... Ξενοφῶντα γενόμενον ἰατρὸν/ θεοῦ Κλαυδίου Καίσαρος.[137] Both aspects, the relative informality of *archiatros* and the fundamental importance of Xenophon's medical skill in and outside Rome are finally verified in the inscription[138] in which the *damos* of Kalymna honors Philinos as uncle "of Claudius' physician" (ἰατροῦ Τιβερίου Κλαυδίου Καίσαρος).

As for Xenophon's distinctly Koan functions, it is equally noteworthy (and was noticed long ago by Herzog)[139] that no list of the great benefactor's specific posts and titles includes his tenure in the highest local magistracy. But we happen to know from the dating formulas of two Kalymnian manumissions that Xenophon was twice *monarchos*.[140] He and his honorers seem never to have alluded to it, however, (in contrast for example with his own brother's practice, cf. above). How should we understand this omission? A chronological explanation, i.e. the (certain) tenure of this office in the Neronian period of his life and retirement to Kos, seems improbable because—as we shall see—two of the four longer honorary inscriptions for him (as well as his self-presentations cited above) also postdate Claudius' death. The explanation rather lies in the relative unimportance of this iterated *monarchia* inside Xenophon's local sphere, in obvious contrast with his accumulation of priesthoods, which we examine next. Furthermore, Xenophon might have exhibited locally a sort of constitutional tact, quite like the Augustan practice with which he must have been acquainted in Rome. It would be perhaps too provocative to emphasize his tenure in the eponymous magistracy as an expression of abiding power.[141] Thus he sought the confirmation of his local authority on safer ground.

Before we proceed to an analysis of Xenophon's various Koan priesthoods, we can now assign a Claudian or a Neronian date to the

---

"officialization" of the *archiatros* post in Late Antiquity).On the Koan background of the title (and here, probably, city office): Sherwin-White, *Cos*, 281-3.

[137] Segre, *I.Cos*, EV 221. Claudius should be dead here (γενόμενον, θεοῦ).

[138] Segre, *TC*, 146. Cf. above.

[139] Herzog, *KF*, 196.

[140] *Segre, TC*, 193.1 (Ἐπὶ Μ τὸ Β Ξενοφῶντος...), 194.1-2 (Ἐπὶ μο(νάρχου) Κλεωνύμου τοῦ Κλευάντου μετὰ μό(ναρχον) τὸ Β Ξενοφῶντα...); on his simple mention as Ξενοφῶντος cf. n. 100 above). There is possibly also a mention of Xenophon as *monarchos* in Segre, *I.Cos*, EV 51[bis]. 6-7 (restored).

[141] Segre, ib., 3-5 has hypothetically restored ...τὸν μόν[αρχον/ καὶ μοναρχή]σαντα πλ[εονά/κις... We could also restore [γυμνασιαρχή]σαντα.

inscriptions where they appear, relying on two criteria: (a) the presence/absence of the title φιλονέρων (on its content see below)—regularly erased—for Xenophon in the original text, and (b) Claudius' mention as *divus*. According to them, Segre, *I.Cos*, EV 219 and 241 (in both Xenophon is φιλοκλαύδιος but not φιλονέρων, in EV 219 Claudius is not *divus* yet) antedate and *PH* 345 (φιλονέρων erased, cf. below) and Maiuri, *NS*, 475 (ll. 2-3: ...τοῦ Αὐτοκράτορος Κλαυδίου Καίσαρος ϑεοῦ)[142] postdate Claudius' assassination and Xenophon's apparently definitive return to Kos.[143] Even this elementary chronological frame, completed by the Neronian date of Xenophon's own dedications mentioned above, seems to let a certain development of his significant priestly offices on Kos gradually emerge.

In the Claudian period Xenophon appears as ἱαρέ[α διὰ]/ βίου Σεβαστοῦ[144] and as ἱερέα διὰ βίου τῶν Σεβαστῶ[ν]/ καὶ Τιβερίου Κλαυδίου Καίσαρος Σεβαστοῦ Γ[ερ]/μανικοῦ αὐτοκράτορος καὶ Ἀσκληπιοῦ καὶ [Ὑ]/γείας καὶ Ἠπιόνης καὶ κατὰ γένος Ἀπόλλ[ω]/νος Καρνίου καὶ Σεβαστῆς Ῥέας.[145]

So we find Xenophon during his residence under Claudius in Rome (at least for most of his time), having first assumed apparently a lifelong priesthood of Sebastos (Claudius) alone and then a lifelong, enlarged priesthood of the Sebastoi (obviously the previous Augusti), Claudius and the local Koan triad of Asklepios, Hygieia and Epione. To the latter a hereditary priesthood of Apollo Karneios and Sebaste Rhea (Agrippina)[146] has been added.

---

[142] The significance of the word is also proved by Maiuri, *NS*, 462.8-11: ...ἱερέα ἐπὶ βίου Τιβερίου Καίσαρος Σεβαστοῦ καὶ Τιβερίου Κλαυδίου Καίσαρος Γερμανικοῦ Σεβαστοῦ ϑεοῦ..., where the omission of ϑεοῦ after Tiberius' name is obviously due to the well-known fact that he was not deified posthumously: *D.C.*, 60.4.6 (cf. 59.3.7, 9.1); *Tac., Ann.*, 4.38; *Dessau* 6088.XXVI, 6089.LIX. Cf. K.Latte, *Römische Religionsgeschichte*, (München 1960) 318 and J.Kirchner on *IG* II-III² 3264. On *divus* Claudius always basic: M.P.Charlesworth, *JRS* 27(1937), 57ff.

[143] Cf. Herzog, *X&N*, 240ff.; Sherwin-White, *Cos*, 151.

[144] Segre, *I.Cos*, EV 241.5-6.

[145] Ibid., EV 219.5-9. The passage right before this on the stone remains enigmatic: Segre has restored (ll. 4-5): ...εὐεργέτην τῆς πατρίδος, (πα)[ρὰ]/ τοῦ Σεβαστοῦ, ἱερέα..., and commented: "v. 4, A, lap.." My own inspection of the stone on Kos has shown that after the A seen by Segre there is the trace of a vertical stroke, and there must have been initially (the right edge of the stone has been later chiseled off) room for about two more letters. As there is also a faint trace of a vertical stroke before A, I ask myself whether the right reading could be simply ἰατ[ρὸν]/ τοῦ Σεβαστοῦ, the later entry ἀρχίατρ[ον] (l. 9) representing just a posterior, higher title (cf. above).

[146] The identification rests on further evidence from Kos: cf. Herzog, *N&X*, 239 with n.3.

When Xenophon retired to Kos under Nero, he seems to have accepted the additional honor (and undertaken the burden) of many more local priesthoods, some of which—as Herzog reasonably supposed—[147] were actual revivals of obsolete local cults. This picture emerges from Maiuri, *NS*, 475[148] mentioning Xenophon as

ἱερῆ διὰ βίου τῶν Σεβαστ/ῶν θεῶν[149] καὶ Ἀσκλαπιοῦ καὶ Ὑγείας καὶ Ἀπιόνας/ καὶ [Κῶ κ]αὶ Μέροπος καὶ Ἴσιδος καὶ Σαράπιδος, ἱερῆ/ καὶ ἀπ[ὸ/ γένους Ῥ]έας καὶ Ἀπόλλωνος Καρνείου[150] καὶ Ἀπόλλω[νος/ Πυθίου ?] καὶ Διὸς Πολιέως καὶ Ἀθάνας Π[ολιά/δος---] θεῶν καὶ Ἥρας Ἑλίας Ἀργίας Βασι/[λίας καὶ θεῶν? Νικ]ομηδείων καὶ Ἀπόλλωνος/[Δαλίου ? καὶ Ἀφρο]δίτας Ποντίας ἱερῆ Σ[εβαστοῦ? / ---δ]υώδεκα θεῶν καὶ ΜΗ[....]/[---]/ΙΣ [..]ΣΕΣΑ (ll. 5-14).

Xenophon's accumulation of priestly offices is impressive and reminiscent of earlier similar Koan examples.[151] What we find in *PH* 345 seems, then, to represent the immediately following phase of his priestly action on Kos: Xenophon is here simply ἀρχιερέα τῶν θεῶν καὶ ἱερέα δι[ὰ/ βί]ου τῶν Σεβαστῶν, καὶ Ἀσκλαπιοῦ, /[καὶ] Ὑγίας καὶ Ἠπιόνης. Dubois,[152] Paton and Dittenberger[153] thought that the term "high priest of the gods" referred to dead emperors and complemented the next, familiar priesthood of Sebastoi etc. in which we should recognize the living emperors. Herzog preferred to see all emperors, dead and alive, included in *theoi*, and assumed that "priest of the *Sebastoi*" referred to a separate priesthood of the reigning Augusti (Nero and Agrippina).[154]

---

[147] Herzog, *N&X*, 241.

[148] This big marble base has been built into the lowest right wall of the passage into the interior fortification area of the Knights Castle, the inscription being on the side inside the wall and visible only through a slot between this and the next stone. I have spent some hours there trying to discern the text and collate particularly the part including Xenophon's priesthoods with Maiuri's edition and the preliminary but sometimes more accurate one by Herzog, *N&X*, 226, n.1. The slightly revised text appearing here is the result of this work.

[149] Almost certainly all Augusti, dead and alive, see below.

[150] Cf. Segre, *I.Cos*, EV 219.8-9, and for ἀπὸ γένους *Syll.*³ 783, 30.

[151] Cf. esp. the earlier case of his possible relative Minnis Praylou discussed above and Xenophon's approximate coeval L.Nonius Aristodamus (Maiuri, *NS*, 462). On the various Koan cults attested here cf. Sherwin-White, *Cos*, 360 and passim.

[152] *BCH* 5(1881), 475.

[153] *Syll.*³ 804, n. 8.

[154] Herzog, *KF*, 195 (cf. id., *N&X*, 240f. where such a separation of priesthoods is also suggested). C.G.Brandis, *RE* II.1(1895), s.v. Ἀρχιερεύς, 480 also accepted that both living and dead emperors were here the content of *theoi* but equated completely the latter with *Sebastoi*, which could only render the one of the two priestly offices redundant.

Both solutions seem to be unsatisfactory: for it is on the one side inconceivable that Xenophon's priesthood of the *Theoi Sebastoi* in Maiuri, *NS,* 475 should be limited to dead emperors. For no complement with the reigning ones immediately followed.[155] Besides, again in *PH* 345, Xenophon is *archiatros* of the *Theoi Sebastoi,* which can hardly refer only to dead emperors, even had Xenophon in the meantime moved to Kos. On the other hand, it seems extravagant to assume a separate high priesthood of all Sebastoi (dead and alive) and another reserved for the reigning ones but without a specific mention of them.[156] I think that the evolution of Xenophon's priesthoods may provide a more natural interpretation. In *PH* 345 all Xenophon's various priesthoods are included and cumulatively upgraded into a general "high priesthood of the gods (: all gods, imperial and local)" so that his basic priestly office combines again the specific cult of all emperors with that of the most important local deities.[157] So the twofold need of finding a loftier title for the great benefactor of Kos and evading an immense list of local priesthoods was satisfied. Xenophon was recognized as the head of religious life on the island, something which perfectly matches his already mentioned, epigrammatic description as ἱερεὺς on Koan coins. Later, when Nero was identified with Asklepios and Agathos Theos, Xenophon himself chose to mention only his priesthood of this cult[158] and omitted the train of priestly offices covering almost all other aspects of the local religious tradition. The emperor and the holy triad of Kos sufficed.

Xenophon's concentration of religious offices may be compared to ithe career of an earlier peer's, Potamon of Mytilene, the famous Lesbian statesman of aristocratic descent and vital liaison of his city and island with both Caesar and Augustus. He was invested with a general priesthood of all cults both in Mytilene and Lesbos. We also know that he was actively engaged as priest and/or high priest in the local cult of Augustus.[159] Such a "personal union" of religious posts reappears in the

---

[155] The apparently secondary mention in l. 12 of ἱερῆ Σ[εβαστοῦ or -ῶν?], cf. above, is not at all certain.

[156] As for example the priesthood of Claudius integrated with that of the Sebastoi in Segre, *I.Cos,* EV 219 quoted above.

[157] The acceptance of such a general high priesthood would also better explain the probably contemporaneous existence of more specialized priesthoods like that of L.Nonius Aristodamus in Maiuri, *NS,* 462. The distinction ib., 5-6: ἐκδύσαντα το[ῖς]/ Σεβαστοῖς καὶ τοῖς ἄλλοις θεοῖς should also refer to past and present emperors on the one side and the rest of the gods on the other. Cf. also on this meaning of *Sebastoi*: Brandis (n. 154), 480-1; Price, *R&P,* 58.

[158] With the concomitant figures of Hygieia and Epione in *AnÉp* 1934, 93.

[159] *IG* XII Suppl. 7.3-4 (+ L.Robert, *REA* 62(1960), 310, n. 2): [...τὸν θέων πά]ντων τε καὶ παῖσαν λάβοντα (sc. Ποτάμωνα Λεσβώνακτος) κατὰ /[γένος --- ταῖς ἱερω]σύναις τᾶς

career of another Lesbian magnate, very probably Xenophon's contemporary, Ti.Claudius Damarchos of Eresos.[160]

This constant prominence and augmentation of Xenophon's role as a (finally central) priestly figure on Kos, however, deserves more comment. It is, of course, not the first time that the imperial cult becomes a channel for provincial ambitions, aristocratic or not. The specific character of Xenophon's case seems to result from his imperial authority, which is no less important than his personal resources, with which he reestablished himself in Koan society. Add to this the difficulty of finding some other both constitutionally acceptable and personally sufficient function for him on Kos. As high priest, uniting in his person both the vital expression of loyalty to the Augusti and due homage to Koan religious tradition, Xenophon very probably found an ideal office that was at once serviceably "clerical" and inoffensively secular. We may also recall how the Ptolemaic governors of Cyprus in the Hellenistic age had finally appropriated, in parallel to their political authority proper, the post of high priest (ἀρχιερεύς) of all cults—nota bene, the highest, dynastic cult found on their island.[161] Granting that direct and significant political power was past history on Kos, religious authority naturally tended to take the place of (not to replace, of course) its extinguished political correlate. What could be saved of old Kos was linked to imperial loyalty. Xenophon was a sensitive Janus—caught between a fatherland no longer important (and probably strong sentiment) and the new Roman order to which he and, largely through him, Kos owed its privileged status.

The list of Xenophon's titles may also give valuable insight into the way(s) he accommodated himself to the world of imperial Kos. A useful historical interpretation might begin with some sort of temporal classification. The "canon" of Xenophon's titles presented in the small dedicative monuments to the "paternal gods" (see below) includes the attribute φιλοκλαύδιος but not the similar φιλονέρων. This must mean that

---

τε πόλιος καὶ τᾶς Λέσβω. On his involvement in the cult of Augustus as lifelong priest (or high priest): *IG* XII.2.154. Cf. R.W.Parker, *ZPE* 85(1991), 119ff. and now Labarre, 109ff.

[160] *IG* XII.2.549, 1-2: Τὸν εἴρεα καὶ ἀρχείρεα τῶν Σεβάστων καὶ/ τῶν ἄλλων θέων πάντων καὶ παίσαν διὰ βίω... That here Sebastoi were all emperors, dead and alive, shows a comparison with ib. 541. Cf. Parker (previous n.) and Labarre, 127. Also relevant the case of Sex.Pompeius Eudamos in Sparta (second/third century A.D.) who was also high priest of the Sebastoi and priest of a long list of local cults: *IG* V.1.559; cf. A.S.Bradford, *A Prosopography of Lacedaemonians (323 B.C.-A.D. 396)*, (München 1977) 166. I thank M.Kantirea for a relevant discussion.

[161] See Bagnall, 48 and more recently A.Mehl, "Militärwesen und Verwaltung der Ptolemäer in Zypern," *RCCM* 38(1996), publ. 1997, 215ff. (238-40) with further bibl.

at least the initial list antedates Nero's reign and represents the earlier phase of Koan reaction to Xenophon's services for the island. So it seems preferable to use the "canonic" titles as the basis for interpretation, integrating at the proper place each one of the rest, which were posterior (φιλονέρων) or remained outside that "public codification"—for reasons we shall also have to examine.

The standard text of the dedications to the *patroioi theoi* for Xenophon's health (fifty eight cases attested so far, see Appendix 3) is:

Θεοῖς πατρῴοις ὑπὲρ ὑγιείας Γαΐου Στερτινίου Ἡρακλείτου υἱοῦ
Ξενοφῶντος, φιλοκαίσαρος, φιλοκλαυδίου, φιλοσεβάστου, δάμου υἱοῦ,
φιλοπάτριδος, εὐσεβοῦς, εὐεργέτα τᾶς πατρίδος.

The obvious and significant, major change, in comparison with similar older texts for Nikias[162] is that the first group of Xenophon's titles refers to his imperial connections. In this public image of the model citizen, however, it is not his medical service at court but the results of that service—being on personal, friendly terms with the emperors—that dominate his ideological picture. This is expressed by three pregnant terms that correspond to finely different aspects of this relation: φιλόκαισαρ, φιλοκλαύδιος, φιλοσέβαστος.

Philokaisar and *philosebastos* are frequently used titles,[163] actually so often added to the names of individuals or public (civic)/private corporations that some interpreters hold that they were no more than simple "adulatory adjectives,"[164] which would deny them any real historical significance. L.Robert should be credited for having opposed

---

[162] A minor difference is that the standard formula in the texts of this form for Nikias was ὑπὲρ/περὶ τᾶς σωτηρίας but in the dedications for Xenophon we see this only once (see Appendix 3, no. 3). Ὑπὲρ ὑγιείας seems naturally to have more of a private than a public character, and to be less dramatic, but we should not press the point.

[163] Basic discussions of them (including a large collection of examples): Münsterberg, 315-321; L.Robert, *Hellenica* 7(1949), 206ff. (esp. 211f.); J.H.Oliver, *The Athenian Expounders of the Sacred and Ancestral Law*, (Baltimore 1950) 87-9; Ch.Dunant-J.Pouilloux, *Recherches sur l'histoire et les cultes de Thasos*, II, (Paris 1958) 120f.; Pleket, *I.Leyden*, 4-10 (starting from the interpretation of the related term φιλοκαισαρεῖς); Fraser, *Kings of Commagene*, 369-371. See also the further examples of both terms cited or quoted below. The Koan testimonies of *philokaisar* and *philosebastos* had been collected by Sherwin-White, *Cos*, 144f., n. 338. We may now add: Segre, *I.Cos*, EV 135, 136, 216, 226.

[164] So e.g. D.Knibbe, *JÖAI* 46(1961-63), Beiblatt, 25 (on the occasion of a *chiliastys philoromaios* in Ephesos): "...eines jener in der Kaiserzeit besonders beliebt gewordenen überschwenglichen Schmeichelepitheta [: φιλορώμαιος, φιλοσέβαστος, φιλόκαισαρ etc.]." He goes on to mention as an impressive example of such a titular accumulation one of the Koan texts for Xenophon (*PH* 345= *Syll.*³ 804).

such superficial judgments and contributed essentially to the elucidation of these and related terms.[165]

Philokaisar seems to be the somewhat earlier term of the two (as *Caesar*, of course, antedates *Augustus*) or, at least, the one with the earlier diffusion.[166] It was an attribute of many client kings (as those of Kommagene and Bosporos) in Augustan and Tiberian times.[167] While in these royal cases the term seems to have alluded to the legal relation of dependence on the Caesar(s) indicated,[168] there seem to have been many equally early examples where *philokaisares* was a civic term by which distinguished citizens were obviously somehow connected with the emperor, though rarely in a specific way. We find them holding various local posts, but, significantly, they seem to be frequently involved in some form of the imperial cult.[169] J.H.Oliver[170] once suggested that the combination of the terms *philokaisar* and *philopatris* could even be the first step in the evolution of the imperial high priests' titulature in Athens, and possibly elsewhere. While this tends, characteristically perhaps, to give the use of *philokaisar* too precise a meaning, the always possible implication of the imperial cult should be kept in mind. Sometimes this becomes more explicit as, for example, on Kos when the

---

[165] *Bull.* 1966, 368: "...nous ne saurions suivre K(nibbe) dans ce qu'il dit des "Schmeichelepitheta" φιλορώμαιος, φιλοσέβαστος, φιλόκαισαρ." Cf. esp. his study cited in the previous n.

[166] Cf. already Münsterberg, 318.

[167] In addition to the literature cited above (n. 163): R.D.Sullivan, *ANRW* II.8(1977), 783; Braund, 105-7 (with n.s, p.116f.); Nawotka.

[168] Cf. again Münsterberg, 317 who first underlined the parallel use of φιλόκαισαρ καὶ φιλορώμαιος in Greek inscriptions (see for example V.V.Struve (ed.), Corpus Inscriptionum Regni Bosporani, Moscow 1965, 44) and *amicus imp(eratoris) populiq(ue) R(omani)* in a Latin one (ibid., 46) for Sauromates I of Pontos in Trajan's times. See also below.

[169] A selection of examples in this latter sense (see also below): *IG* V.1.59, 551, 553 and *SEG* 34.307, 313 (Sparta, quite usual the further combination of φιλόκαισαρ with φιλόπατρις here and in many of the next examples, also sometimes with υἱὸς πόλεως); *IG* V.1.1449 (Messene, a φιλόκαισαρ ὁ ἱερεὺς αὐτοῦ, i.e. of Nero); *I.Ephesos* 3801 (for an archiereus of Asia under Claudius); *IBM* 894 (for an archiereus with the gentilicium Julius in a decree of Halikarnassos for Augustus); *I.Stratonikeia* 1024 (the bearer, a Ti.Claudius, was also ἱερατεύσαντος τῶν Σεβαστῶν); *OGIS* 583 (Lapethos, a priest of Tiberius); *FdD* III.3, 181 (=*Syll.*³ 813 A); *SEG* 7.825 (Gerasa, for the *agonothetes* of a local festival for Trajan praised διὰ τὴν ὑπερβάλλουσαν αὐτοῦ πρός τε τὸν οἶκον τῶν Σεβαστῶν εὐσέβειαν..., the honorand apparently never having been personally acquainted with the emperor; only his relations with governors and procurators are mentioned); ibid. 17.596 (a similar case from Attaleia, third cent. A.D.?).

[170] l.c. (n. 163). Cf. the view of Dunant and Pouilloux (n.163) on the connection of the same titles with the formative period in the development of the imperial cult and its representatives on Thasos during the first century A.D.

title *philokaisar* is attributed to the head of a local association of frippery dealers in the text of a dedication to Augustus identified with Hermes.[171]

Philokaisar, however, seems fundamentally to have expressed the titular's devotion to the *kaisar/-es*, this being postulated by the inherent force of the first part of the compound.[172] Furthermore, the gradual formation of the family of the *kaisares* rendered the term as applying to loyalty to the whole family. *Kaisar* remained for a long time in the Greek East the standard way of referring to the emperor, rivaled only by *autokrator* and later by *basileus*,[173] while *Sebastos* remained always the term for referring either to the founder of the principate, Augustus himself, or an actual title of the emperor(s) as a *living institution*.[174] I do not know of any case (and I could not imagine one) in which a Greek would address a Roman emperor in the early centuries "ὦ Σεβαστέ." *Kaisar* was much more of a personal, real name and so the term *philokaisar* was ideally suitable to express a devotion primarily to the person(s) and not the institution.

---

[171] Maiuri, *NS*, 466, on which see above, p. – with n. 93.

[172] Cf. below on various such compounds with the names of Roman sovereigns. Of course, this form and idea ("very favorable, devoted to" without an implication of cult) of compound was not new but rooted in classical and hellenistic Greek tradition, regarding especially cities, rulers, and men of letters. Thus we find e.g. φιλαϑήναιος, φιλοϑήβαιος et simm.; φιλόκυρος, φιλαλέξανδρος, φιλαρσάκης (all already in Strabo) and, of course, various such dynastic titles as φιλάδελφος, φιλοπάτωρ et simm.; φιλόμηρος, φιλευριπίδης et simm. (all the examples from *LSJ*, s.vv. where the respective source/s are cited). That such compounds could have been used in the pre-Roman age as a distinctive expression of the devotion to a ruler as an institution and as a person is shown by *Diod.*, 17.114.2: ...ἐπεφϑέγξατο (sc. Ἀλέξανδρος) Κρατερὸν μὲν γὰρ εἶναι φιλοβασιλέα, Ἡφαιστίωνα δὲ φιλαλέξανδρον. The basic significance of the *philo*-compounds survives much later as best exemplified in the description of Sarapis himself as φιλόκαισαρ in an inscription from Coptos of Severan date: B.A.Van Groningen, *Mnemosyne* 55(1927), 265. On the other hand, a possible religious connation in the devotion expressed by this sort of compound predating Roman times can be seen in such cases as, for example, the φιλοβασιλισταὶ of Ptolemaic Egypt—cf. M.Launey, *Recherches sur les armées hellénistiques*, (Paris 1987²) II.1029f.—with which we could then compare the φιληραϊσταὶ of Samos and the φιλάρτεμις Salutaris cited below or the φιλοδιόνυσοι of *Didyma* 502 (second cent. A.D.) or, even more appropriately, the φιλοκαισαρεῖς of the inscription of Ilion (Pleket, *I.Leyden*, no. 4: first cent. A.D.). A late antique application of such a usage is then e.g. the expression φιλοχρίστου Ἰουστινιανοῦ in *IG* IV.205 (sixth cent. A.D.).

[173] See the still useful delineation of the semantic content of these terms in Greek texts of the Roman period by Al. Wifstrand, Autokrator, "Kaisar, Basileus. Bemerkungen zu den griechischen Benennungen der römischen Kaiser," in: ΔΡΑΓΜΑ. (M.P.Nilsson... dedicatum, ed. K.Hanell et al.), 1939, 529-539. Further: Mason, 119-21.

[174] This emerges most clearly, I think, from the frequent collective use of the plural (οἱ) Σεβαστοί: e.g. in *Syll.*³ 814.45, 820.9; Oliver, *GC*, 29.6-7, 38.17,46.4. [Ὁ] ϑεὸς Σε[β]αστὸς ibid., 75.II.41 (a letter of Hadrian to the Delphians, 125 A.D.) was obviously Augustus. Cf. Mason, 144f.

A telling detail in this respect is that *philosebastos* is used only later with a frequency paralleling that of *philokaisar* but also applied, far more often than its "twin title," to larger bodies such as cities, constitutional organs of cities (demos, boule, gerousia etc.) and associations of various kinds.[175] A good example comes from Kos itself where Sosikles son of Menippides, himself styled as *philokaisar*, is the priest of φιλοσεβάστου Δάμου Κῴων.[176] The same impression is conveyed exactly by a passage in the famous donation of Salutaris at Ephesos: in a context where almost everyone and anything wears the badge of *philosebastos* (as very usual in this city), Salutaris himself distinctively appears as φιλάρτεμις καὶ φιλόκαισαρ,[177] both terms obviously bearing out a much more personal and genuinely religious devotion than *philosebastos*, which seems to stay on a somewhat more distant and official (though, of course, not negligible) level. Nevertheless, this does not at all impede a connection with the imperial cult for *philosebastos*, too, as many examples may show—notably in an inscription from the Heraion of Samos on which we find in the year 71 after Augustus' *apotheosis* (: 85 A.D.) a νεοποίης εὐσεβὴς bearing the dual title φιληραϊστὴς φιλοσέβαστος.[178] As we also happen to know on Samos of a priestess τῆς Ἀρχηγέτιδος Ἥρας καὶ Θεᾶς Ἰουλίας Σεβαστῆς (:Livia),[179] it should be clear that both cults, Hera's and Augusta's ran parallel to their priests' respective devotional titles. On Kos itself we find a priest of Tiberius, worshipped as Zeus Kapetolios Alseios, with the titles φιλ[ο]καίσαρος φιλοσεβάστου[180] and a collegium of three *napoai* at Halasarna dedicating a statue of Sebasta

---

[175] On *philosebastos* applied to cities etc. see above all L.Robert, in: J. des Gagniers (et al.), *Laodicée du Lycos. Le Nymphée*, (Québec 1969) 281-9; id., *Hellenica* 7(1949), 212. A further selection of examples: *I.Pergamon* 432: φιλοσέβασ[τον κοινὸν τῶν κατὰ τὴν] Ἀσίαν [Ἑλλήνων]. *IG* XII.7.266 (Minoa/Amorgos): ἡ φιλοσέβαστος Μεινωητῶν βουλή. *IGRR* IV.932 (of the *gerousia* of Chios), 1223, 1248, 1249 (of the *boule* of Thyateira). *SEG* 28.1115, 1119 (of the *demos* and a *phyle* in Eumeneia/Phrygia). Also this usage of the term is especially frequent in Ephesos: *SEG* 77.419d (of the *polis*); *I.Ephesos* 449 (of the *demos*), ib. 21 and 449 (of the *boule* and the *demos*), 532 (of the *boule*, so also in *SEG* 37.886), 535 (of the *gerousia*, so also in *SEG* 71.568), 293 (of the οἱ τοῦ προπάτορος θεοῦ Διονύσου Κορησείτου σακηφόροι μύσται).

[176] *PH* 362, probably first century A.D.

[177] *I.Ephesos* 27.451-2 (p.198). Cf. also ibid. the decree no. 449 (under Domitian) where *philosebastos* is attributed to the *boule*, the *demos* (cf. above) and the collectively (not individually) named *strategoi* of the city while the *grammateus* of the people, fully named, is *philokaisar*.

[178] *IGRR* IV.1732. Cf. the comment of the *editio princeps* by M.Schede, *MDAI(A)* 44(1919), 39.

[179] *IGRR* IV.984.

[180] Segre, *I.Cos*, EV 135.2.

Homonoia Drusilla and being collectively called φιλοκαισάρων.[181] In other Koan examples, as for example in the collective attribution of the title *philokaisares* to a group of three generals honored after their period of service,[182] the term may have a more formulaic and general connotation.[183]

So both titles, not an invention of Xenophon's age, already had (and would continue) a history on Kos and the rest of the Roman East. An old and relevant question here is how someone received these titles. There seem to be mainly two theories: either they were conferred by the emperor[184] (as the title *amicus Caesaris/principis*, postulated as an equivalent for them in all cases) or they were granted by the cities to their citizens who had distinguished themselves through some special connection with the emperor.[185] The first alternative proves impossible if we consider the great numbers of these titulars and the further attribution (especially of *philosebastos*) to corporations etc.[186] The case of the client kings, for whom *amicus Caesaris* sometimes actually equals *philokaisar*,[187] seems to be an early and particular part of the development, belonging rather to the sphere of expressly inter-state relations and consequent concession of titles. The second alternative seems much nearer the truth, and the view has been held that popular proclamations were the usual mode of such awards as it is attested for cognate terms, for example *philopatris*.[188] The end of a fragmentary,

---

[181] Herzog, *Hal.*, no. 5 (p. 493). Drusilla's name had been erased but was still legible in Herzog's time.

[182] *PH* 65.1.

[183] On the other side, the more personal flavor of *philokaisar* seems also confirmed by its parallel development into a Greek personal name (Φιλόκαισαρ): Fraser, *Kings of Commagene*, 370, n. 27.

[184] Münsterberg, 315-*316* (with earlier literature).

[185] Most recent and authoritative expression of this view by Fraser, *Kings of Commagene*, 370 who thinks, however, that Xenophon as *philokaisar* is to be classified in a wide category of "notable public figures and especially client-rulers," having earned this title from "the Roman authorities." I think a civic award of this title on Xenophon, too, is more probable. Imperial favor was the precious political metal necessary but it could be coined into Greek titles *locally*, either by client kings themselves, as the highest authority in their states, or in the case of an outstanding citizen, by his own city. (Of course, there was perfect understanding with both emperor and honorand). Cf. below.

[186] Even an eventual mediation of the provincial representatives (governors etc.) of the emperor in the local award of the titles could not sufficiently explain the diffusion of the latter.

[187] Cf. n. 168 and Braund, 106.

[188] So Fraser, *Kings of Commagene*, 370, n. 28 utilising L.Robert, *Études épigraphiques et philologiques*, (Paris 1938) 140 (a mention of φιλόπατρις φωνηθείς in an inscription of Chios) and id., *Hellenica* 13(1965), 215f. with n. 4 (combination of the latter with *Luc.*, *Peregr.* 15 on the reaction of the *demos* of Parion to the announcement of a donation by

apparently unpublished honorary inscription for a Koan benefactress, lying today in the courtyard of the *Casa Romana*, clears up the point: to reward the lady's services ...ὁ δᾶμος ἐψαφίσατο χρηματίζεν αὐτὰν εὐσεβῆ ἡρωίδα φιλόπατριν.[189] Obviously, these three designations (*eusebes, herois, philopatris*) were titles officially conferred through a popular vote. Whether this always occured only in the form of popular proclamations, or these latter possibly culminated from an act of the assembly might be a matter of (perhaps varying) style. There seems to be no reason to suppose that there was a procedural difference in regard to the awarding of *philokaisar* and similar "imperial" titles in Greek cities. Thus the important fact emerges that the possession of these titles on a local level was not simply the imprint of the imperial power-nexus on provincial societies—the people of a polis were also allowed some sense (better: illusion) of autonomy in keeping the formal right to confer titles testifying loyalty to the Sebastoi. A little strange though this may appear, it was nonetheless quite clever as an injection of vitality into local politics to involve the citizenry in rendering such loyalties into socially accepted titles on the peripheral, but not at all insignificant, civic level.

On the other hand, the proliferation of these "imperial titulars" in the cities obviously created the need of a new term by which to honor someone more closely connected with a specific emperor (or even actual co-emperor). So the properly personal friendly relation with, and devotion to, a particular emperor found its expression in further *philo*-compounds, continuing a relevant tradition of the Greek (see above). We find such an association of φιλαγρίππαι συμβιωταί, obviously devoted to Augustus' viceroy, in Smyrna (?).[190] Philo[191] has Macro, the praetorian prefect, assert he had sufficiently proved φιλόκαισαρ ἰδίως καὶ φιλοτιβέριος εἶναι ("to be not just a friend of the Caesar(s) but especially of Tiberius"). There is then only one φιλογάιος in an Ephesian name list

---

Peregrinus : ...ἀνέκραγον εὐθὺς ἕνα φιλόσοφον, ἕνα φιλόπατριν, ἕνα Διογένους καὶ Κράτητος ζηλωτήν).

[189] This is the conclusion of the preserved text (sixteen lines), covering the lower part of a broken marble stele (h. 64, w. 59.5, th. 24 cm; the left and right margin take the form of a decorative cornice, so the written surface is just 47x40 cm). The honorand's services concerned the provision of a whole series of cult objects (apparently for a temple), so (ll.4 ff.): ...καὶ χλαμύδα Ἀνουβια[κὴν]/ καὶ βωμὸν χάλκεον καὶ τρά/πεζαν μαρμαρίναν καὶ θυ/μιατήριον ἀκρόχαλκον καὶ/ τρίποδα νίγρινον καὶ θρό/νον πύσινον (?) σὺν ὑποποδί/ω καὶ ἀγαλμάτια λεῖα πέντε/ καὶ παραπετάσματα τρία/ καὶ κρατῆρα ὑελοῦν/ ὁ δᾶμος... The lettering would agree with an early imperial date. On the popular award of such titles cf. now also the case of Kleanax φιλοπάτωρ in Kyme (2 B.C.-2A.D.): *SEG* 32(1982), 1243.26-28.

[190] Pleket, *I.Leyden*, no. 5 (p.11). Cf. the testimony of a συμβίωσις τῶν φιλοσεβάστων published and commented by C.Habicht, *Pergamon* VIII.3, no. 85 (p.117).

[191] *De leg. ad Gaium*, 37.

of Caligula's times in which all persons included are collectively designated at the end as οἱ φιλοσέβαστοι.[192] Polemo II of Pontus, a close friend of Caligula, from whom he received his throne,[193] appears also as φιλογερμανικός in the date of a manumission from Gorgippia.[194] Herod of Chalkis is styled as φιλοκλαύδιος on some of his coins.[195] Still later a procurator of Commodus and high priest in Egypt styles himself as φιλοκόμμοδος καὶ φιλοσάραπις,[196] while—not to lose sight of the basic undertone of familiarity in such compounds—one of Commodus' deliciae was called Φιλοκόμμοδος, δεικνυούσης τῆς προσηγορίας τὴν στοργὴν τὴν ἐς τὸν παῖδα τοῦ βασιλέως as Herodian explains.[197]

Against this background, it is quite natural, but nonetheless significant, that Xenophon was also φιλοκλαύδιος[198] and later on φιλονέρων.[199] *Philoklaudios* appears in the "canon" (see above). In Segre, *TC* 111 (cf. above) both titles were inscribed and survived. *Philoneron* existed in *PH* 345 (erased)[200] and *AnÉp* 1934.93 (also erased).[201] It is further remarkable that *philoklaudios* appears in the "canon" between *philokaisar* and *philosebastos*. It seems apt to say that all three terms in this arrangement expressed the combined familiarity and loyalty of Xenophon to the family of Caesares, Claudius personally and the institution of the Principate. The friendlier one might appear to various aspects of imperial power, the more elevated one's local status and dignity were.

---

[192] L.Robert, *Hellenica* 7(1949), 207. Cf. also Robert's remarks, ibid. 210f. on the really exquisite titles σεβαστονέως and σεβαστολόγος.

[193] D.C., 59.12.2.

[194] *IPE* II.400 (41 A.D.; Polemo's name has been later erased to be replaced by that of Mithridates (II). Cf. Braund, 105+116(n. 2, giving a wrong citation).

[195] Burnett, *RPC*, 4778, 4779 (43/4 A.D.).

[196] H.Hunger, *AAntHung* 10(1962), 154f.

[197] 1.17.3.

[198] The imperial credit for this civic political capital appears in Claudius' second and third unpublished letters to the Koans (see below, p. 138ff.) where we find a mention of Στερτινίου Ξενοφῶντος/ τοῦ ἰατροῦ μου καὶ φίλου (ll.6-7 of the second letter) and [Στερ]/τινίου Ξενοφῶντος [τοῦ ἰατροῦ μου καὶ φί]/λου ἀεὶ φιλοπάτριδο[ς] (ll. 9-11 of the third letter). The juxtaposition of Xenophon's devotion to his emperor and his homecity here is noteworthy. It is, of course, a fine irony of imperial history that one of two men in all who gained a public recognition of their special "friendliness" to Claudius was the emperor's Tacitean poisoner (*Ann.*, 12.67). Cf. Herzog, *X&N*, 231-6.

[199] The only so far attested case of such a titularly coined familiarity with this emperor.

[200] There seems to be no sufficient reason for supposing, however, that an earlier engraved φιλοκλαύδιον had been replaced by φιλονέρωνα at this point as Paton, ibid. assumed just on the ground that on the "impression" of the stone he was able to study the available space "suits the former better than the latter." The *editio princeps* by M.Dubois, *BCH* 5(1881), 474, n. 1 does not mention any traces of a double erasure but simply supposes (as verified by later finds) a succession of titles in Xenophon's nomenclature.

[201] Xenophon styles *himself* (dedicator!) here simply as φιλονέρων.

Xenophon's Roman connections were also twice (in the two documents mentioned last) expressed with the oldest pertinent title φιλορώμαιος. As both these cases are post-Claudian (cf. above) and in the latter, Xenophon's own dedicative text, *philoromaios* is placed first, before *philoneron*, *philokaisar* and *philosebastos*, there might be an effort here to emphasize the great Koan's firm bonds with Rome, beyond any change of ruler.[202]

Between Xenophon's titles of imperially and locally centered distinction belongs εὐσεβής. This is very probably a hint at his various priestly positions discussed above; *eusebeia* was, of course, the virtue par excellence for a priest.[203] Piety to all gods, imperial and local, was certainly an asset of Xenophon's personality; thus it appears independently exalted in the "canon." Xenophon himself did not fail to include this attribute in his own edition of his titulature (*AnÉp* 1934.93, cf. above). Claudius probably also mentions Xenophon's *eusebeia* in a restored passage of the first of his three unpublished letters to the Koans (see below, p. 138ff.).

We next address the portion of the title list that brings Xenophon nearer his native island with its political traditions. In a significant way, it helps mark the points of similarity and difference in the polis-centered praise of him and Nikias, his unspoken predecessor in local excellence. Immediately after the titles that celebrate various facets of his familiarity with the imperial house, Xenophon appears in the "canon" as δάμου υἱοῦ, φιλοπάτριδος and (after εὐσεβοῦς) εὐεργέτα τᾶς πατρίδος, which concludes his *Bürgerspiegel*. We may recall that these are all old conceptual insignia of Nikias. The last one remains virtually the same (only τᾶς πατρίδος replacing τᾶς πόλιος), Xenophon's quality as Koan *euergetes* crowns and epitomizes at the same time his historical role in Koan eyes (cf. above). On the contrary, we may notice that place and value of the rest have substantially changed. The subordination of Kos to Rome is now openly expressed in Xenophon's usual hierarchy of titles for distinction near the emperors comes first.[204] Unavoidably, the old

---

[202] However, we should also notice that in *PH* 345 *philoromaios* appears last in the series of "Roman" titles, just before *philopatris*. Compare also the remarks above on the absence of this element from Nikias' titulature.

[203] Thus for example the instigator of the above-mentioned reform of the Halasarnan priest-list, Aristion son of Chairippos, appears himself with the label εὐσεβής (Herzog, *Hal.*, no.4, priest no. 38). The same title is attached to the *neopoiai* at the Samian Heraion known from *IGRR* IV.991. The actions of a priest were also often praised with the adverb εὐσεβῶς as (i.a.) in the Koan examples *PH* 119; Maiuri, *NS*, 462; Segre, *I.Cos*, EV 226.

[204] The only exception is *PH* 345 where δάμου υἰὸν comes after the Roman posts but before the Rome-centered titles.

designations "son of the *damos*" and *philopatris* look insignificant in comparison with those of Nikias' age—especially the first, as already noticed in the longer discussion of its attribution to Nikias (see above). It cannot have retained the same meaning and force. This is here clearly a supplementary titular filiation (Xenophon's real father is always mentioned first), which takes us from the simulation of a real relation to the Damos, (and consequent foundation of a heroic identity in Nikias' case), to the level of a simple element of the honorary political vocabulary in the imperial East. It is perhaps equally significant that what was by now simply a title could be also omitted, while the Roman titles remained—as in Maiuri, *NS,* 459 (the honorary inscription for Xenophon's mother, cf. above). Besides, it might be noteworthy that Damos as a deity, although mentioned in connection with other local priests of his age,[205] is absent from what we know of Xenophon's own priesthoods.

Xenophon as *philopatris* needs only two more points of comment: (a) Claudius himself mentions (and advertises in a way) this quality of his favorite doctor in his third unpublished letter to the Koans (see below). The emperor apparently regarded it as vital to confirm this element in the public image of such a useful human bond between the imperial center and periphery. (b) *Philopatris* appears also in many other similar honorary texts for imperial magnates in the Greek East in combination with (and regularly in hierarchical subordination to) the "Roman" titles *philoromaios/philokaisar/philosebastos.*[206] An alternative conjunction of "son of the people/city etc." and these latter titles is also frequent.[207] The significance of these phenomena should be clear: love of the fatherland and filial care of one's homecity could be now only guaranteed if, and to the degree, a civic statesman could exhibit firm loyalty to Rome and receive corresponding Roman (in the best case: imperial) favor.

The only title of Nikias' canon interestingly absent from Xenophon's is *heros.* As analyzed above, the other post-Nikian examples of its attribution on Kos may show that, as a term of public distinction, it was not lavishly bestowed, but was rather conservatively and selectively used for really important Koans. At least some of its original value must have been preserved. It is therefore noteworthy that this attribute does accompany Xenophon's name in one of his own dedicative texts (*AnÉp* 1934.93) and also in three of the honorary texts for him (*PH* 93; Segre,

---

[205] So in Maiuri, *NS,* 462.

[206] Cf. n. 169 above.

[207] Cf. on Kos itself the cases of Nikagoras son of Eudamos, C.Hetereius P.f. Lautus and L.Cossinius L.f. Bassus cited above (p. 52, n. 119).

I.Cos, EV 241; Segre, *TC*, 111, cf. above on all these texts). The authors of these honors are public bodies (the people/the city of Kos, the council and the people of Kos, the deme and residents of Kalymna respectively). In all four passages *heros* appears side by side with *euergetas* (in *PH* 93 these two terms alone summarize his personality). As the date of *AnÉp* 1934.93 and Segre, *TC*, 111 is Neronian and also *PH* 93 looks rather like a thanksgiving (εὐχαρ[ιστίας] χάριν) to Xenophon for his contribution to Koan welfare,[208] we may see a later, crowning honor in this title. However, its bestowal cannot postdate Claudius' death since Xenophon is *philoklaudios* only in Segre, *I.Cos*, EV 241. A title that could have been perhaps provocative (as compared to Nikias' earlier entitlement?) at an early date for Xenophon in the interest of Kos, was eventually granted by the city and born by him with unaffected pride in the mature years of his career. The dedicative text of *PH* 93 mentions Xenophon's name in the dative (...Ξενοφῶντι) so the verb to be restored is probably καθιέρωσεν as in the similar dedication to Nikagoras son of Eudamos.[209] This seems further to imply real cult honors for Xenophon as *heros*, alive or dead.[210]

To sum up, Xenophon's titulature, provides clear evidence that the advent of a new era on Kos: accommodation and influence with Rome is the condition openly celebrated in the new type of *euergetes* that Claudius' doctor represents, while the traditional civic distinctions are relegated to a secondary position. Even the "revised" *euergetes'* local piety may appear because it is integrated into the cult of the gods, the imperial ones significantly leading the list.

---

[208] Cf. Herzog, *N&X*, 241.

[209] Herzog, *KF*, 212, p. 135; cf. above.

[210] Cf. above on this ambiguity in some uses of *heros* and also the probable restoration of the same term for Xenophon (here certainly dead) in the honorary decree for his descendant, known from Herzog, *N&X*, 246, n. 2 (cf. above, p. 77).

D. M.Aelius Sabinianus: Titulature and public position on Kos, profession, date and possible connections. M'.Spedius Rufinus Phaedrus and the Koan Spedii.

The next important public figure on Kos to be considered is M.Aelius Sabinianus, who seems to rival in the second century A.D. Xenophon's authority on Kos in the first. What we knew of him until now consisted mainly in another small series of the small dedicative monuments to the "paternal gods," of the type already examined in connection with Nikias and Xenophon. The standard text of these dedications is: Θεοῖς πατρῴοις ὑπὲρ ὑγείας Μάρκου Αἰλίου Σαβ(ε)ινιανοῦ, υἱοῦ πόλεως καὶ γερουσίας, εὐεργέτα τᾶς πατρίδος.

Paton, Herzog, and Maiuri were aware of few such documents (see Appendix 4) and none commented on the person they concerned. Conversely, when one of the small dedications for Sabinianus was found in the excavations of the *Casa Romana*, L.Laurenzi,[1] reached the radical conclusion, that in this man "si crede di poter riconoscere un parente dell'imperatrice Sabina" (cf. below). Even after Segre, *TC*, 202 published a Kalymnian manumission dated ἐπὶ μο(νάρχου) Αἰλίου Σαβεινιανοῦ and identified this *monarchos* with the honorand of the dedications mentioned above, no further notice has been made of him. S.Sherwin-White has not mentioned him in her synthesis of Koan history, and J.Benedum in an almost contemporaneous article on a new dedication for Sabinianus (see Appendix 4), reached only the negative conclusion that he should not be confused with a Fabius Sabinianus known from Iasos.[2]

After Segre, *I.Cos* increased the number of the private dedications for Sabinianus from seven to twenty three (Appendix 4) the situation has considerably changed. Furthermore, the first time we have now also an honorary text for him inscribed on the base of his statue erected by the *gerousia* of Kos (see below). Habicht has remarked, on the basis of the significantly increased number of the private dedications and their formulaic similarity with those for Nikias, that this Sabinianus should possess an analogous position in Koan society; he could be "ein Herodes

---

[1] "Attività del Servizio Archeologico nelle Isole Italiane dell'Egeo nel biennio 1934/35," *BA* 30(1936) 129ff. (140).
[2] Benedum, 239.

Atticus im kleinen."[3] Evidence currently available seems to confirm this impression, offering important details and allowing room for further possible connections.

As for Sabinianus' small private dedications, we should specify first that their preserved number is now approximately the same as that of Nikias' (twenty-three to twenty-two respectively) and about half of those for Xenophon (fifty-eight), as tabulated in the Appendices 2-4. If we compare these numbers with the four known cases of similar dedications for M'.Spedius Rufinus Phaedrus (see below and Appendix 4), the text of which, apart from the honorand's name, is identical with that for Sabinianus, we may conclude that the latter's importance and recognition on imperial Kos recalled rather the position of his glorious forerunners in local politics than that of his possible contemporaries or successors.

Equally instructive is comparing the dedicative text to the "paternal gods" for Sabinianus with those for Nikias and Xenophon. It strikes one immediately that the term "son of the people" (υἱὸς τοῦ δάμου) has not even been given a subordinate place in the dedications for Sabinianus: it has been simply replaced by the new distinction "son of the city and the gerousia" (υἱὸς πόλεως καὶ γερουσίας). That in one of the twenty three dedications[4] the old label survives in conjunction with the gerousia (δάμου καὶ γερουσίας υἱοῦ) is even more symptomatic of the change implied. "Son of the damos" is clearly an outdated element, practically a relic, of political portraiture. The (great) euergetes of Kos, Sabinianus, as his only other distinction in these texts emphasizes, is not adorned even with a mere titular-like mention of the Koan damos (as it was still the case with Xenophon). Instead he is now simply one of a number of imperial magnates of the Greek world (see above) who styled themselves as "son of the city," "son of the boule," "son of the gerousia" etc.

Despite van Rossum's[5] useful and important dissertation, we still cannot understand exactly the role(s) of the various gerousiai in Greek cities of the Roman Empire. One thing seems certain: they were regularly local elite bodies with apparently religious duties and/or educational character, such as supervision of a gymnasium, probably even more aristocratic in concept and essence than some cases of boulai in the imperial period.[6] That the emperors corresponded with gerousiai, and

---

[3] Habicht, I.Kos, 87, although he somewhat underestimates (nineteen) the new total of private dedications for Sabinianus.

[4] Segre, I.Cos, EV 71.

[5] J.A. van Rossum, De gerousia in de griekse steden van het romeinse rijk, (diss. Leiden 1988), in Dutch with an English summary: pp.238-242.

[6] Cf. especially the institution of the patrobouloi, sons of council-members (bouleutai) who were allowed to participate, without formal membership yet, in the proceedings of the councils, and so prepared to succeed their fathers later as councillors: see Nigdelis, 191f. (with the earlier literature).

often dealt with requests from and about them,[7] shows how important a "para-public" position this institution had for the. Roman view point. What we knew about the Koan *gerousia*[8] has now been considerably enriched. The second of the three unpublished letters of Claudius to the Koans (see below, p. 138ff.) concerns the award of some privileges to the Koan *gerousia* through the usual mediation of Xenophon. The grateful reaction of the body to Xenophon's munificence towards Kos is contained in the very fragmentary decree (Segre, *I.Cos*, EV 9). This *gerousia* on Kos seems to date at least from the beginning of the Empire. There is probably some evidence of her activity already under Augustus in Segre, *I.Cos*, EV 373: [Ἀ γερουσί]α Γάιον/ [Καίσαρ]α Σεβαστοῦ/ [Καίσαρ]ος υἱόν.[9] There is now also a very interesting document about the *gerousia*'s responsibilities in Segre, *I.Cos*, ED 230 (dated there "I sec. d.C."). The *gerousia* erected here a list of persons, obviously important citizens and probable benefactors of the city and itself in previous generations, whose honorary statues (ἀνδριᾶσι) the body somehow "consumed in the emergency faced" (ἁ γερουσία... κατεχρήσατο ἐς τὸν ἐπιστάντα καιρόν). Habicht notices the unique character of this document and points to a probable identification of some names listed here with Koan notables of the first half of the second century B.C.[10] This must mean that the Koan *gerousia* was officially invested not only with the care for the preservation of these statues (and, if needed, with a similar dispositional authority), but also, in a way, with the collective memory of the whole city. We may also conclude that its origin was possibly earlier than the Augustan age. However, the function of the *gerousia* as a further significant organization of public interest (and possibly involvement) on imperial Kos evidently emerges here, and is probably summarized in the twin filiation of Sabinianus as "son of the city and the *gerousia*." We may also notice that in the text of the private dedications Sabinianus is εὐεργέτας τᾶς πατρίδος, while in the new honorary document of the *gerousia* for him (see below), he appears as εὐεργέτης τῆς πόλεως καὶ ἑαυτῆς (sc. τῆς γερουσίας). The content of "fatherland" seems equated with city and gerousia combined.

I am tempted to recognize here the end of a distinct development of terms and realities: the successful local politician of later imperial Kos did

---

[7] The case of the Athenian *gerousia* in the late Antonine period is an instructive (though also insufficiently known) example: cf. the dossier Oliver, *GC*, nos. 193-203.

[8] A concise picture in Sherwin-White, *Cos*, 222f.

[9] A restoration [ἁ βουλ]ὰ may be excluded, as there seems to be no certain case of a Koan monument erected by the council alone. On *PH* 118 cf. Paton's comment, ibid. On the involvement of the *gerousia* on Kos (as elsewhere) in the imperial cult cf. Segre, *I.Cos*, EV 255 (Vitellius).

[10] Habicht, *I.Kos*, 86.

not lay any more emphasis on projecting his ideal relation to the Koan *damos*. The more impersonal and constitutionally neutral term of the *polis*, as well as the selectively constituted and highly active and respectable local *gerousia*, were sufficient substitutes if he wanted to advertise his public favor. The Koan *demos* survived as a name and constitutional appearance (so e.g. in a perhaps somewhat later Ephesian inscription)[11] but the eroding of its real power seems to be reflected in this evolution of political-ideological terminology.

Two of the new private dedications for Sabinianus offer another insight: they combine the standard text with the representation of a snake—in relief[12] or engraved.[13] We have already seen the meaning of this element on some similar monuments of Xenophon's—[14] so the conclusion may be reached that Sabinianus was also a doctor. Thus he may be compared to Xenophon in regard to his social position on Kos. The outstanding political success of an important doctor was iterated. The wealth of a good doctor (as we know of Xenophon)[15] probably facilitated his career as a local benefactor.

The date and connections of Sabinianus should also be examined. Segre concisely and uniformly labeled the private dedications for Sabinianus "II sec. d.C.." His different dating of *I.Cos*, EV 71: "I sec. d.C." (if it is not a misprint) may be explained by the unusual conjunction of *damos* and *gerousia* in his title noted above. It is clear, however, that this inscription cannot be separated from the rest by a century. I wonder whether Segre was also somewhat influenced in the aberrant dating of that single document for Sabinianus by his already established position on the date of the *monarchos*, Aelius Sabinianus, in the series of the Kalymnian manumissions. It was his theory that the dossier of these manumissions (edited, also posthumously, in the *TC*, nos. 152ff.) should fall inside the period from Tiberius to about the end of Claudius.[16] So Aelius Sabinianus, listed as *monarchos* in one of these documents, also belonged in that period. A consequent uncertainty has attached to Sabinianus' date. The new honorary inscription of the Koan *gerousia* for him and the examination of other, already published documents definitely prove, I think, that his context in Kos is the second century A.D. (if not still a little later).

---

[11] R.Heberdey, *Forschungen in Ephesos*, II, (Wien 1912) no. 55 (p.171), where δῆμος Κῴων and πόλις Κῴων are alternating terms.

[12] Segre, *I.Cos*, EV 71.

[13] Ibid., EV 281.

[14] See above p. 95, n. 135.

[15] *Pl., NH,* 29.5.7-8. Cf. above.

[16] Segre, *TC*, pp. 170-2. The only later, systematic study (from a juristic point of view) of the same material by Ant.Babakos, Σχέσεις οἰκογενειακοῦ δικαίου εἰς τὴν νῆσον Κάλυμνον τὸν Aʹ μ.Χ.αἰῶνα, (Athens 1963) 23 accepted Segre's date.

The new document for Sabinianus has been found in the city of Kos (not *in situ*)[17] and lies now in the Castle of the Knights. It is inscribed on the front face of a base of greyish marble (h. 64 cm, w. 58 cm, th. 36 cm), preserving on its upper surface two small almost square dowel holes, probably for the fastening of the superimposed statue. The text reads:

Ἡ γερουσία Μᾶρκον/ Αἴλιον Σαβινιανὸν/ τὸν τῆς πόλεως καὶ/ ἑαυτῆς
εὐεργέτην εὐ/χαριστίας χάριν, γυμνα/ σιαρχοῦντος Λουκίου/ Φαννίου
Βάσσου Ἐγνα/τιανοῦ, ἐπιμελητεύ/οντος Μάρκου Σπεδί/ου Βηρύλλου,
ἐργεπιστα/τήσαντος Αἰλίου Ἀλε/ξάνδρου.

At the end of l. 1 a *hedera* ("ivy-leaf") and at the end of l. 3 another sign (like a tau "fallen" to the left) serve decorative-symmetrical purposes. The letters are carefully written and apicated. The middle bar of alpha is broken, omicron is as big as the other letters. The circle of omega (also as big as the other letters) opens at the bottom to continue in the form of two short, horizontal lines. The circle of phi is oval-shaped and its vertical line longer than the usual height of the rest letters. The most similar example of lettering I could find among illustrated Koan inscriptions is *PH* 130= Segre, *I.Cos*, EV 206, of probably Neronian or post-Neronian date (the honorand is priest of Asklepios Caesar). However, here and in *PH* 94= Segre, *I.Cos*, EV 233 (for Xenophon's brother) several letters suggest a distinctly older dating.[18] So a date in the second century A.D. for the new inscription is probable and can only be corroborated by a study of the letter forms in the rest of the documents illustrated for Sabinianus.[19] We should, of course, consider that these latter, because of their character, represent a regularly lower level of execution than the monument erected by the Koan *gerousia*.

Some further prosopographical and onomastic observations on the persons mentioned in the new text for Sabinianus may strengthen the proposed rough dating. Two officials of the *gerousia*, L.Fannius Bassus Egnatianus[20] acting as gymnasiarchos (γυμνασιαρχῶν) and M.Spedius

---

[17] Its find (1991) in a late antique context in the southeastern part of the city (on the way to Kako Prinari), approximately at the limit of the ancient city and its modern extension in this area, has been noticed by Ersi Brouskari in a report to be published in the *Chronika* of *AD* 1996. Her report will include a photograph. I thank her for this information and also for the permission to study the inscription and present its text here.

[18] In the first inscription the kappa, the phi and the omicron. In the second one the horizontal bar of pi does not project on the sides, while the general form of the letters is still more of a "square" than tending to oblong shapes.

[19] Segre, *TC*, 202, pl. CXV; *id.*, *I.Cos*, II. pls. 90 (EV 71), 93 (EV 86, 88), 135 (EV 281, 282), 137 (EV 287, 292), 140 (EV 304, 305, 306, 307, 308), 142 (EV 313), 143 (EV 323), 146 (EV 336, 338), 147 (EV 342).

[20] I can find no other Fannii on Kos but I wonder whether there could be some ultimate connection with C.Fannius C.f. στρατηγὸς ὕπατος who sends a letter to the Koan

Beryllus as *epimeletes* (ἐπιμελητεύων), and Aelius Alexander, an obviously subordinate superintendent of the technical work (ἐργεπιστατήσας),[21] were involved in Sabinianus' honor. M.Spedius Beryllus must be related to M.Spedius Beryllus Allianus Iulianus of *PH* 103 (cf. above, p. 88 on this man's relation to the Claudii Iuliani): not only the combination of gentilicium and cognomen,[22] otherwise unattested on Kos, but also the apparently similar social position bring the two Spedii close to each other. The one was here *epimeletes* of the *gerousia* while the other was hereditary priest "in accordance with a divine order."[23] So we should either identify them or suppose that the polyonymous priest was the grandson of the *epimeletes*. That Bassus bears the *agnomen* Egnatianus while Beryllus the *epimeletes* has none, makes a relationship of grandfather to grandson, between the latter and the priest, look more probable. Now, the lettering of *PH* 103 presents a form of omega more elaborate than in Sabinianus' inscriptions: the upper part of the letter is separated from the two short horizontal bars below and shaped like an ellipse opening and twisting inside at both ends below (somewhat recalling the volutes of the Ionian capital).[24] This almost calligraphic form of the letter appears e.g. also in *PH* 99, a dedication for Geta; ibid. 102, an honorary monument independently datable after Commodus; ibid. 129, most probably datable after the *Constitutio Antoniniana* on the ground of Αὐρ. Εὐφροσύνου in ll.8-9; ibid. 141(honorary monument of a *familia gladiatorum* for their patron, the Asiarch Nemerius Castricius L.f. Paconianus and his wife *Aurelia Sappho*), not earlier than the second half of the second century A.D. because of its type and the *gentilicium* of Sappho.[25] There are many similar examples of omega in Koan texts that also seem to date from such

---

archontes (*Jos., AJ* 14.233) to facilitate some Jews' transit through Kos (this Fannius, and the incident, is rather to be dated to 161B.C.: Sherwin-White, *Cos*, 222f. with n. 292). Egnatii on Kos: Herzog, *KF*, 61; probably also *PH* 361 and Segre, *I.Cos*, EV 364.

[21] That he has the same gentilicium as Sabinianus but no praenomen and the kind of his engagement here may even suggest that he was a freedman of the honorand.

[22] Beryllus is also a rare cognomen on Kos, the only other case I know of being P.Ropillius Beryllus in the Greek inscription Herzog, *KF*, 122. See below on its significance.

[23] *PH* 103.2ff.: ἐπὶ ἱερέως κατὰ θείαν κέλευσιν ἀπὸ γένους Μάρκου...

[24] Cf. the facsimiles of this and the next inscriptions from *PH*.

[25] See Campanile, no.54 (p. 70f.).

a late period.[26] These similarities should put the date of the polyonymous priest Beryllus approximately into the third century (first half?) and his grandfather the *epimeletes* somewhere in the second half of the second century A.D. This should then also be the approximate date of M.Aelius Sabinianus.[27]

In further support of this, we may notice that *cognomina* or *agnomina* in -ianus, derived from respective *cognomina* or *gentilicia*, seem to appear as a distinct onomastic phenomenon on Kos about the middle of the first century A.D. They become fashionable no earlier than the second. Apart from the first members of the Claudii *Iuliani* (see above), we should count among the earliest examples: Λεύχιος Κοσσίνιος Λευκίου υἱὸς Βάσσος Οὐ(α)λεριανός[28] and Πό(πλιος) Βισέλλιος Βαβυλλιανός[29] in the first century A.D.; then Πωλλίων Σεργιανός, twice priest of Apollo at Halasarna at rougly the turn from the first to the second century A.D.;[30] still later Μ. Αἰφίκιος Φαβιανὸς gymnasiarch in the second/third century A.D.,[31] the polyonymous Ti.Claudius Alcidami f. Tullus Iulianus Spedianus Allianus,[32] the similar and roughly contemporaneous case of M.Spedius Beryllus Allianus Iulianus, Nemerius Castricius L.f. Paconianus (both latter cited in this section) etc.[33] So a date around the later second century A.D. would suit Sabinianus onomastically, too.

---

[26] So Segre, *I.Cos*, EV 94, 220, 236, 249, 261, 264 (with the respective plates in vol. II). It is frequent among these examples that the two small horizontal lines are, even more elaborately, apicated at the ends.

[27] This conclusion has its importance for the dating of the Kalymnian series of manumissions published by Segre (cf. above), whose time-span for these now proves to be too short. It should be also evident that e.g. Segre, *TC*, 167 (cf. 168-172), dated ἐπὶ μο(νάρχου) Φλαουίου Κλωδιανοῦ, is Flavian at the earliest.

[28] *PH*130 (he is here mentioned as priest of Asklepios Caesar, which points to the period of Nero, cf. ibid. 92). Cf. Segre, *I.Cos*, EV 206 and above (p. 52, n. 119) on his name.

[29] Segre, *I.Cos*, ED 228.11; most probably of the Flavian period, cf. p. 86 above.

[30] Herzog, *Hal.*, no. 4, priest nos. 124 and 131 (ca. 97 and 104 A.D. respectively). He is probably a descendant (son?) of the earlier priest ibid., no. 104 Λεύ(χιος) Σέργιος Λευ(χίου) υἱὸς Πωλλίων. Should the younger Pollion be the son of a Roman and a Greek and thus possibly no Roman citizen himself (as his name form seems to indicate), the *agnomen* Sergianus would have additional significance.

[31] Segre, *I.Cos*, EV 250 ("II-III sec. d.C."). Cf. also the case of a Φλαβια[νόν] restored in Segre, *I.Cos*, EV 147.5 ("II sec. d.C.") and possibly ibid., 160.

[32] *PH* 135, cf. p. 87 above.

[33] The existence of two persons simultaneously with such *agnomina* (Sabinianus, Egnatianus) in the honorary text of the *gerousia* for Sabinianus somehow also indicates an onomastic fashion. The tombstone *PH* 306: Σπεδίου Ἐπαφροδείτου Ὀφελλιανοῦ could belong to a freedman of the Spedii preserving their polyonymous habits.

A further basic onomastic remark, reserved for this context, concerns the *gentilicium* of Sabinianus, Aelius. There are few other (and not earlier) Aelii on Kos,[34] so it is most probable that Sabinianus' *nomen gentis* should ultimately go back to Hadrian or one of his (adoptive) imperial relatives and successors. Having said this, we may enter the final prosopographical quest for Sabinianus. It is certainly possible that

the name Sabinianus could antedate the possession of Roman citizenship and then derive from a person with some other *gentilicium*.[35] On the other hand, it is equally possible that such a *cognomen* could be derived not only from some related Sabinus but also from a Sabina, for example in the case of Ti.Flavius Sabinianus, the son of Ti.Flavius Diomedes and Claudia Leontis quae et Sabina in *I.Stratonikeia*, I, p.67. So Laurenzi's old and bold assumption of a relation with Hadrian's empress cannot be excluded.

Sabinianus' *praenomen*, however, is Marcus while the Hadrianic Aelii's typical *praenomen* was that of Hadrian himself: Publius. Hadrian's planned successor was a Lucius and his eventual one (Antoninus Pius) a Titus. So an immediate connection with any of these imperial personalities seems impossible. Of course, we cannot exclude the possibility of a change of *praenomen* in Sabinianus' family after an original enfranchisement due to one of those Aelii. On the other hand, at least some M.Aelii must have received their Roman citizenship from M.Aurelius who bore as Caesar (139-161) the name M.Aelius Aurelius Verus Caesar,[36] and sometimes appeared even as Augustus in the onomastic form M.Aelius Aurelius Antoninus.[37] A closer link with Sabinianus could then be M.Aurelius' youngest daughter Aurelia Vibia Sabina[38] (born ca. 172 A.D.),[39] who outlived Septimius Severus, whose sister she had been officially recognized to be. We should also consider that some link between M.Aurelius and L.Verus with Kos may be supposed on the basis of the fragmentary inscription *PH* 101 that Paton preferred to restore as containing mention of these two emperors.

Should we then connect the doctor M.Aelius Sabinianus with the imperial patronage of M.Aurelius and/or his youngest daughter in whose honor his cognomen would have been coined? We still know too little to

---

[34] I can find only *PH* 188 and 261, neither of which should antedate the second century A.D.

[35] In the area of the islands we know e.g. Τ. Φλαούιος Σαβεινιανὸς ὁ καὶ Διονύσιος honored as *heros* by the council and people of Chalkis in *IG* XII.9.947. We should also consider an eventual change of *gentilicium* in adulation of a new imperial family.

[36] P.v.Rhoden, *RE* I.2(1894), s.v.Annius (94), 2284.

[37] Dessau, 360; cf. Holtheide, 108.

[38] P.v.Rohden, *RE* II.2(1896), s.v. Aurelius (263), 2544.

[39] As estimated by W.Ameling, *Boreas* 11(1988), 69.

be categorical either way. However, at least some hint at such a prestigious connection might have been expected in Sabinianus' titulature. But what we know of it (even in the new text of the Koan *gerousia*) seems to be of exclusively local relevance. Xenophon's later peer on Kos had to appear stripped of imperial titles. Thus, although Sabinianus' *praenomen* and *nomen* may go back to M.Aurelius' times, his cognomen could find another plausible and "non-imperial" interpretation.

We should also note here that the names in -ianus, already examined from more than one aspect above (p. 84ff.), could also express some sort of devotion to[40] or, in some cases, an intellectual apprenticeship to, a person. In this latter sense we know for example that the disciples of the jurist Masurius Sabinus (first half of the first century A.D.) were known as *Sabiniani* (the counter-school were the *Proculiani*). [41] Our Sabinianus was no jurist but we know of a Sabinus (Σαβῖνος) who was an important doctor.[42] He is mentioned by Aulus Gellius[43] (ca. 180 A.D.) and Galenos,[44] the latter having been educated about the middle of the second century A.D. at Pergamon by his disciple Stratonikos. So Sabinus' *floruit* should be roughly placed in Hadrianic times. He was esteemed as a commentator of Hippokrates. A connection between this Sabinus and the Koan Sabinianus would then also be possible on professional, onomastic, and chronological grounds. However, we should content ourselves at present with simply pointing to it. There are still too many pieces missing from M.Aelius Sabinianus' puzzle.[45]

As we have seen, M.Spedius Beryllus was *epimeletes* when the Koan *gerousia* honored M.Aelius Sabinianus. This man, his probable grandson,

---

[40] This idea presents itself not only in the frequent derivation of such names for slaves/freedmen from their masters' own names—see I.Kajanto, *The Latin Cognomina*, (Helsinki 1965) esp. 35—but also in the naming of political or religious groups after their own "masters," so e.g. Albiniani, Nigriani, Cassiani (*Tert., Ad Scap.*, II.5) and, of course, Christiani.

[41] See Ar.Steinwenter, *RE* IA.2(1920), s.v. Sabinus (29), 1600f.; W.Kunkel, *Römische Rechtsgeschichte*, (Köln [8]1978) 107; most recently T.Honoré, *OCD*[3] s.v. Masurius Sabinus, 935f.

[42] H.Gossen, *RE* IA.2(1920), s.v. Sabinus (25), 1600; K.Deichgräber, *Die griechische Empiriker-Schule*, (Berlin 1965[2]) 25-9.

[43] III.16.8:...Sabinus medicus, qui Hippocratem commodissime commentatus est...

[44] V.119 (Kühn): ...εἷς τῶν ἐν Περγάμῳ διδασκάλων ἡμῶν Στρατόνικος τοὔνομα, μαθητὴς Σαβίνου τοῦ Ἱπποκρατείου... and XVI.196 (ibid.): ...Ῥοῦφος δὲ ὁ Ἐφέσιος καὶ Σαβῖνος ἐκ τῶν νεωτέρων... Rufus of Ephesos belongs probably to Trajan's times: H.Gossen, *RE* AI.1 (1914), s.v. Rufus (18), 1208.

[45] For the sake of completeness I may also cite the apparently important son of a Sabinianus, a *hostis publicus* whose property had been confiscated (early third century A.D.?): the succession of his *iura patronatus* is treated in *CJ* VI.4.1 of 210 A.D. (cf. Frg.Vat. 29= *FIRA*[2], II, p.468).

and another Spedius seem to have had important social roles on imperial Kos. We also noted above that the least numerous group of dedications to the "paternal gods" for the health of a local notable concern M'.Spedius Rufinus Phaedrus (four cases, see Appendix 4). The form of the text is the same as for Sabinianus; that is, Phaedrus was also "son of the city and the *gerousia*" and "benefactor of the fatherland." Thus the constitutional and social conditions for Phaedrus' honors should be also approximately the same. His meager epigraphic record looks rather like the dwindling phase of a long tradition, so I would be inclined to date him after Sabinianus. A comparison of the general style of lettering in his few inscriptions with those for Sabinianus on the basis of Segre's photographs (and a partial personal examination) seems to favor the same conclusion, but one cannot be certain.[46]

What we may finally infer is that there seem to be some indications of humble origins for the Koan Spedii. In *PH* 309[47] we have the tombstone of M.Spedius Naso and his wife Spedia Elpis (her name in characteristically inverse order in the Greek text) whose occupation is expressly stated: πορφυροπώλου, πορφυροπώ[λιδος]. They were obviously engaged in the flourishing and lucrative trade of purple, which was connected with the local silk industry.[48] We may combine this with the fact that the Spedii are one of the Roman *gentes* on Kos who are also attested on Republican Delos.[49] An origin from Italian *negotiatores* in the East seems then probable. On the other hand, there seems to be in this family a predilection for personal names (*cognomina*) borrowed from the vocabulary of precious stones.   This is the case not only with *Beryllus* itself (beryllus= βήρυλλος, a green-blue precious stone)[50] but also with the

---

[46] It is further possible to recognize in Rufinus Phaedrus a descendant of M'.Spedius Faustus (same *praenomen* and *nomen* !) who served twice as priest of Apollo at Halasarna in the first half of the first century A.D.: Herzog, *Hal.*, no. 4, priest nos. 66, 74.

[47] Sherwin-White, *Cos*, 232, n.65 dates it "c. i B.C.-i A.D.."

[48] Cf. ibid. 231f., 242 (on the relation to the Koan silk) and 383 (on the fame of the latter and its importance for the establishment of the Roman community on the island).

[49] See ibid. 252, n. 182. Cf. also the general remark by O.Salomies on the existence of Spedii in both Macedonia and Asia in Rizakis, *R..Onomastics*, 125.

[50] The word seems to appear first in the later Greek (cf. *LSJ*, s.v.) and is probably of eastern origin (the stone reputedly came from India or other regions of the East, cf. H.Blümner, *RE* III.1 (1897), s.v. Beryllos (3), 320f.). I was not able to find any other use of it as a proper name in the area of the islands (no entry in Fraser-Mathews) and there is only a Σαίδιος Βήρυλλος known from Athens in the first half of the third century A.D.: M.J.Osborne-S.G.Byrne, *A Lexicon of Greek Personal Names, II. Attica*, (Oxford, 1994) s.v. It seems to have been more widespread in southern Italy but mainly in the imperial period: P.M.Fraser-E.Matthews, *A Lexicon of Greek Personal Names, III.A,* (Oxford 1997) s.v. (p.90, four examples). Cf. also W.Pape-G.E.Benseler, *Wörterbuch der griechischen Eigennamen*, I(1870³), s.v. and n.52 below.

cognomen of Σπεδίας Ἀδαμανδίου,[51] that is Spedia Adamantion ("the small diamond," a typical use of a neutral diminutive as a female pet name). It is well known that such "mineral" names were very often given to slaves, and so to freedmen (Beryllus was such a favorite name among them).[52] This could very well have been the case with the last mentioned Spedia. The rise of the Koan Spedii could then be simply another case of gradual social mobility on provincial level. Not only the family of Sabinianus but also that of Rufinus Phaedrus would seem to suit well the cost and taste of *Casa Romana* on Kos.[53]

---

[51] Maiuri, *NS*, 654 (a tombstone). Cf. Fraser-Mathews, s.v. Ἀδαμάντιον. It is far less probable that Ἀδαμανδίου should be a patronymic genitive. It is instructive to compare with this case, also in social respect (see below), the Phrygian Σμαράγδιον ("the small emerald") in Maiuri, *NS*, 239 (also a tombstone).

[52] J.Baumgart, *Die römischen Sklavennamen*, (diss. Breslau 1936) 40f. (having counted thirteen examples of Beryllus and two of Berullus with such a social position). Beryllos who appears as teacher (παιδαγωγός) of Nero and in his office *ab epistulis Graecis* in *Jos., AJ* 20.183f. (cf. W.Henze, *RE* III.1(1897), 319f.) should also most probably be a slave or freedman. Cf. also for example the Ἀδάμας Ὀδρύσης in *IG* XII.2.246 (Paros, fourth century B.C.) who could very well be a (typically) Thracian slave or ex-slave and the Thracian eunuch of Kotys *Adamas* in *Arist., Pol.*, V.1311 b 24-25.

[53] L.Laurenzi, *BA* 30(1936), 140 had also noticed that the small dedication for Sabinianus from the excavations at the *Casa Romana* was found not on the pavement of the building but in the probably disturbed stratum above it. So a closer connection between Sabinianus, his epoch and the house on the basis of this find is impossible. However, the taste of an "imperial elite" and the date (mosaics of the third century A.D.) of the house recently suggested by M.Albertocchi (during the First International Congress on Ancient and Medieval Kos, convened there in May 1997) are not at all unsuitable for the above tentative connections. Cf. also M.Albertocchi, "An example of domestic garden statuary at Cos: the Casa Romana," in: I.Jenkins & G.B.Waywell, *Sculptors and Sculpture of Caria and the Dodecanese*, (London 1997) 120-6 (esp. 124), and p.150 below.

E. Fluctuations of favor. Concluding remarks towards a reconstruction of the course of Koan relations with Rome and the consequent status of the island from Mithridates to late antiquity.

A reconstruction of the main stages in the political and social history of Kos as a satellite under Roman hegemony and then as a more or less integrated part of the Roman Empire, even a rudimentary one, must remain incomplete and uncertain on significant points. Despite new evidence analyzed above, too many gaps persist to learn more about various phases and aspects of that development. What follows is a consciously modest attempt to set the results of the partial studies above into the framework of what we do know from other sources about Kos or of Koan relevance in this period. That may provide an interim balance of research and possibly a guide for future studies.

That the experience of the First Mithridatic War was crucial for setting Rome's relations to the Greek cities in the East on a more realistic and sometimes even brutal context should have been relatively clear,[1] but it has recently been exposed with new force and cogency.[2] For the first time in the evolution of her eastern policy, Rome was confronted, through Mithridates, on a grand scale, with hate and aversion against anything Italian. The king's success (and the Romans' failure) was based specifically on a widespread reversal of the climate in Greek-Roman relations, almost at the antipode of Flamininus' era. Certainly, there are many aspects of the problem: only a few cities and principally the lower social layers among Mithridates' eventual allies were internally and militantly anti-Roman.[3] As it has already been observed[4] (and is a priori

---

[1] The advent of a new era in the Roman treatment of the Greek East is e.g. partially assumed in H. Bengtson, *Grundriß der römischen Geschichte*, (München 1982³) 197: "...unter seiner (: Sullas) Ägide haben sie (: seine Soldaten) in Griechenland und in Kleinasien geraubt und geplündert, wie dies bisher undenkbar gewesen war." On his settlement of the East and its consequences cf. the concise picture by J.-M.Bertrand, in: C.Nicolet et al., *Rome et la conquête du monde méditerranéen, 2: Genèse d'un empire*, (Paris 1978) 800-807. Particularly on the epochal character of his measures for the cities (and the drastic reduction, ca. by one half, of the *civitates liberae*): Bernhardt, *I&E*, 114-133; W.Dahlheim, *Gewalt und Herrschaft. Das provinziale Herrschaftssystem der römischen Republik*, (Berlin 1977) 226-236.

[2] By Kallet-Marx, esp. 282-290 (cf. esp. his concluding phrase: "Roman rule, such as it emerges from the pages of Cicero, is largely the product of the First Mithridatic War.")

[3] Cf. the picture drawn by McGing, esp. 108-118.

[4] So esp. Bernhardt, *Polis&RH*, 63f. (cf. his view: "Die Passivität der meisten Städte wurde zweifellos vom Bewußtsein ihrer militärischen Schwäche mitbestimmt..."). Kallet-Marx, 153-160 has adopted and elaborated this point but probably exaggerated in

probable on the grounds of these same cities' necessarily and constantly re-adjusting loyalties on the chessboard of the earlier, Hellenistic monarchies), many cities had no real chance to move against the flow, or rather the torrent, of Pontic advance. In such historical situations, as many later examples may show, even half-hearted compliance with the final loser's wishes cannot be easily expiated. The logic of power and the legitimation of a new, post-war order often demand expressions of heroism in situations where simple human reason would see no room but for the language of dire necessity. Perseverance in friendship towards Rome was something the imperial state meticulously registered and duly reciprocated; its mention has already been noticed as a recurring phrase in Roman decrees and epistles settling questions of the East after the First Mithridatic War.[5] To have remained "up to the end" (διὰ τέλους) a friend of the Romans was obviously a basic condition for achieving a privileged status after the war. In the SC de Asclepiade there is even an explicit connection of a city's free status with this constant loyalty: one jurisdictional option for Asclepiades and his fellow captains of Roman merit was to appear in court Ἐπὶ πόλεως ἐλευθέρα[ς] τῶν διὰ τέλους ἐν τῇ φιλίᾳ τοῦ δήμου τοῦ Ῥωμαίων μεμενηκυιῶν.[6]

Kos evidently lacked such flawless credentials. She was not alone in this or in the ensuing diplomatic mobilization to secure a status partly undeserved by those rigorous standards. Many cities will have emphasized episodes of the preceding war that suited their post-war claims. A good case in point is Aphrodisias. Ambassadors of this inland Karian city resumed contact with the Roman general Q.Oppius residing on Kos (see above, p. 17f.) after 85, expressing their joy over his reappearance on the scene of action[7] and renewing an earlier friendly climate in the city's

---

presenting any anti-Roman feelings and actions in the Greek cities during the war as simply "dictated" by the Pontic king; cf. G.Reger's review of his book, *Bryn Mawr Classical Review* 97.2.6.

[5] Kallet-Marx, 282 with n. 81 (citing the evidence of Sherk, *RDGE*, 18, 22, 23). The same spirit underlies Sherk, ibid. 20 C. 3-6 and 21.II.3 that concern the Thasians' commitment in the same period, as well as Sulla's own phrase in his speech to the representatives of Asian cities in *App., Mithr.*, IX. 62:. οἱ μὲν ἐπηγάγεσθε Μιθριδάτην, οἱ δὲ ἐλθόντι συνέθεσθε (the negative of correctness towards the Romans is conceived here as either encouragement and support of Mithridates' invasion from the beginning or some sort of compromise with him at a later stage of the war, that is again lacking *unfailing* loyalty to Rome).

[6] Sherk, ib. 22. 19-20. The respective, partly restored phrase in the Latin version of the text, ibid. 8-9: "[...in civitate leibera aliqua/ earum, quae perpe]tuo in [amicitia p(opuli) R(omani) manse]runt...."

[7] Reynolds, doc. 3.16f.: ...χαίρειν ὑμᾶς με/γάλως ἐπὶ τῇ ἐμῇ παρουσίᾳ. Oppius had been kept hostage by Mithridates and liberated after the peace of Dardanos: *App., Mithr.*, III.20, XVI.112.

relation to him. They had enthusiastically tried to support him through the prompt dispatch of a civic militia while he was besieged by Mithridatic troops in Laodikeia on the Lykos in 88. Oppius answered with a letter fully certifying the Aphrodisians' loyalty to Rome (and himself) in that beginning phase of the war, and accepted their request to assume the role of their *patronus* in Rome. While the Aphrodisians inscribed on their "archive wall" in the theater both their original and emotional decree of help to Oppius[8] as well as his post-war letter,[9]— which seemed to be a certificate of pro-Roman feeling and action—there is no allusion there or elsewhere to the conduct of the city after Oppius' capture in Laodikeia and the establishment of Mithridatic domination in their area. Furthermore, some vital interest of the Aphrodisians seems to lie behind Oppius' promise "to explain" their acts during the war to the senate and the people when he returns to Rome.[10] The Aphrodisian cause in the imperial city was probably in dire need of a positive report by a high Roman official to redress the balance of favor or disfavor they accumulated for what they did or omitted during the same war. Finally, it is noteworthy that Octavian later conferred the status of *civitas libera* to Aphrodisias for the city's brave resistance to, and hardships experienced at the hands of, his enemies.[11] Reynolds[12] ponders the possibility that Aphrodisias was no *civitas libera* in the period between Sulla and Octavian but examined other possibilities as well. Even if Aphrodisias finally secured a free city status after 85 B.C. (it was then lost again before Octavian's grant, in the hands of Cassius and Brutus?),[13] the city's somewhat concerned approach of Oppius after Sulla's victory may show that any evidence of pro-Roman conduct available was useful at that time. We can also hardly believe that Oppius' patronage would have

---

[8] Reynolds, doc. 2.

[9] Ibid., doc. 3.

[10] Ibid., ll. 44–48: ...ὅπως τε τῇ συνκλήτῳ τῷ τε δήμῳ τὰ ἀφ' ὑμῶν πεπραγμένα ἐστίν, ὅταν εἰς Ῥώμην παραγένωμαι, διασαφήσω. The words used by Oppius strongly recall the pattern in *Pol.*, 22.14.4, although the latter is negatively colored: Philip V fears here in 184 B.C. the unfavorable information on his conduct as a Roman ally that Onomastos might give in Rome (παραγενηθεὶς εἰς τὴν Ῥώμην...πάντα διασαφήσῃ τοῖς Ῥωμαίοις). A lack of first-hand and significant information in Rome is implied in both cases.

[11] Reynolds, doc.s 8 (SC de Aphrodisiensibus), 10 (Octavian's letter to Stephanos), 13 (Octavian/Augustus' letter to the Samians; ll. 2-3: ...τὸ φιλάνθρωπον τῆς ἐλευθερίας οὐδενὶ δέδωκα δήμῳ πλὴν τῷ τῶν Ἀφροδεισιέων ὃς ἐν τῷ πολέμῳ τὰ ἐμὰ φρονήσας δοριάλωτος διὰ τὴν πρὸς ἡμᾶς εὔνοιαν ἐγένετο). On the identification of this latter war, the respective enemies (Labienus) of Octavian/Augustus (appearing here as Αὐτοκράτωρ Καῖσαρ θεοῦ Ἰουλίου υἱὸς Αὔγουστος) and the date of the document see Reynolds, p. 105 but also E.Badian, *GRBS* 25(1984), 165-9 and, independently, G.Bowersock, *Gnomon* 56 (1984), 52 (both suggesting a date after Actium).

[12] Reynolds, p. 4f.

[13] Cf. *Reynolds*, ibid.

been so important for Aphrodisias if Sulla himself or the senate had already formed a picture of unequivocal Aphrodisian loyalty in the war. We should not forget at this point that Sulla had at least some connection with the city through the local cult of his own divine patron, Aphrodite. He had even offered there an axe as an ex-voto in accordance with a favorable oracle he had received during his operations in Greece.[14] Apparently, even the divine patronage of the city might not suffice to balance some of its war record.

Finally, there is at least an indication of Aphrodisian involvement in a common effort of the *koinon* of Asia to attain some alleviation of their onerous provincial burdens handled by the *publicani* (the relevant decree of the *koinon* should date from the seventies B.C.).[15] This could mean that, even with the eventual retention of the free status after Sulla, the city had nonetheless to share the common provincial fate of heavy Roman taxation. This is uncertain, however, since the Aphrodisian ambassadors sent by the *koinon* to Rome seem to have also been citizens of Tralleis. Their election for this mission could thus be irrelevant to the actual status of Aphrodisias and merely due to their important Roman connections.[16] That the city decided to inscribe the honorary decree of the *koinon* for these Aphrodisian-Trallian citizens could also be an expression of pride in its important diplomatic role between the province and Rome, although a closer interest of the city in the aim of that embassy seems more straightforward.

A similar ambiguity of status seems to be reflected in what else is known about Kos between the time of Sulla and the Second Triumvirate. As we saw above (p.28) in the analysis of the relevant passages of the *Lex Fonteia*, Kos must have been a *civitas libera* during Antonius' administration of the Roman East. However, we cannot be sure whether Kos enjoyed this status without interruption between ca. 85 and 40 B.C. We also saw above (p. 18ff.) that Chairylos tried to have the ancestral Koan autonomy reaffirmed by Rome after the city's compromising entanglement with Mithridates, with no obvious results. The question of Koan status must have been raised in Rome then but we still cannot say with certainty how it was finally resolved, despite subsequent Koan services to the Romans.[17]

---

[14] *App., BC*, I.XI.97. Cf. Reynolds, p.3.

[15] Reynolds, doc. 5. Cf. the comm. ibid. and Campanile, 14f.

[16] Also to the prestige of Aphrodisias itself in Rome, cf. Bernhardt, *Polis&RH*, 295.

[17] Such a case was the participation of a Koan ship (with captain and crew) in the naval operations of A.Terentius A.f.Varro, the legatus of Murena and probable successor of Lucullus in the command of the Roman fleet off Asia after Sulla's departure (ca. 84 B.C.), known from a dedication at the sanctuary of Zeus Ourios at the north exit of

If we look for further evidence on Koan status in the sources, we find only some indications of the financial burden Kos had to bear during the period of growing Roman control of, and demands on, the Greek cities after the *Mithridatica*. First, the evolution of Koan coinage seems instructive: despite remaining uncertainties about the beginning date of the late Hellenistic tetrobols of Kos[18] I see no reason to reject Kroll's dating of its end to ca. 88 B.C.[19] Subsequent coin issues in silver (drachms, hemidrachms) or bronze are rather rare.[20] Thus Nikias' coins appearing later (probably in the late forties/early thirties B.C.), seem to represent almost a new beginning in Koan numismatic production. We should perhaps not overlook the point that this apparent new issue of Koan coinage was also its definitive restriction to a bronze one.[21] Although the coins were relatively large, this change is evidence of a gradual, relative impoverishment of the Koan state.

Inscriptions add occasional insights, although necessarily partial and/or fragmentary ones. Thus Sulla's well-known letter to the archons, the *boule*, and the *demos* of Kos on the local publication of the Dionysiac artists' privileges[22] seem to have never been set clearly enough into the proper context of Kos' parallel obligations towards Rome. Sulla granted a united[23] Dionysiac guild in Asia a renewed, circumstantial exoneration

---

Bosporos: *IG* XII.8.260= *IGRR* I.843. Cf. Magie, 238, 1118f. (n. 20); Sherwin-White, *Cos*, 139; Habicht, *I.Kos*, 88 with n. 29. The target of these operations may have been the pirates in the Aegean and adjacent seas, the activities of which Murena tried to check: cf. Magie, 240f.; McGing, 133. That the Koan contribution to Varro's fleet could well be an obligation of a non-free city is shown by the case of Miletos that provided Murena with ten ships "*ex pecunia vectigali...*, sicut pro sua quaeque parte Asiae ceterae civitates" (*Cic., In Verr.*, II.I.89); cf. Magie, 1121f. (n. 27).

[18] *Kroll*, 84 accepted the date ca. 145 B.C. as a *terminus post quem* for their appearance. H.Ingvaldsen (Oslo, cf. p. 21, n.62 above) kindly informed me in a letter of 13.1.1997 that his work on Koan coins convinces him of a much earlier date.

[19] Kroll, 85: "The historical situation provides no conclusive reason for an interruption in coinage which might serve as a *terminus ante quem* for the tetrobol series[...] Nevertheless, as Head remarks, it is scarcely likely that the Asklepios silver went on after the Mithradatic War. Apart from considerations of style, there is the circumstance that it is a substantial coinage and its largest issues[...] are the latest in date. It is quite improbable that such sizable strikings would have been put out in the post-Mithradatic period." *Contra*: Sherwin-White, *Cos*, 23, n.57.

[20] *PH*, p. 318; *BMC Caria*, pp. 210-3 (nos. 165ff.); Head, *HN*, 634. Cf. Burnett, *RPC*, p. 452.

[21] Duly noticed by Kromann, 213.

[22] Sherk, *RDGE*, 49 (now also Segre, *I.Cos*, ED 7). The inscription is still at the magazine of inscriptions at the Knights Castle where I was able to study it in December 1997 (cf. p. 7 above). On its content cf. also esp. Sherk, *Cos* and Sherwin-White, *Cos*, 140 with n. 306, 316f.

[23] Sherk, *RDGE*, p. 265 with n. 2 has assumed a re-unification of the guilds of the Dionysiac artists ἐπὶ Ἰωνίας καὶ Ἑλλησπόντου and περὶ τὸν Καθηγεμόνα Διόνυσον under Sulla whose friendly relation and even familiarity with the *Dionysou technitai* is well-

from many forms of civic liturgies—at least some of them consisting in offering various services to Rome (military service and accommodation of Romans are expressly mentioned). His relevant letter to the artists and a parallel decree of the senate had been appended to his letter to the Koans and published together in the latter's city. Obviously, the beneficiaries of his grant had some special reason to ask through an ambassador, the citharist Alexander of Laodikeia, for the dictator's personal intervention to attain the publication (and implementation) of their privileges on Kos. As Sherk has already supposed,[24] the Koans may have tried to circumvent respecting guild members' immunity. These would have been residents or possibly citizens of Kos. What distinctly emerges is the effort of the Koan state to include as many people as possible in supporting its current communal tasks towards Rome.[25]

At least one of these tasks reappears in a Koan inscription of the first century B.C. as a separate category of civic obligations, immunity from which is this time granted by the Koan state itself. Segre, *I.Cos*, ED 180[26] is the text of a civic statute regulating various aspects of the cult of Herakles Kallinikos. One of them is the sale of its relevant priesthood, and we find among the privileges to be enjoyed by the priest-to-be: ...ἀπολελύσθω δὲ καὶ σιτοφυλακίας καὶ ὑ[πο]/δοχᾶς Ῥωμαίων καὶ ἐπιμηνιείας πάσας ἐφ' ἃς [αἱ]ρεῖται [ὁ δᾶ]/μος (ll. 18-20). Obviously, the "reception of (hospitality to) the Romans" had already established itself among the essential but burdensome, liturgic offices of the city.[27] It would thus be a not negligible secondary motive for a priest-to-be to know he would be freed of it, too.

Finally, we have in Segre, *I.Cos*, ED 193 ("I sec. a.C.") a tantalizingly fragmentary document the subject of which seems to be a loan given to the city by a private creditor (the Aristokritos twice

---

known (*Plut., Sulla*, 26, cf. 36). S.Aneziri, Die Vereine der Dionysischen Techniten in der hellenistischen Zeit, (diss. Heidelberg 1997), ch. A.III.3 has now reviewed the evidence and rejected the idea of a splitting of the united Asian guild between 133 B.C. to Sulla's time. The fact remains that the organization and circulation of these guilds were very useful for Roman propaganda purposes during and after the First Mithridatic War, and so worthy of support.

[24] Sherk, *Cos*, 215 (cf. id., *RDGE*, p.266).

[25] See further below on the style of Sulla in addressing here the Koans.

[26] See also the comments of Habicht, *I.Kos*, 88 on this text.

[27] On the historical development of such "host obligations" in the Greek cities of the Hellenistic and early Roman periods cf. now the special study by D.Hennig, "Die Beherbergung von "Staatsgästen" in der hellenistischen Polis," *Chiron* 27(1997), 355-68 (on the Koan case here discussed: 364). The evidence he assembles and interprets shows even more clearly how onerous this "friendly hospitality" was felt to be. That the aftermath of the First Mithridatic War represented a new strain on the Asian cities in this respect, too, is well-known: *Plut., Sulla*, 25.

mentioned?). There appear sums in "denarii," 1.2; a "capital" (κεφάλαι[ον], 1.3; a "not contemptible man" (μὴ εὐκαταφρόνητον ἄνδρα), l. 6; "a bond" (χειρόγραφον), ll. 7 and 14; "private persons and slaves sent (by someone) to demand" (the sum of the original loan? the interest?), l. 8; "the city's money," l. 12; a "creditor" and perhaps a mention of "the whole senate" (ὅλης τῆς σ[υν/κλήτου]), ll. 13-14. Unfortunately, we cannot say more here except that the city seems to have serious problems with an influential creditor, and some Roman involvement in this strife seems possible. The document seems to be simply another view of a city critically burdened in the first century B.C., a period of serious difficulties for many other Greek cities as well.[28]

Of course, all these glimpses of Koan problems in the first century B.C. cannot prove or disprove the level of its autonomy after Sulla. The most that can be said is that even if Kos remained a city officially free from Roman intervention and regular taxation, a *civitas libera et immunis*, (on the necessity or not of this twofold connection, see below), what it had to sustain was not (or at least was not perceived as) minimal. Furthermore, we should not underestimate, I think, the level of Sulla's intervention in behalf of the Dionysiac artists mentioned above. S.Sherwin-White[29] has concentrated her attention on that part of his letter to the Koans in which the dictator "asks" the Koans to find the most prominent place for the publication of the documents on the artists' immunity.[30] What she describes, however, as a "language...of advice and not command as to a subject community" comes just after his announcement in the same letter that he had already allowed Alexander of Laodikeia (see above) to erect a stele with his guild's privileges on Kos.[31] The city is simply asked to look for the proper place for this

---

[28] In regard to the financial burdens of the Greek cities of Asia after 85, we may recall especially the dramatic description of their indebtedness in *App., Mithr.*, IX.63. Segre, *I.Cos*, ED 192 looks also relevant. It has been attributed by its editor to Halikarnassos on the grounds of a characteristic similarity of style (introduction of new entries in the text by the word ἄλλο) also appearing in *IBM* 893 from the same city. If Segre is correct, it is very interesting to find in this inscription (dated also "I sec. a.C.") again evidence of onerous taxation and contributions to the Roman wars in the area (cf esp. the mentions of εἰσφορά in ll. 5, 12, 24, φόρων, l. 32; ἡγουμένων διὰ τὸν πόλεμον, l. 6, and τὰς τῶν ἡγουμένων ἐπιφ[ανείας?], l.31, clearly pointing to the Romans).

[29] Sherwin-White, 140. Sherk, *Cos*, 212, n.5 was much nearer the point: "The phrase used by Sulla is the usual one employed by the Senate or the higher magistrates in giving instructions to provincial governors on special legates[...]Courteous but firm."

[30] Sherk, *RDGE*, 49. A.13-15: ... ὑμᾶς] οὖν θέλω φροντίσαι ὅπως [ἀπο/δειχθῇ παρ' ὑμεῖν τόπος ἐπισ]ημότατος ἐν ᾧ ἀναθή/[σεται ἡ στήλη ἡ περὶ τῶν τεχνιτῶ]ν.

[31] Ibid. 8-11: ...ἐπέτ[ρε/ψα στήλην] παρ' ὑμεῖν ἐν τῷ ἐπισημοτάτῳ τόπῳ ἀναθή[σεσθαι ἐν ᾗ] ἀναγραφήσεται τὰ ὑπ' ἐμοῦ δεδομένα/[τοῖς τεχνίταις] φιλάνθρωπα. The letters ΕΠΕΤ at the end of l. A.8 are still visible on the stone.

monument. There is no similarity here with Augustus' style in his letter to the free city of Knidos.[32] Closer parallels are to be found, not at all surprisingly, in Sulla's language to the cities of Asia after his victory, documented by Appian,[33] and in M.Antonius' epistle to the Koinon of Asia on the privileges of "the world association of the victors in sacred contests and those where a wreath is the prize."[34] In the first instance Sulla, after having rebuked the Asian cities for their repeated ingratitude to Rome (during the challenge of Aristonikos and then Mithridates) and dismissing a proper retaliation as unworthy of the Romans, builds his harsh fiscal condemnation of the cities on four verbs in the first person singular:

> ἐπιγράφω πέντε ἐτῶν φόρους ἐσενεγκεῖν...καὶ τὴν τοῦ πολέμου δαπάνην..., διαιρήσω ταῦθ' ἑκάστοις ἐγὼ κατὰ πόλεις,...τάξω προθεσμίαν ταῖς ἐσφοραῖς, ...τοῖς οὐ φυλάξασιν ἐπιθήσω δίκην ὡς πολεμίοις.

The delegates of the cities assembled at Ephesos could not negotiate at all; they were subsequently sent back to collect the sums specified. Sulla decided, the cities' task and responsibility was merely to execute his orders. Despite the difference of the setting, the essential style is the same—and significant. M.Antonius' later announcement about the associated game winners' privileges to the cities of the Koinon of Asia is also similar. The triumvir ingenuously expresses the renewal and extension of the association's privileges as his personal grant (συγχωρῶ, 1.19; ἐπεχώρησα, 1.31) and classes his letter to the Koinon of Asia as mere notification: ὑμῖν δ(ὲ) γέγραφα περὶ τούτων (l. 33). Although it is not certain that free cities would not have participated in this forerunner

---

[32] As assumed by *Sherwin-White, Cos,* 140, n. 306. Augustus' letter to the Knidians (Sherk, *RDGE,* 67) presents a distinctly more indirect and polite style in regard to the local implementation of his decision: ἀλλὰ νῦν ὀρθῶς ἄν μοι δοκεῖτε ποιῆσαι τῆι ἐμῆι [περὶ (?) τού]/των γνώ(ι)μηι προνοήσαντες καὶ τὰ ἐν τοῖς δημ[οσίοις]/ ὑμῶν ὁμολογεῖν γράμματα. Furthermore, the Augustan period represents an advanced stage in the relations between *civitates liberae* and Rome, and Augustus expressly mentions that he heard both sides' arguments (some privates' and the Knidians') before he reached his "view" (γνώμη) on the point. Finally, as Millar, *ERW,* 443 correctly remarked, "though Augustus advises them [: the Knidians] to make their public records agree with his verdict, he does not order its public display" (the inscription has been found on Astypalaia where the surviving defendant of the case seems to have retreated after Knidos). Cf. on all points the comm. by Sherk, loc. cit.

[33] *Mithr.,* IX.62. It seems to be an understatement to call Sulla's speech a "harangue": J.G.F.Hind, *CAH²,* IX.162.

[34] Sherk, *RDGE,* 57 (the Greek title of the association: ἡ σύνοδος τῶν ἀπὸ τῆς οἰκουμένης ἱερονικῶν καὶ στεφανειτῶν).

of the later provincial council of Asia,[35] Antonius' style of addressing it seems to have corresponded principally to the rank and file among its members, that is, cities subjected directly to the Roman provincial administration.

Thus we may be trying to define things more precisely and distinctly than the reality of post-Sullan conditions in the Greek cities warranted. Even if Kos remained both "free" and "tax-free" (*civitas libera et immunis*)[36] after Sulla, what would that mean? A good example is Gytheion,[37] a city of the Lacedaemonians/Eleutherolakones (of at least equally pro-Roman tradition)[38] and apparently a "free city,"[39] which was also bending, during the first years of the Third Mithridatic War and M.Antonius Creticus' operations against Aegean pirates, under the weight of what is usually described (with Strabo's term for Sparta's obligations towards Rome) as φιλικαὶ λειτουργίαι, "friendly services."[40] The meaning of such "privileged conditions" had probably depreciated as much as the corresponding value of Greek *amicitia* in Roman eyes after the Mithridatic turbulence. "Freedom" might be retained (as for example Athens, a city most unworthy of it) or it might be restored after some appeals. But it could be most probably curtailed either directly through regular provincial taxation or indirectly through various "offers." Some of its most essential components, and the tact of Roman promagistrates[41] would be even less guaranteed in such cases than before. A *koine* of Roman behavior towards Greek cities was seemingly emerging, in which privileges tended to degenerate into simply titles.

Koan formal autonomy under M.Antonius should then be assessed either as ongoing since approximately the aftermath of the First Mithridatic War or as recently recovered. The latter alternative would perhaps better explain Nikias', Antonius' man on Kos, initial popularity.

---

[35] Free cities' participation at least in the common obligations of the Asiatic Koinon of the imperial period seems to have been optional: cf. esp. Reynolds, docs. 14 and 21 (with comm.). On the republican Koinon of Asia see still J.Deininger, *Die Provinziallandtage der römischen Kaiserzeit*, (München 1965) 14ff.

[36] On the necessity or not of this *joint* status see below with n. 75.

[37] See *Syll.*³ 748 (= L.Migeotte, *L`emprunt public dans les cités grecques*, (Québec 1984) no.24 with precious comm.).

[38] Cf. most recently on the problem of the epigraphically known League of the Lacedaemonians and its apparent successor since Augustan times, the League of the Eleutherolakones, and their relation to Sparta and Rome, the concise picture given in P.Cartledge-An.Spawforth, *Hellenistic and Roman Sparta*, (London 1989) 99f.

[39] On the status of Gytheion vis-a-vis Rome in this period the best remarks are still by Accame, 131f. (but cf. 74!), accepted by Bernhardt, *I&E* 194, n. 523.

[40] *Str.*, 8.5.5 (C 365 fin.).Cf. *Bernhardt, IF*, 196ff.

[41] Cf. the terms ἐπιτασσόμενα, ll.18/9, and ἐπιτάξαντος, l.25, in the decree of Gytheion for the brothers Cloatii cited (n. 37).

The episode of Turullius, Antonius' general, who could not be deterred by any formal protection from felling wood for his master's fleet even in the holy grove of Asklepios,[42] dramatically shows the inherent problems of such privileged relations. Siding with Antonius and his men too closely meant not only profiting from his favor but also enduring the sacrifice of Koan sacred objects (and ideas) to his needs.

On the other hand, the aspects of Nikias' personality and ideological portrait analyzed above appear still very "hellenocentric." The connection with Rome and the triumvir's favor although a vital element, was apparently still incompatible with the official self-image and pride of the Koan city. Nikias' case also proves in this to be less atypical than we might first think. There are at least two partly comparable contemporaries of his: Hybreas of Mylasa and Anaxenor of Magnesia on the Maeander. Both were connected with M.Antonius and played an important role in and for their cities during his command in the East. Anaxenor of Magnesia on the Maeander[43] was a citharoede, known from Strabo[44] and Plutarch[45] as tax-collector and favorite of Antonius in Asia and commander of a detachment of Roman soldiers. However, nothing of all this appeared in the honorary inscription[46] on the basis of a bronze statue erected for him by the Magnesians. There he was simply the excellent cithaoede, implicitly compared through a Homeric citation with Demodokos "whose voice resembled that of the gods,"[47] a distinctly heroic trait.[48] A honorific picture of Anaxenor in the city, mentioned by Strabo in the passage cited, presented him in his purple attire as priest of Zeus Σωσίπολις ("City-Savior").[49] Strabo's testimony seems to suggest that at least one of these honors postdated Anaxenor's connection with Antonius.[50] So the integration of his projected image into the traditional values of the city seemed complete even after his Roman advancement.

---

[42] D.C., 51.8.3: Καῖσαρ δὲ τὸν μὲν Τουρούλλιον ἀπέκτεινε (καί, ἔτυχε γὰρ ἐκ τῆς ἐν Κῷ τοῦ Ἀσκληπιοῦ ὕλης ξύλα ἐς ναυτικὸν κεκοφώς, δίκην τινὰ καὶ τῷ Θεῷ, ὅτι ἐκεῖ ἐδικαιώθη, δοῦναι ἔδοξε)... Cf. Sherwin-White, Cos, 141.

[43] Cf. Magie, 428; Bowersock, A&GW, 10.

[44] 14.1.41 (C 648).

[45] Ant., 24.2.

[46] Syll.³ 766 (cf. Strabo's passage, n. 44).

[47] ...Θεοῖς ἐναλίγκιος αὐδῇ (the end of a distichon cited from Od., IX. 3-4).

[48] Cf. the formula Θεοῖς ἐναλίγκιος ἥρως used to honor a governor in a late antique text from Stratonikeia: I.Stratonikeia 1018.

[49] On this Magnesian cult: Joh. Schmidt, RE IIIA.1(1927), s.v. Sosipolis (2), 1170f. A political allusion in the bestowal of this priesthood on Anaxenor cannot be excluded, especially if we consider some evidence of the use of the adjective σωσίπολις for distinguished benefactors of Greek cities: cf. L.Robert, Bull. 1959, 259 (p. 213).

[50] Str., l.c. (n. 44) mentions as the principal sources of Anaxenor's fame and advancement the theater and Antonius (ὅτι μάλιστα !), and adds, somewhat with the sense of a local

Hybreas'[51] identity and public image is also relevant; the natural interpretation of his onomastic form in some epigraphic testimonies[52] on him and his son shows, I think, that he did not even possess Roman citizenship (like Caesar's and Augustus' friend Potamon in Mytilene). Nevertheless, it has been made plausible in a recent study[53] that his portrait appeared on some rare silver coin issues of Mylasa. He was further worshipped as a *heros* in his city (not necessarily right after his death),[54] and he possibly possessed there a *heroon*.[55] Although of modest origins (his father seems to have been a small wood merchant),[56] he managed through his rhetorical and political skill to succeed as dominant figure at Mylasa his rival Euthydemos whom he once called "a necessary evil"[57] for the preservation of their *polis*. Moreover, Strabo ascribes to both these political stars of ca. triumviral Mylasa monarchic traits (even expressly a "tyrannical" one in Euthydemos' case), endured by the city because of their political talent in leading the citizens through

---

reaction to this wider success of the Magnesian citizen: καὶ ἡ πατρὶς δ' ἱκανῶς αὐτὸν ηὔξησε...

[51]*Str.*, 14.2.24 (C 659-660); *Plut., Ant.,* 24; *I.Mylasa* 534-536; the still unpublished inscriptions from Mylasa mentioned first by L.Robert, *AJA* 39(1935), 335 (cf. id. *Hellenica* 8(1950), 95f.; apud: A.Akarca, *Les monnaies grecques de Mylasa,* (Paris 1959) 28f., n.2; *AC* 35(1966), 419f.(= *OM* VI, 43f.). Cf. L. Radermacher, *RE* IX.1(1914), s.v. Hybreas (1), 29-31; Bowersock, *A&GW*, 5f., 45; Berve, *Tyr.,* 438, 726.

[52] The already mentioned (previous n.) three inscriptions from Mylasa are dedications (the first by a gladiatorial association, οἱ κυνηγοί, the second by a similarly large but otherwise unspecified group of people, the third by a man and his sons) for a person appearing uniformly in the genitive as Γαΐου Ἰουλίου, Λέοντος ἥρωος υἱοῦ, Ὑβρέου ἥρωος, ἀρχιερέως διὰ γένους (so the punctuation of L.Robert, *Les gladiateurs dans l'Orient grec,* (Paris 1940) no. 175, p. 179 - cf. p. 330 -, adopted in *I.Mylasa*). However, with enduring respect for Robert's authority, I find it difficult to accept that the titular use of hero (cf. above) was here applied to the apparently insignificant father (see below) of our Hybreas. I think that the natural reading of the name is Γαΐου Ἰουλίου Λέοντος ἥρωος, υἱοῦ Ὑβρέου ἥρωος, ἀρχιερέως διὰ γένους. This is also consonant with the otherwise predominantly Greek onomastic forms of these texts. We should understand that C.Iulius Leon, Hybreas' son, first found access to the Roman citizenship, and was honored as hero in Mylasa before or after his death just like his father. This interpretation would also better explain the mention οὗ προστάτης Ὑβρέας Λέοντος appended to the name of one of the dedicants in the first of these inscriptions (*I.Mylasa* 534.14). This should not be the honorand in a simpler, Greek name form but his father, the statesman of the Antonian era.

[53] R.H.J.Ashton, "A New Silver Issue from Mylasa," *NC* 1990, 224f.

[54] Cf. the discussion above, p. 55 ff.

[55] L.Robert, apud Akarca (n. 51) also mentioned an epigraphic testimony of a "priest of *heros* Hybreas" and made a concrete proposal for the identification of a funeral monument at Mylasa as Hybreas' *heroon*.

[56] *Str.,* 14.2.24 (C 659):...Ὑβρέᾳ δ' ὁ πατήρ, ὡς αὐτὸς διηγεῖτο ἐν τῇ σχολῇ καὶ παρὰ τῶν πολιτῶν ὡμολόγητο, ἡμίονον κατέλιπε ξυλοφοροῦντα καὶ ἡμιονηγόν.

[57] Ibid. : Εὐθύδημε, κακὸν εἶ τῆς πόλεως ἀναγκαῖον· οὔτε γὰρ μετὰ σοῦ δυνάμεθα ζῆν οὔτ' ἄνευ σοῦ.

contemporary troubles.[58] Although Hybreas' renown seems to have survived undiminished the political change after Actium (he is credited with having a critical relationship with M.Antonius in the latter's heyday),[59] there are in his career many obvious points of similarity with Nikias' position on Kos.[60] The Koan "tyrant" may have been simply less careful in compromising himself under M.Antonius so that his dramatic, belated *damnatio memoriae* was perhaps simultaneously something of a clever Koan *auto-da-fè* towards Octavian.

Whether the Koan status changed after Octavian's victory is the main question. I think we are on safe ground at least in regard to the fiscal obligations of the island towards Rome. Strabo[61] mentions in his entry on Kos an instructive exchange between the city and Augustus. When he received from them Apelles' painting of Aphrodite Anadyomene (to dedicate it to Caesar in Rome) he reduced the tribute the Koans would have paid (τοῦ προσταχθέντος φόρου) by one hundred talents. Bernhardt's view[62] that the above terms meant here not plain taxation, but simply the "friendly services" a *civitas libera et immunis* still owed to Rome, cannot stand. An assessment of the Koan monetary obligations is here manifestly implied. Therefore Kos cannot be regarded as *immunis* under Augustus and, since we know of the celebrated later acquisition of *immunitas* under Claudius, it is very plausible that for the whole period in between Kos was not freed from Roman provincial taxation. Can these fiscal duties have overlapped the same period as Kos' unfree status?[63] Had Kos been so heavily punished for its Antonian-

[58] Ibid.:...ταχὺ δὲ αὔξησιν ἔσχε (sc. Ὑβρέας) καὶ ἐθαυμάσθη ἔτι μὲν καὶ Εὐθυδήμου ζῶντος, ἀλλὰ τελευτήσαντος μάλιστα, κύριος γενόμενος τῆς πόλεως. Ζῶν δ' ἐπεκράτει πολὺ ἐκεῖνος, δυνατὸς ὢν ἅμα καὶ χρήσιμος τῇ πόλει, ὥστ', εἰ καί τι τυραννικὸν προσῆν, τοῦτ' ἀπελύετο τῷ παρακολουθεῖν τὸ χρήσιμον.

[59] Plut., Ant., 24. Cf. Magie, 1278, n.1.

[60] A point of onomastic similarity may also exist with Augustus' friend of dynastic aspirations in Laconia and the Peloponnese, C.Iulius Eurycles (cf. above, p. 42 with n. 69). Although he appears with his full Roman name in some official documents like IG V.1.970 and SEG XI.923 (=Oliver, GC, 15, I), a new honorary inscription for him (base of a statue?) erected by Sparta presents his simple Greek name form (Eurykles son of Lachares). Apparently, his Roman identity was not always the proper one to emphasize.

[61] 14.2.19 (C 657/8). Cf. Sherwin-White, Cos, 145f., 227.

[62] Bernhardt, IF, 201f. (with n. 74). Cf. my n. 75 below.

[63] Until now the two main theses were those of: (a) Sherwin-White, Cos, 146ff., denying that Kos was *civitas libera* between Augustus and Titus but accepting its general *immunitas* since Claudius. She actually elaborated on Herzog, N&X, 215, though cf. ibid., 230 with n. 2 pondering a restitution of *libertas* together with *immunitas* by Claudius (cf. Neppi Modona, 52, 55). (b) Bernhardt, IF, 201-3 (n. 74) choosing the *libertas* of Kos between Augustus and Vespasian (and successfully refuting S.Sherwin-White's counterarguments), though combining it with a "restricted immunity" until Claudius and a "full one" from that time on (see my n. 75 below). Höghammar, 31ff. is a full

Nikian past?[64] To answer these questions we may again gather and try to interpret correctly various testimonies.

The first to examine is the poorly preserved honorary Koan decree for Augustus from Olympia (*IvOl* 53), already cited above (p. 91) because of one of its proposers, C.Iulius Caesar's priest Eudemos son of Epikrates. The text is in the *koine* with some Dorisms, probably to suit the "panhellenic" place and character of its publication. Despite Herzog's second-thought doubts about its Koan origin,[65] the view seems preferable that there is no reason to dissociate this text from Kos. The comparison of the honorand with Merops, the mythical founder of Kos, is clear enough (ll. 22/3).[66] The decree should express, in bombastic style, the Koan gratitude to Augustus for his help to the city after an earthquake (l.7: ...τῆς δὲ τῶν σεισμῶν περιστάσ[εως]), some time after his Cantabrian expedition of 26 B.C. (l. 13).[67] We may note that Augustus is here (ll. 6-7) presented also as πλήονα τῶν [ἄ]λλων ἐπὶ τῆς Ἀσίας Ἑλλή[νων] εὔνοι/αν εὐεργεσίαις τῆ] ἡμετέρᾳ πόλει μεγ[ά]λαις ἐπισφραγιζόμενος. In other words, Kos seems to compare its own (more favorable) treatment by Augustus with that experienced by the rest of the Greek cities in Asia. The connection with Asia reappears in a later passage.[68] Does this mean that Kos understands itself to be here a part of the administrative unit of the *provincia Asia*?[69] I can see no compelling reason for such a conclusion. It is obvious that the natural catastrophe hit not only Kos but a larger area of the Asian coastline, as is often the case in history. Consequently, the framework into which Kos sets itself should be rather a geographical/geophysical than an administrative one, and thus irrelevant to the actual political status of the island during the period in question. Kos found itself in the same sort of trouble with the cities of the province but was not necessarily in the same status with them.

The inclusion of Kos in another Augustan measure of 12 A.D.

---

acceptance of the first position, while Sherwin-White, *RFPE*, 245 has already estimated that Kos "was tributary though free in the Augustan period."

[64] The testimony of *D.C.* 51.2.1: καὶ ὃς (: Octavian after Actium) τὰς μὲν πόλεις χρημάτων τε εἰσπράξει καὶ τῆς λοιπῆς ἐς τοὺς πολίτας σφῶν ἐν ταῖς ἐκκλησίαις ἐξουσίας παραιρέσει μετῆλθε... should probably be interpreted against the whole picture of Augustus' diplomatic leniency in the East after his victory, as reconstructed by Bowersock, *A&GW*, 85ff.

[65] *N&X*, 216, n.6.

[66] Cf. on and against Herzog's later views on this inscription L.Robert, *Hellenica* 2(1946), 146, n. 2 and *BCH* 102(1978), 401; also Höghammar, 33.

[67] Cf. Höghammar, ibid.

[68] L. 24: ...ἐπ[ὶ τῆς] Ἀσία[ς ? ῥα]στώ]νης π[ρο]νοῆσαι.The context remains too fragmentary.

[69] So Sherwin-White, *Cos*, 146 with n. 345.

seems to be more revealing. Cassius Dio[70] reports that the emperor tried in that year to tighten control of exiles in the empire. These often left their place of banishment or, if they remained there, they lived in luxury. To limit transgressions of the first kind, Augustus decreed that in the future all exiles should stay only on islands at least four hundred stadii (ca. 70 km) away from the mainland. However, he excepted from this rule Kos, Rhodes, Samos and Lesbos. Dio admits his incapacity to understand this exception. However, a basic reason for the different treatment of the four islands[71] must have been that Augustus considered them very secure places for exiles. In other words, he had complete confidence not only in their loyalty to him, but probably also in their determination not to imperil their status through involvement in subversive actions. Therefore, it is quite natural that Rhodes, Samos, and the main city of Lesbos, Mytilene (probably also Methymna), are all known to have possessed the status of *civitates liberae/foederatae* in this period.[72] I cannot see why Kos, mentioned first in Dio's passage, should not have maintained the same conditions of both trust and concomitant privilege.[73] So the only logical inference possible is that Kos was a *civitas libera* in 12 A.D.

About ten years later, in 23 A.D., Tiberius let the senate recognize the *asylia* of both the Heraion of Samos and the Koan Asklepieion, as

---

[70] 56.27.2-3: ἐπειδή τε συχνοὶ φυγάδες οἱ μὲν ἔξω τῶν τόπων ἐς οὓς ἐξωρίσθησαν τὰς διατριβὰς ἐποιοῦντο, οἱ δὲ καὶ ἐν αὐτοῖς ἐκείνοις ἁβρότερον διῆγον, ἀπηγόρευσε (sc. Augustus) μηδένα πυρὸς καὶ ὕδατος εἰρχθέντα μήτε ἐν ἠπείρῳ διατρίβειν μήτε ἐν νήσῳ τῶν ὅσαι ἔλαττον τετρακοσίων ἀπὸ τῆς ἠπείρου σταδίων ἀπέχουσι, πλὴν Κῶ τε καὶ Ῥόδου Σάμου τε καὶ Λέσβου· ταύτας γὰρ οὐκ' οἶδ' ὅπως μόνας ὑπεξείλετο... The reading Σάμου is here Boissevain's reasonable emendation of Σαρδώ (Sardinia) in the manuscripts.

[71] Cf. B.Levick, *Historia* 28(1979), 376, n. 96 remarking: "It is tempting to think that the restrictions were imposed to anticipate or check activity by political exiles..." and D.Kienast, in: *Klassisches Altertum, Spätantike und frühes Christentum (Festschrift A.Lippold)*, hrsg. von K.Dietz u.a., (Würzburg 1993) 204: "Vor allem diese letzte Bestimmung zeigt, daß damals offenbar die gesamte römische Welt durch Unruhen gefährdet war, deren Urheber oft genug innenpolitische Gegner des Augustus oder seines präsumptiven Nachfolgers waren." At the same time, the exception could well have meant a privilege for these islands where the usually affluent Roman exiles were sent—as noted by Höghammar, 32f.; A.J.Papalas, *Ancient Icaria*, (Wauconda/Ill. 1992) 136f.

[72] Bernhardt, *I&E*, 190 (Rhodes), 201 (Samos), 187 (Mytilene). Methymna had an old *foedus* with Rome (*Syll.*[3] 693, ca. 129 B.C., cf. Bernhardt, *I&E*, 109 with n. 108 and most recently Kallet-Marx, 187 with n. 17), and there seems to be no reason for a later change of its status vis-a-vis Rome (some doubt in Bernhardt, *I&E*, 126).

[73] So also Bernhardt, *IF*, 203 (n.74). However, I cannot see any evidence for an institutionalized privilege of some cities in the Roman world to accept exiles, for which he uses (also Bernhardt, *I&E*, 229, cf. 99) the term "ius exilii" (perhaps misleadingly: on the usual sense of the **personal** *"ius exilii"* cf. concisely A.Berger, *Encyclopedic Dictionary of Roman Law*, (Philadelphia 1953) s.v., 528).

already noted above in the context of Chairylos' and Xenophon's careers (pp. 16f., 76). The equally unreserved confidence in Koan loyalty expressed through this distinction, the high praise bestowed on the island's past record of devotion to Rome according to Tacitus[74] and, last but not least, the parallel application and success of Samos who was already a *civitas libera*, may confirm the above conclusion. At the beginning of Tiberius' reign Kos should have retained this status. What we know further in connection with Koan status in later years does not conflict with this conclusion as we shall presently see. Kos was most probably a free but non tax-free *polis* in the early empire.[75] We should

---

[74] *Ann.*, 4.14. We recall that the episode with the Koan refugees at the Asklepieion appears only here in our ancient tradition.

[75] Bernhardt, *IF* has presented in detail the thesis that a *civitas libera* was automatically also *immunis*, in the sense that it was freed from direct Roman taxation, from the republican period until late antiquity. He tried to explain the obvious difficulty thus remaining in the sources, that some "free cities" still appear there without "immunity" (immunitas, ἀτέλεια) or acquire it afterwards, by assuming a distinction between a "restricted immunity" in the above sense (: from the direct taxes of the ordinary *civitates stipendiariae*), properly called ἀνεισφορία in the Greek sources, and a "full one," ἀλειτουργησία in precise Greek, freeing a city from all forms of financial obligations and services to Rome, such as billeting of troops, provision of food etc. This latter concept of immunity should be identified with the *plenissima immunitas* mentioned in *Dig.*, 27.1.17.1 (for Ilion). Thus a "free city" should possess always the first and sometimes the second, higher form of immunity. Bernhardt's theory has certainly the allure of a neat solution. However, various points remain uncertain or point directly to the possibility of Rome's combining the grant of *libertas* with the demand for taxes so that the old view, since Mommsen (cf. also the still useful study by A.H.M.Jones, "Civitates liberae et immunes in the East," in: *Anatolian Studies Presented to W.H.Buckler*, (Manchester 1939) 103-117), holding the *immunitas* (with whatever extent) to be a separate and eventually separable privilege seems to me still preferable. Apart from the above rejected equation of φόρος/-οι with forms of real services to Rome (the various *philikai leitourgiai* of the "free cities") we should especially consider that: (a) The practice of levying direct taxes on "free cities" under the Republic does appear in our sources, though connected with emergencies. The first such case fits exactly into the aftermath of the First Mithridatic War according to *App., BC*, I.102, a later one appears ib., V.6 (during Antonius' rule in the East). If we also take into account that *Cic., Off.*, 3.87 ascribes to Sulla a policy of selling the status of *libertas* to some cities, that is probably demanding the payment of their direct taxes to Rome in a single rate (he also demanded five years' taxes in advance from the rest of the cities: *App., Mithr.*, IX. 62), we may realize that no principle of leaving the "free" untaxed is discernible. (b) In regard to the evidence of Reynolds, doc. 13, in which Augustus seems to regard the freedom from taxes as a natural concomitant of civic *libertas*, I think that Badian's reserves, *GRBS* 25(1984), 169f. are justified. How can we know that the Samians had not asked him for *libertas* and *immunitas* (cf. the connection οὐδὲ in the Greek text), that is, as two cognate but separate privileges, to receive finally neither? (c) As Ferrary, *P&I*, 7f. (n. 7) remarked, Plinius' usage of *immunis* in the sense of a "full immunity" is neither consistent nor compatible with the usage of Cicero in the speeches against Verres. (d) Even the example given in *Dig.*, 27.1.17.1 for the extent of the Ilians' "plenissima immunitas," their exemption from the obligation to undertake a *tutela* of non-Ilian children, seems to suggest a specific rather than general type of privileged status. (e) The celebration of

then also conclude that Nikias' posthumous condemnation was not accompanied by a parallel loss of political-legal status of his city. Augustus, who was more than once celebrated as *ktistas* and whose cult was possibly conjoined with that of Asklepios on Kos,[76] was apparently able to show once more a lenient face to one of Antonius' partisan cities in the East.[77] Local self-government under some distant Roman control could continue, although combined with direct taxation (until Claudius' reign, see below). However, equally important will have been for Augustus the possibility of indirect control on Kos through local distinguished citizens. It is useful to recall here the impression (p. 46 above) of a certain continuity in local administrative careers bridging Nikias' and Augustus' periods. The emblems might change but Augustus seems to have been wise enough again not to renounce the further collaboration of well-established local cadres.[78]

If Kos thus experienced in the Augustan-Tiberian phase of the principate a relative state of respect and even distinction, the apex of privilege was reached with Claudius through Xenophon. This is an exemplary case of how important the mediation of a Greek of high imperial standing could prove to be for the corresponding status of his homecity. Thanks to Xenophon's assiduous persuasion, Kos achieved the vital complement of its desired status: *immunitas*. According to Claudius (as reported by Tacitus) the Koans should in future, freed from any tribute, devote themselves fully to the role of keepers of their holy island.[79] This was in 53 A.D., just one year before Claudius' dramatic

---

ἀτέλεια alone on some coins of the *civitas libera* Alabanda in the Augustan period (Head, *HN*, 607, legends ΑΤΕΛΕΙΑΣ, ΑΤΕΛΕΙΟΣ; cf. Bernhardt, *IF*, 195) is much more understandable if that immunity was an extra privilege, perhaps recently acquired. (f) Especially intriguing and unclear is the case of cities that managed to have their "free city" status restored after some departure in their loyalty to the Romans. Their reacquisition of a local government according to their *patrioi nomoi* was up to a point expedient to Rome itself, ever unwilling to swell its provincial administration. Taxation was probably another matter.

[76] Patriarca, no.10= Höghammar, no. 69, an honorary inscription (base) for an author of *enkomia* ἔς τε τὸν κτίστα[ν] τᾶς πόλιο[ς] Σεβαστὸν Καίσαρα καὶ τὸς εὐεργέτας Τεβέριον Καίσαρα... Maiuri, *NS*, 462.12-3 (post-Claudian, cf p.97 with n. 142 above) mentions Σεβ[ασ]τὰ Ἀσκλαπίεια μεγάλα: cf. Herzog, *N&X*, 217 (tracing this back to Augustus); Sherwin-White, *Cos*, 358 (stressing the general connotation "imperial" of the epithet *sebastos* added to the name of festivals but also the post-Augustan date of the other testimonies on the syncretism between the cult of the emperor with that of Asklepios on Kos).

[77] Cf. Bernhardt, *I&E*, 177ff. (esp. 182).

[78] Bowersock has well demonstrated this policy in regard to the dynasts of the East in *A&GW*, 42ff. Cf. now also the concise picture by B.Levick, *CAH²* X(1996), 649f.

[79] *Tac., Ann.*, XII. 61. 2: "...dixit (sc. Claudius)...precibusque eius (sc. Xenophontis) dandum, ut omni tributo vacui in posterum Coi sacram et tantum dei ministram insulam colerent."

end. We may be a little surprised at his relatively late grant of such a crowning privilege. Xenophon's achievement of a position of influence with the emperor must have immediately postdated the British expedition (see above, p.74f.). Thus almost a decade intervened between what might be called a potential and an actual state of Claudian favor towards Kos.

The emperor's three new letters to the Koans, repeatedly alluded to above, fall exactly into that intervening period and, despite their state of preservation, may help us understand better the development of Claudius' attitude to Kos.[80] The first letter, dated to Claudius' seventh *tribunicia potestas*, that is 47/48 A.D., is the answer of the emperor to a decree of the Koans delivered to him by a Koan embassy headed by Xenophon himself. The content of the decree seems to have been Koan congratulations to Claudius for his British victory—on the occasion of which sacrifices and other celebrations on Kos are mentioned. The emperor refers explicitly to Xenophon's both exemplary piety to him and vigilant care for Kos, and apparently assures the Koans that the "outstanding gifts" (δωρεαῖς μεγίσταις, col. II.35) to the island in the past would be preserved and perhaps enlarged (εὐερ]/γεσίας προσεξευρί-σκοντ[α ?, col. II.35/6]. After this preparatory and reconnoitering approach, the correspondence between the emperor and the Koans continued with two more letters, both dated to the next year (48/49).[81] In

---

[80] My knowledge of these letters rests on: (a) the apograph of Herzog, now kept at the *IG* in Berlin (and prepared for publication with all his other Koan *inedita* by L.Hallof) kindly communicated to me by K.Hallof; (b) the personal study of the stone that I finally rediscovered in the magazine of the Koan Castle in May 1997. The inscription had also been seen and numbered as ED 147 by Segre, *I.Cos*, I (a photograph ibid., II, pl. 43) but he has apparently not transcribed the text. The extant fragment of the original marble stele (81x79x7cm) preserves a part of the edge below and above but is broken on both the left and the right side, almost vertically up to about the middle of the whole height and from there on in an oblique way towards the upper central part. So the upper part of the stone takes on a trapezoidal shape. On the lower part of the back face two small square holes are preserved: perhaps they facilitated the fastening of the stele on a wall. On the front face, further worn in the long period since Herzog's original find, the text is arranged in three columns. We have the extra right and lower part of a first column (traces of twenty lines, ca. the last ten letters of each preserved), the whole area of a second column (thirty lines of about thirty five letters each) and the left and mainly lower part of a third column (traces of ca. twenty seven lines, each with just one to eleven letters preserved up to line fourteen and ca. fifteen letters in the sequel). So we have in all a text of seventy-seven lines the reading of which is very difficult because of the state of the stone. On many points, however, it is still possible (on the original and my squeezes), and especially valuable where Herzog's apograph does not offer a convincing text (on such a case see below).

[81] The second letter is dated by δημαρχικῆς ἐξουσίας τὸ/ ὄγδοον (col. II.42-3). The third letter should reasonably fall either in the same or in one of the following years. Herzog's restoration of the relevant passage (col. III.68/9) also as δη[μαρχικῆς ἐξουσίας τὸ ὄγδο]/ον must be correct because all legible beginnings of lines (I checked it myself) are entire syllables. So e.g. [ἔνατ]/ον may be excluded.

the first of these, the second of the series, Claudius appears to respond to a request of Xenophon concerning some privileges for the Koan *gerousia*: its members (τοὺς τοῦδε/ μετέχοντας τοῦ συστήματος, ibid. 48/9)[82] should be freed from the obligation of housing (Roman) official guests (...τᾶς ξενοδοχίας ὀχλήσεως..., ibid. 50). Most intriguing is the final letter preserved. Although we have only nine lines in all after the introductory and dating formula, and of these only a left vertical strip of ca. fifteen letters per line is legible, we get some insight into a difficult situation that caused Claudius' repeated communication with the Koans in the same year. The reason for this letter seems to have been a political conflict that had flared up on Kos (ἀ]/κμάζουσα στάσις, ibid. 77/8). Claudius presents the "always patriotic" (αἰεὶ φιλοπάτριδο[ς], ibid. 76) Xenophon fearing that this situation could lead to more serious trouble (δείσαντος μήποτ[ε].../ μείζονος κακοῦ αἰτ[ία γένηται (sc. ἡ στάσις) ?], ibid. 77, 79). The emperor's reaction to Xenophon's fears (and most probably the realization of the latter's suggestions *ad rem*) seems to have remained at the beginning of this letter. It may have meant the prohibition of some form of dangerous activity in the city but the more precise form in which we should restore the text here is uncertain.[83] What should become clear is that the current political climate on Kos was not at all calm so that an imperial intervention instigated by Xenophon was thought necessary. Therefore, the late addition of *immunitas* to the city's privileges may have been simply reasonable: Kos probably had to persuade both emperor and counselor a little more that it was politically prudent enough and worthy of further distinctions. Xenophon's role as a Koan patriot of Roman principles becomes hereby all the more interesting.[84]

---

[82] Herzog had read this point as τοὺς ΕΠΥΥΣΤΟΥ ἀλλὰ/μετέχοντας τοῦ συστήματος...

[83] However, a crucial word in col. III. 73 is ΑΡΑΣ read by Herzog as ἀράς. I think that this is a participle, ἄρας, and could give the clue to a reading as, *exempli gratia*, [τὰς ἑταιρεί]/ας ὑμῶν ἄρας ἀεὶ νευ[ούσας πρὸς ταραχήν].

[84] This climate of political agitation in the city is clearly a further indication that Kos was already a *civitas libera*: cf. a somewhat similar situation of *stasis* on Antonine Rhodes as depicted in Aelius Aristides' Ῥοδίοις περὶ ὁμονοίας (Keil XXIV). In regard to the Claudian period itself, we should also not forget the political climate on Rhodes that led to the events (44 A.D.) described by *D.C.* 60.24.4: τῶν τε Ῥοδίων τὴν ἐλευθερίαν ἀφείλετο, ὅτι Ῥωμαίους τινὰς ἀνεσκολόπισαν. The restitution of Rhodian liberty also took place late in Claudius' reign with the famous advocacy of Nero (53 A.D.): *Tac., Ann.*, 12.58; *Suet., Nero*, 7 (the event wrongly dated two years earlier); *IG* XII.1.2.12-14. Cf. F.Hiller v.Gaertringen, *RE* Suppl. V(1931), 810; H.H.Schmitt, *Rom und Rhodos*, (München 1957) 189. On Xenophon's adoption of Roman principles cf. the penetrating remarks by F.Millar, *A Study of Cassius Dio*, (Oxford 1964) 189f.: "...there can be no doubt that for the leading families in the Greek East, posts in the Roman governmental hierarchy were the objects of ambition and the crown of social prestige [...] To gain these

The constant interest of the imperial center in Koan developments under Claudius can now also better explain a well-known document from Kos, not seen so far from this perspective: Corbulo's letter to the Koans.[85] Cn.Domitius Corbulo[86] is known as proconsul of Asia under Claudius and a fragmentary letter of his addressed (as Claudius' letters) to the archons, the *boule*, and the people of Kos is preserved there. The subject of the letter must be an appeal of a Koan citizen submitted directly to the emperor, that is, without the proconsul's previous examination of the cause for this appeal. The appellant seems to have acted so in connection with (against?)[87] a relevant decree of the city, and "in a malicious, obstructive attitude" (ἐπηρείας/[χάριν], l. 13).[88] The proconsul begins his letter by referring to his responsibility, frequently publicized before, to examine the causes of such appeals before they reach the emperor. So, if the present appellant wishes his case to follow the normal method of appeal (obviously to be respected), he has now to deposit with the proconsul the sum of earnest (2,500 denarii) that the latter had fixed for such cases, that is, as a surety against litigants who eventually would not appear at a trial. The inscription might be taken as evidence that Kos was no *civitas libera* at that time since the provincial governor could insert himself in this way as an intermediate authority between the emperor and the city. The crucial fact is, however, that the governor does not appear here as a substitute for civic jurisdiction but

---

they must have acquired not only Latin but certain governmental skills and attitudes of mind."

[85] The basic edition of this text should now be Segre, *I.Cos*, ED 43 (previously accessible in the advance publication in *PP* 30(1975), 102ff.). I was able to check his readings against the proposals of J.H.Oliver, *AJPh* 100(1979), 551-4, who was unable to see the stone, in the original, also at the magazine of the Knights Castle. Two significant results of my examination are that: (a) the first preserved letter of l. 4 is rather a lambda, only looking like an alpha because of a later, horizontally engraved line (part of a cross) in this section of the text. So Oliver's version for ll. 4ff. seems basically correct and we should read them as: [Οὐκ ἀλυσιτε]λὲς ἡγησάμην πολλάκις/ [καὶ πόλεσ]ι παραστῆσαι, [ὅ]σα ἐν ἐμοὶ μά/[λιστα, ὅτι ἃ] ἄξια δύναται νομι[ί]ζεσθαι/ [κρίσεω]ς εἶναι θείας τοῦ Σεβαστοῦ, /[πρότερον πρὸ]ς τοὺς ἐπὶ τῶν ἐπαρχει/[ῶν πέμπεσθαι ἐν ται]/ς ἐντολαῖς ἐπι/[τέτακται... (b) There seems to be neither a trace of, nor room for, restoring a nu at the end of l. 16, so Segre's reading should stay vs. the alternative restoration of Oliver. On the content of the text in connection with the problem of the emperor's issue of *mandata* to proconsuls in the early empire cf. also G.Burton, *ZPE* 21(1976), 63-8.

[86] Cf. concisely on him now A.Momigliano-G.E.F.Chilver-M.T.Griffin, *OCD*[3], s.v., 492f.

[87] *Segre, I.Cos*, ED 43.10-12: [...νῦν δ' ἐξ ὑμετ]έρου ψηφίσμα/[τος ὁ δεῖνα ἔκκ]λησιν ἔθετο ἐπί/ [τὸν Σεβαστὸν...The situation would be still clearer if we restored [...νῦν δὲ καθ' ὑμετ]έρου ...

[88] Cf. *LSJ*-Revised Supplement (1996), s.v. ἐπήρεια. The other side of the story is most probably the appellant's distrust both of the civic iurisdiction and the governor's stance in his case. Oliver's (cf. n. 85), alternative restoration, ἐπηρείας [ἔργο]ν, and comment on

only as the first possible contact with the imperial administration in a case where one of the persons involved had already decided to embark on an appeal to Roman authorities.[89] The point seems to be the hierarchization (and eventual decentralization) of the appeal procedure—a recurring problem in the empire[90]—rather than any formal "provincialization" of Kos. At the same time the inscription shows two further important things: first, that even a *civitas libera* was counted potentially among the nearest governor's responsibilities; this relationship could be activated if the working of the city ceased to function in a "self-sufficient" way, as for example in this case of discontent with civic decisions.[91] To express it differently, a "free city" was as little or as much subordinated to provincial Roman authorities as it could do without them or not. Second, this apparently abortive attempt of a Koan citizen to come into direct contact with the emperor's justice, by-passing what could be the standard procedure, cannot have been unrelated to the frequent, direct channel of communication between Rome and Kos. What seems to have been the normal procedure for Koan problems reaching Claudius through Xenophon (and probably his own people on the island), however, was blocked if someone else aspired to a similar and immediate access to imperial interest. Such cases were diverted and decided first (and possibly finally) at the proconsul's court. This clear pattern of direct and indirect access to Rome may suit very well the new information on internal dissent on Kos in the same period. Some Koans were controlled on a provincial level before the central imperial authority became involved. Xenophon's key role and fears on Koan discord under Claudius may have found a discreet expression here, too.

Koan relations within the larger organizational framework of the *provincia Asia*, without any necessary formal integration into it, are

---

this point seem to be no progress. The bracket after χάριν has been inadvertently omitted in Segre, ibid.

[89] Sherwin-White, *Cos,* 146f., though inclined to conclude from this text that Kos was no *civitas libera* at that time, has to admit (in the face e.g. of Hadrian's instructions in his Athenian "oil-law," Oliver, *GC* 92.55f.) that the governor's "competence over appeals is not of itself proof of the Coans' incorporation in the province of Asia." It is characteristic that Oliver (n. 85), 553 would better understand the interaction of city and governor in this case if Kos were a "free city."

[90] Cf. recently K.Buraselis, The Roman World of Polyainos, *Archaiognosia* 8 (1993-94), publ. 1995: 130ff. (with further bibl.)

[91] Cf. the cases on a similar subject already studied by J.H.Oliver, "The Roman Governor's Permission for a Decree of the Polis," *Hesperia* 23(1954), 163ff. (one of his conclusions, 167: "...The free cities (*civitates liberae*) were not bound to consult the governor as frequently as the other cities, but though they did not ask his permission for their enactments, they may have been just as eager as any other polis to enlist supporting action from the Roman government.")

further reflected (a) in the designation of one of Xenophon's relatives, although probably not himself a resident of Kos, to the post of the high priest of Asia (see above, p. 81); (b) somewhere in the period between ca. 70 and 90 A.D., in the Ephesian list[92] of Asian cities and communities arranged according to *conventus/dioikeseis* and accompanied by short entries of various duties in money. The character of this list remains, despite all efforts,[93] enigmatic. I find it impossible to accept D. Knibbe's[94] reservedly expressed theory, however, that the document represents a kind of "inventory of the *fiscus* of the province Asia" at some point of the period mentioned. We find notably among the *poleis* of the list Samos, Chios, Mytilene, and Kos. Samos[95] and possibly Kos, as we shall presently see, lost their *libertas* and probably also their tax-free status under Vespasian. We know nothing concrete about the other two. Chios especially had a long-standing, stable record as a "free city" since the First Mithridatic War,[96] and there seems to be no reason to suppose a later interruption of it.[97] So we should rather see in the inclusion of these four cities in the list a partial proof that its purpose was different, possibly an officially established, central record of local, civic taxes or a list of contributions to a provincial scheme surpassing the distinction between *civitates liberae* and *civitates stipendiariae* (imperial cult?).[98] In either case, Kos is found again participating in the common life of the Asian cities without any indication that things went farther than that.

The only probable testimony of a rather short change of status for Kos in the Flavian period is an entry of the list of priests of Apollo from Halasarna the *terminus a quo* and the beginning part of which have been

---

[92]Original publication by C.Habicht, "New Evidence on the Province of Asia," *JRS* 65(1975), 64ff. Now also *I.Ephesos* 13= *SEG* 37.884. Cf. the next notes.

[93] I know of two major attempts at a general interpretation of this intriguing document so far: F.Gschnitzer, "Beurkundungsgebühren im römischen Kaiserreich. Zu IvE I a 13," in: *Symposion 1985. Vorträge zur griechischen und hellenistischen Rechtsgeschichte* (hrsg. von G.Thür), (Köln 1989) 389-403, trying to interpret the list as a central tabulation of various civic taxes in the province; D.Knibbe, "Zeigt das Fragment IvE 13 das steuertechnische Inventar des *fiscus Asiaticus*?," *Tyche* 2(1987): 75-93, the content of which is already indicated in the title question (cf. below).

[94] Previous n. His tentatively expressed views have already been criticized by H.W.Pleket, *SEG* 37(1987), 884, comm. Also reserved: R.Gordon et al., *JRS* 83(1993): 141.

[95] *Suet., Vesp.*, 8.4. This short list of cities that lost their *libertas* under Vespasian includes Rhodes, a neighbor of Kos.

[96] Sherk, *RDGE*, 70. Cf. Bernhardt, *I&E*, 128, 157, 187f. with n. 488.

[97] It is noteworthy that Chios and Kos present exactly the same two categories of entries (πάντων - εἰς γερουσίαν), the latter occurring only here in the whole text. The sums mentioned are different for each island.

[98] The former view has been proposed by Gschnitzer, cf. n. 93. The second is adumbrated but not adopted, ibid., 402.

examined in the chapter on Nikias (p. 41ff.). As already noticed there, the first entry of this list has been dated by Hiller to 27 B.C., on the ground of the addition following the name of the priest P.Hetereius Hilario, no. 106: ἐπὶ τούτου οἱ νόμοι ἀποκατεστάθησαν. Although some doubts might remain with regard to the character of these "laws" (sacred or public), Hiller's solution—to recognize here a restitution of Koan *patrioi nomoi*, that is a return to the status of *civitas libera*, is more probable, especially if we consider the tendency to "enlarge" personal entries in various lists of officials in order to glorify the person catalogued by listing him chronologically with a generally important (and favorable) event.[99] If we accept the date initially preferred by Herzog for the inception of the list, 30 B.C., this restitution should fall inside Vespasian's reign, in 76 A.D. We know that Rhodes lost its liberty under him but very probably regained it under Titus.[100] Hiller identified Titus' first year, 79 A.D., with the year no. 106 in the Halasarnan list. This can be only a relative chronology; the change may well have happened some years later and the beginning of the list postdated 27 B.C. At least, I cannot see any compelling reason to connect the year no. 1 in the list with Augustus' assumption of his new, dynastic name and constitutional position. However, Vespasian's removal of *libertas* from many Greek cities, for example Koans' neighbors, the Rhodians, and the restitution of status in apparently later Flavian times in the Halasarnan list, make it probable that Kos experienced a similar fluctuation of imperial favor and local status. What we know now about the island's unrest under Claudius—and the climate of Nero's period cannot have diffused political animosities in any Greek city—may corroborate this impression. Thus, we may now, after the development delineated above, dispense with the alternative possibility once endorsed by S. Sherwin-White,[101] that Kos was not a *civitas libera* in the period from Augustus to

---

[99] Cf. esp. Chaniotis, *H&H*, 189f.

[100] See n. 95 on the Rhodian loss of *libertas* under Vespasian. Its restoration under Titus may be concluded from *IG* XI.1. 58.9-11 (honorary decree for a Rhodian τυχόντα τῶν καλλίσ/των γραμμάτων ἀπὸ τοῦ θεοῦ Σεβαστοῦ (: Titus, l. 5f.) ἐν/ τῷ τᾶς πρυτανείας καιρῷ; on the special significance of expressions like *kallista grammata* et simm. cf. p. 20f. above). Whether this grant/promise of a grant by Titus was first enacted under Domitian (so esp. A.Momigliano, *JRS* 41(1951), 150f.) or the similar mention ἐφ' οὗ ἀπε[κα]/τεστάθη ἁ πάτριος πολει/τεία(ς) added to the title of a Roman official co-dedicating a monument to Domitian and Domitia (identified with Homonoia) in *Syll.*[3] 819 (= A.Bresson, *Recueil des inscriptions de la Pérée rhodienne (Pérée intégrée)*, (Paris 1991) 132) represents another restitution of Rhodian liberty after the trouble witnessed by Plut., *Mor.*, 815 D (οἷα Περγαμηνοὺς ἐπὶ Νέρωνος κατέλαβε πράγματα, καὶ Ῥοδίους ἔναγχος ἐπὶ Δομετιανοῦ...) should still be uncertain.

[101] Cf. n. 63 above.

Titus. A shorter interval of direct subordination to provincial authorities seems to suit our present evidence better.

In Severan (rather Caracalla's) times Kos is honored in a decree of Ephesos[102] as [τὸ]ν ἐπιφανέσ[τ]ατον/ [τῶν ἐν Ἀσίᾳ πόλ]εων, ἐλεύθερο[ν/ καὶ αὐτόνο]μον κατὰ τὰ δόγμ[α/τα τῆς ἱε]ρᾶς συνκλήτου, τὸν/ [ἀδελ]φὸν αὐτῆς (sc. τῆς Ἐφέσου) Κώιων/ [δῆ]μον... So the Koan *libertas* survived at least until this date. As already noticed above, the festive mention of the Koan *demos* is probably in contrast with the constitutional reality on Kos in Sabinianus' and Phaedrus' times. In a similar way, if Heberdey's restoration [τῶν ἐν Ἀσίᾳ πόλ]εων is correct, the *eleutheria* (and probably the *autonomia*) still distinguishing Kos were no longer any real obstacle in referring to the city simply as one of "the cities in Asia." At least some degree of administrative inclusion in the province, the result of a long development, seems to be here combined with old terms of privileged exclusion from it. I cannot resist, in their case, the impression of gradually waning titular values—perhaps only potentially preserving a part of their old substance.[103]

The administrative connection of Kos with Asia has appeared especially in Corbulo's letter and the Flavian catalogue of the Asian cities' (local?) taxes discussed above. The inclusion of Kos in administrative units comprising the *provincia Asia* or parts of it, however, becomes for the first time evident in a bilingual (Latin-Greek) inscription found on the island, probably of Trajanic or Hadrianic date, where an imperial freedman appears as "proc(urator) XX her(editatium) regionis Kariaes (*sic*) et insularum Cycladum."[104] A further imperial *libertus*, a *subprocurator* this time, is found on Kos entrusted with the collection of the *vicesima hereditatium* in the later second century (under M.Aurelius and L.Verus or the early Severans).[105] It may be concluded that the island was the seat of the regional office of the vicesima for "Karia and the Kyklades," Kos being obviously reckoned as a part of

---

[102]R.Heberdey, *Forschungen in Ephesos*, II, (Wien 1912) no. 55 (p. 171f.), cf. no. 56 on the date. Could the mention of *senatus consulta* refer back to the period of the Republic? Cf. also p. 114 above.

[103] Cf. Reynolds, doc. 14 (Aphrodisias and Trajan), 21 (Aphrodisias and Gordian III) with the editor's comments.

[104] Maiuri, *NS*, 562. The area of his office in the Greek version: περιόδου Καρίας καὶ νήσων Κυκλάδων. His name and status, *M.Ulpius Aug. lib.*, give the approximate date. Cf. esp. Pflaum, *I.Kos*; Nigdelis, 223.

[105] Herzog, *KF*, 165 (p. 106f.)= *CIL* III, Suppl. 2.14199⁵. The date may be concluded from the mention: ...*Augustor(um) n(ostrorum)* lib(erto); cf. Herzog, ibid.: "Terminus post quem ist das Jahr 161."

either of them.[106] We meet then between 198 and 209 Q.Cosconius Fronto who was "proc. Augg. item ad vectig. XX her. per A[s]iam, Lyciam, Phrygiam, Galati[am], insulas Cyclades."[107] Thus we find again Asia and the Kyklades together (Kos very probably included here, too) as part of one of the larger administrative areas of the vicesima covering more than one province. A more specific attachment of the islands off the western coast of the *provincia Asia*, possibly a part of the same "Cyclades," to the administrative organism of the province is implied earlier in two instances of M.Aurelius' times. First, in the mission of C.Vettius Sabinianus Iulius Hospes, who had held the post of *legatus provinciae Asiae*, as *legatus Augusti ad ordinandos status insularum Cycladum*;[108] a little later in the case of L.Saevinius Proculus serving (and possibly just completing Vettius' work) as *legatus pro praetore Asiae et insularum Cycladum*.[109] So the final, Diocletianic inclusion of Kos (and the other Aegean islands) as parts of the *provincia insularum*[110] in the larger entity of *dioecesis Asiae* should be the natural conclusion of a longer administrative development. Geographic-administrative simplicity has eventually won over the tradition of old boundaries, mainly of political origin, between Europe and Asia in an age of superimposed Mediterranean peace.

Another subject to touch upon in this final attempt at a historical sketch of some main points in the development of the island under Roman sway and domination is the course of Graeco-Roman symbiosis and gradual synthesis on Kos. To treat the subject extensively, however, we should rather await the publication of the rest of the prosopographical material in the *Nachlass* of Segre (tombstones) and Herzog. Only then can we have a picture as complete as present evidence allows of constant and changing characteristics in the structure of Koan population during

---

[106] Cf. already Herzog, *KF,* p.107: the freedman (Hermes) was "wohl Vorstand des koischen Hilfsbureaus (statio) der Erbschaftssteuerbehörde von Asia." The geographic term *Kyklades* may be used here in a later, more expanded sense: cf. *St. Byz.,* counting among the Kyklades Nisyros, that is the island just opposite to the south side of Kos, as well as Telos, Kasos, and Lesbos (s.vv.).

[107] Dessau 1359 (from Sardinia). On the date: Pflaum, *I.Kos,* 66 (the co-reigning emperors must be Septimius Severus and his sons).

[108] *AnÉp* 1920. 45, 16-18 (from Thuburbo Maius in Tunisia). Cf. on this and the next case Nigdelis, 222.

[109] *AnÉp* 1969/70.601 (from Ankara). Cf. the earlier testimony of his career: *AnÉp* 1924. 77(= *I.Ephesos* 3037), 9-12.

[110] *CIL* III.460 (from Kos): "provin[c]. ins. num. [mai]est. q. eor. dic."; cf. already *PH,* p. xli; Sherwin-White, *Cos,* 152. Cf. also the publication by Degrassi, *ILIC,* no. 3 (p.210) of a dedication to Mars pater Gradivus from the period of the Tetrarchy by "...Agathus Gennadius, v(ir) p(erfectissimus), p(raeses)...," who was already and more exactly known

the entire Roman period: from Republican times when Roman influence increased, accompanied by the gradual settlement of Romans on the island (as it happened at many other places, too), down into the Empire. For the time being it would be perhaps wiser to limit oneself to some general and preliminary remarks, somewhat in the sense of an "interim report."

S.Sherwin-White has already offered a useful outline of the history of the Roman community on Kos[111] and stressed, among other things, the relative contrast in the numbers of the Roman presence on Kos and Rhodes in the period ca. 100 B.C.- 100 A.D.[112] Romans who settled on Kos are much more numerous, although the question remains about how many of them counted from the Augustan period on are to be traced back to Italian/Roman families having immigrated to Kos in Republican times. For we may conclude that there already was a Roman community on Kos before the First Mithridatic War (cf. above), but we are still unable to ascertain its direct development or not until the later presence of Roman families on the island.[113] The considerable extent of Roman habitation on Kos in the imperial period, however, is possibly connected, at least in part, with the involvement of the island in Mithridates' fight against Rome. A comparison with the partly parallel case of Lesbos,[114] where the principal city, Mytilene, stood on the Pontic side until well after the end of the First Mithridatic War,[115] may illustrate the point. Mytilene is equally characterized by the frequent presence of Romans who even predominate in some catalogues of names of the late Republican/early imperial period.[116] We might think that areas which had more or less compromised themselves against Rome in the Mithridatic period were subsequently more exposed to the pressure, and probably the need, to

---

as "...Aurel(ius) A[g]athus [G]ennadius, v(ir) p(erfectissimus), praes(es) prov(inciae) insul(arum)..." from an inscription of Mytilene, CIL III.450.

[111] Sherwin-White, Cos, 250-5.

[112] Ibid., 253. Cf. now the observations of A.Bresson, "L`onomastique romaine à Rhodes," in: Rizakis, R.Onomastics, 225-238.

[113] Cf. Sherwin-White, Cos, 252.

[114] Cf. already Herzog, Hal., 492 (where, however, just the economic component of the immigration is noticed).

[115] Liv., per. LXXXIX; Suet., Caes., 2. On date and captor (rather 79 B.C., Minucius Thermus) recently and best: Ar.Keaveney, Lucullus, (London 1992) 185-7 (cf. Magie, 245f.+1124f., n.41 for the older views).

[116] Cf. L.Robert, REA 62(1960), 279ff., 300; Th.Sarikakis, "Τὰ ῥωμαϊκὰ ὀνόματα τῆς Λέσβου," Archaiognosia 8(1993-94), publ. 1995, 97-104, esp. 100f.; K.Buraselis, "Stray Notes on Roman Names in Greek Documents," in: Rizakis, R.Onomastics, 59-61. Cf. now also Labarre, 107-109 (discussion of the Roman presence on Julio-Claudian Lesbos, rather overstating the importance of the frequent imperatorial gentilicia in regard to the overall estimate of real Roman settlement on the island and its development) and 129-136 (list of Roman names with commentary).

accept a significant Roman element into their population. This acceptance could be simultaneously a sort of expiation, especially if it concerned surviving members of earlier resident families in these cities, and a relative reinforcement for the latter, vis-a-vis Roman authorities in the East. We may cite as an appropriate example the text of a dedication of the Roman negotiatores on Kos to the city of their residence: "[C(ives) R(omani) qui C]oi negotiantur/ [civitatem] Coam pietatis in/ [C.Iulium Cae]sarem ponti/[ficem maxim]um, [pat]rem pa/[triae deum]que et benevol/[entiae erga] se caussa."[117] The Koans are here characteristically praised both for their piety to Caesar and their goodwill towards their Roman "guests." It is clear that the existence and relations of this Roman community to the Koans were the best proof and guarantee of Roman control over Kos. Certificates of loyalty to Rome, here personally to Caesar, could be best issued by its private, "unofficial" representatives on the island, the apparently happy successors of the Roman generation imperiled, perhaps partly protected and then certainly evacuated from Kos at the approach of Mithridates about forty years earlier.

If this factor may have contributed to the numbers of Romans on Kos in late republican/early imperial times, K.Höghammar has pointed to another connection.[118] She noticed that Romans begin to appear as priests of Apollo in the relevant Halasarnan list (cf. above) during approximately the last decade of the first century B.C.,[119] that is, in a period when Kos should have been struck by two serious earthquakes.[120] The damage and probable impoverishment of Koan families may well have opened the way to social prominence on Kos for Roman residents willing to undertake costly offices—as priesthoods certainly were.

There is perhaps a little more to say on this Roman connection with Halasarna. The frequent appearance of Romans in the list of Apollo priests (40 out of 125 name entries, that is about one third of the total) may be paralleled by the even higher Roman percentage in the list of

---

[117] Degrassi, *ILIC*, no. 1 (p. 203); republished by A.Donati, "I Romani nell'Egeo. I documenti dell'età repubblicana," *Epigraphica* 27 (1965), no. 16 (p.40); Höghammar, no. 11. Cf. Sherwin-White, *Cos*, 140.

[118] Höghammar, 33.

[119] The first being Μᾶρκος Σθένιος Λευκίου υ(ἱ)ὸ(ς), priest no.17 (ca. 11 B.C.). Chronology should not be pressed too far: cf. above, p. 43, cf. p. 143.

[120] The first earthquake struck the *provincia Asia* in 12 B.C. according to the testimony of D.C. 54.30.3. That Augustus generously undertook to pay the whole tribute of the province for that year from his own money shows the extent of the destruction, thus Kos will have also been a victim of the latter. In the second case, we have an express reference to Kos in ca. 6 B.C. by Eusebios, Chronik (ed. Schoene), II.145 (i): "in insula Coo terrae motu plurima conciderunt" (year 2011, in the Latin version of Hieronymus); cf. Herzog, *KF*, 149 with n. 1.

new members entering the *presbytika palaistra* of Kos (Flavian period, cf. p. 86f. above). Here they make up more than half the total.[121] This similarity in the density of the Roman presence between the city of Kos (where this would appear more natural) and the country demes is significant. As we know from the honorary decree of the *demotai* of Haleis joined by the Romans and other resident foreigners (Augustan period),[122] at least some of the Roman families had established connections with the Koan countryside as landowners (ἐνεκτημένοι).[123] A not adequately emphasized piece of evidence in this respect is priest no. 125 in the Halasarnan list, Λού(κιος) Οὐιψτάνιος Λου(κίου) υἱὸς Φιλόφρων, ὃς μετὰ τὸ μο(ναρχῆσαι) Κῴων ἱεράτευσε γεννηθεὶς ἐν Ἀλασάρνῃ. Most probably he is the hellenized scion of an initially Roman family on Kos who is proud of his "having been born at Halasarna."[124] In other words, the "demotic" connection of the Roman element on Kos indicates the nature and the extent of its settlement on the island but also the kind and the depth of local bonds that have gradually emerged.[125]

Another remarkable point is that Kos conveys imperial gentilicia relatively less often than many other Greek places under Roman domination. There is a wide variety of "private" ones, some of them even rather uncommon in the Aegean.[126] Thus it seems that the degree of mutual Romanization and Hellenization that took place was owed at least not less to private settlement and the establishment of private relations à la longue durée than to imperial generosity to individuals. This is especially true in the case of members of a pre-existing or newly ascending but still indigenous aristocracy. In this peaceful and notable

---

[121] Cf. Sherwin-White, *Cos*, 253f.

[122] *PH* 344= *IGRR* IV.1087.

[123] Cf. now the study of Romans with land property in Eleia by S. Zoumbaki, "Ῥωμαῖοι ἐγγαιοῦντες. Römische Grundbesitzer in Eleia," *Tyche* 9(1994),213-218.

[124] His date as priest should be ca. 98 A.D. So he could very well be a descendant of Μᾶρ(κος) Οὐιψτάνιος Κρίσπος in Segre, *I.Cos*, ED 228.9-10 (Flavian period) whose name is still purely Roman. Cf. Herzog, *Hal.*, 490 (he merely commented on the combination of the deme priesthood and a real residence in the city in Philophron's case, too).

[125] We may also adduce here as relatively early examples of such an integration: (a) the addition (in the first century B.C.?) of a Ὀρδιώνιος Σπό[ρ]ου υἱὸς and a Δέκμος Γράνιος Δέκμου υἱὸς Βάσσος to a demotic list at Isthmos of ca. the beginning second century B.C.: Carratelli, *Isthmos*, p. 177, XI c,nos. 24, 25, cf. Sherwin-White, *Cos*, 251f., n.176; (b) the four bearers of Roman gentilicia (Κοσσουτία, l. 9; Μετείλιος, l. 15; Πώλλα Καικιλία, l. 16; Ῥοπίλιος Ἀγαθό[πους ?], l.22f.) in a list of contributors of early imperial date (?) at the deme of Hippia: Herzog, *KF*, 175, p.118, cf. Sherwin-White, loc.cit.

[126] For example the just mentioned Vipstanius and Hordionius, or Septicius (Herzog, *Hal.*, no. 4, priests nos. 127, 128, probably brothers).

synthesis "from below" we might recognize one of the characteristic traits of Koan society in Roman times.

Kos's continuous Asclepiad and medical tradition may have been a further probable attraction for some Romans, a factor hitherto unnoticed. Men like Xenophon and Sabinianus (see above) were a kind of living advertisement for the social importance of a physician's craft, which could be apparently still studied on Kos. The point becomes clear when an iconographic detail of the Halasarnan list of Apollo priests is correctly interpreted. The names of the priests under the nos. 85, 91, 94, 98, 105, 113 and 116 are followed on the stone by the representation of a staff with serpent. Herzog connected this sign in his original publication with the mention added to the name of the priest no. 74 (ca. 47 A.D.), namely that the latter's priesthood had coincided with the festival of the Great Asklepieia.[127] He supposed that the addition of that sign after some names in the list alluded to a similar coincidence (as this would mean additional largesse from the priests in question, and should so be appropriately highlighted).[128] However, he admitted himself that no convincing cycle of that festival could be established on the basis of the distribution of the entries labeled thus in the list. Fortunately, we were now able to see that on Kos also the staff—with—serpent symbol[129] appears to denote the medical profession of a man (see above on such representations on some of the votive monuments to the "paternal gods" for Xenophon and Sabinianus). It is reasonable to suppose, then, that the appearance of the same symbol after some names in the Halasarnan list is the professional mark of these persons, probably in their dual function as Asclepiads. A certain confirmation of this is priest no. 116 (ca. 89 A.D.) Γ.Στερτίνιος Ἡγουμενός who should be one of the few later direct members of Xenophon's family (cf. above, p. 78). That among the seven so recognized doctors, who assumed at some point of their careers the Halasarnan priesthood of Apollo, there are no less than three bearers of purely Roman names (no Greek *cognomen*) is equally important.[130] The appeal of medical education in a milieu of Asclepiads should probably be seen as a factor in Roman immigration or sojourn on Kos.

---

[127] Herzog, *Hal.*, no. 4, p. 484: Μάνιος Σπέδιος Φαῦστος τὸ δεύτερον κατὰ Ἀσκλαπῖα τὰ μεγάλα.

[128] Ibid., p. 490: "...Wenn nun von da an einzelnen Namen der Schlangenstab des Asklepios beigefügt wird, so liegt die Annahme am nächsten, daß damit diese Panegyris bezeichnet werden soll."

[129] On relevant examples from other places cf. Benedum, 240.

[130] No. 85: Κό(ιντος) Πλώτιος Κο(ίντου) υἱὸς Ῥοῦφος (ca. 58 A.D.), no. 94: Αὖλος Μανίλιος Αὔλου υἱὸς Ῥοῦφος (ca. 67 A.D.), no. 105: Γά(ιος) Κάσιος Γα(ίου) υἱὸς Ποῦλχερ (ca. 78 A.D.).

To sum up, by connecting the essential nature of all these remarks on the Graeco-Roman symbiosis on Kos with some of the artistic masterpieces of the island's imperial period, specifically the decoration of the splendid houses of the third century A.D. in the city like the "Roman House" (*Casa Romana*) or the "House of the Rape of Europa," it should not surprise us how skillfully elements of Greek, and especially Koan, tradition were combined there with prevailing tastes of the wider "imperial culture."[131] This process of inter-cultural dialogue was a very fine and multifaceted one. Kos found its own way to bring nearer Hellenism and Rome.

---

[131] Cf. above, p. 121 with n. 53 and F.Sirano, "Il mosaico della Casa cosiddetta del Ratto d'Europa a Coo," in: *Associazione Italiana per lo Studio e la Conservazione del Mosaico. Atti del 1° Colloquio* [1993], (Ravenna 1994) 541-577 (esp. 573 with n. 129, giving further bibl.).

Appendix 1:

Παραφυλάξαντα τὴν Κώων πόλιν.

Evidence on Kos
during the First Mithridatic War
in a new inscription from Patara

Christian Marek has recently published the honorary inscription on a statue base from Patara in Lycia.[1] It belongs to the well-known category of monuments erected by soldiers/sailors for their officer/captain during a war.[2] In this case a citizen of Patara, Krinolaos, son of Artapates, is honored by the Lycian troops who served under his brave command as *strategos autokrator* "when the allied contingent was sent by the Lycian League to Rhodes during the war that broke out against king Mithridates."[3] Marek has correctly recognized and analyzed the historical context as Mithridates' famous and finally unsuccessful attempt to seize Rhodes during the First Mithridatic War. After this reference the honorific text adds an obviously also memorable service of the Lycian general: παραφυλάξαντα δὲ καὶ τὴν Κώων πόλιν (ll. 9-10). It is clear that this should be also part of the same context, but its exact significance and place in the sequence of events needs a closer study.

It is not difficult to understand that Krinolaos and his men had somehow watched over the city of Kos. If this means that they had been on the island to assist the Koans *before* Mithridates' triumphant arrival there (see above), they could not have achieved very much. There would have been then no reason to include this rather inglorious element into Krinolaos' highlighted deeds. The editor of the inscription has already seen this, and tried to connect Krinolaos' service with a sort of task of watching the Koan harbor as base of the Mithridatic fleet. His Lycian contingent should have spied the movements of the enemy situated at Kos and so helped avert any attack on Rhodes from that direction[4]. However, the text makes explicit that Krinolaos' watching duty concerned not the harbor but *the city* of Kos. So the only possibility that

---

[1] "Der Lykische Bund, Rhodos, Kos und Mithridates. Basis mit Ehreninschrift für Krinolaos, Sohn des Artapates, von Patara," *Lykia* II.1995 [1997]: 9-21 (10).

[2] Cf. the examples collected ibid., 12 (n.11). A variant of this category includes dedications of the—actually again honorary—monument to a divinity: cf. M.Guarducci, *Epigrafia greca*, II, (Roma 1969) 156f.

[3] ...ἐπὶ τῆς πεμφθείσης Ῥοδίοις συμμαχίας ὑπὸ τοῦ κοινοῦ τῶν Λυκίων εἰς τὸν ἐνστάντα πόλεμον πρὸς βασιλέα Μιθριδάτην ἡγησάμενον ἐπάνδρως , ll. 5-9.

[4] Ibid., 19. He compares this defensive function with the προφύλακες mentioned in *App., Mithr.* 26. However, προ-φυλάσσειν has a distinctly different meaning.

remains is to examine whether the Lycians can have undertaken such a duty *after* Kos was freed from the Mithridatic troops. Marek discarded such a solution as it seemed to him, quite understandably, to contradict the Koans' change of camp, expulsion of the Mithridatic force stationed there—after Lucullus' ships appeared near the island—and final participation in the Roman operations against Samos. At first sight there seemed admittedly to be no reasonable place for Krinolaos and his Lycians in this picture.

It will now help to look for the exact sense that παραφυλάσσειν could have in that specific situation. This verb is an interesting *terminus technicus* of the Hellenistic military and political vocabulary. Polybios uses it many times[5] to denote the presence of an additional (this is the actual meaning of the preposition παρά !), friendly/allied garrison to protect a city threatened by an external attack, the potential aggressors sometimes being a combined force of foreigners and a local "fifth column." Some examples are: in spring 208 Philip V sends a small force to help the city of Peparethos (τοὺς παραφυλάξοντας τὴν πόλιν) upon the information that Attalid troops have landed on the homonymous island (10.42.1). About the end of 172 the Roman envoys in Greece preparing the ground for the war against Perseus let an Achaean force come to Chalkis to secure the city (παραφυλάξοντας τὴν πόλιν) until the Roman army appears (27.2.11). The fine, and propagandistic, difference between φρουρεῖν and παραφυλάσσειν becomes clear when Philip V at Nicaea (ca. November 198) faces the Aetolian argument with the assertion that he has withdrawn his men from Lysimacheia "who were no occupying force but a friendly garrison" against the Thracian menace: ...οὐ τοὺς φρουροῦντας αὐτήν, ὡς σύ φής, ἀλλὰ τοὺς παραφυλάττοντας (18.4.6). A well-known dramatic example was the case of the Achaean παραφυλακή of three hundred men sent to Mantineia at the latter's request to have their liberty and safety protected (παραφυλάσσοντες τὴν ἐκείνων ἐλευθερίαν ἅμα καὶ σωτηρίαν) against the Aetolians, the Spartans and inner strife; these Achaean guards were later slaughtered at a pro-Spartan coup in the city (2.58).

Apart from these eloquent examples in Polybios the term παραφυλακή is attested with a similar meaning in epigraphic texts. So a decree of the city of Ilion (*OGIS* 443) honors the commander of a protecting garrison (εἰς παραφυλακὴν τῆς πόλεως) sent there at Roman request by the community of the Poemaneni in 80/79 B.C., that is in a period of intense activity by pirates in the Aegean.[6] In a honorary decree of Arsinoe (Tokra) from the second/first cent. B.C. (*SEG* 26.1817) we find among the services of a local benefactor the

---

[5] Cf. now especially the entries παραφυλακή, παραφυλάττω in: G.Glockmann a.o., *Polybios-Lexikon*, II.1 (παγκρατιαστής - ποιέω), Berlin 1998, cols. 128-130. Cf. also F.W.Walbank, *A Historical Commentary on Polybius*, I, (Oxford 1970²) 156 (on *Pol.*, 2.5.6).

[6] Cf. Magie, 240; Kallet-Marx, 305.

mention: ἐπέδωκε χρήματα κατὰ τὰν τῶ πολέμω περίστασιν ἐς τὰν παραφυλακὰν τᾶς πόλιος (ll.20-23), where we should very probably see his financial contribution to the reinforcement of the menaced city's protection by a mercenary garrison.

Kos certainly also needed such a friendly protection to secure the just re-established pro-Roman regime on the island after Lucullus' appearance and the expulsion of the Mithridatic soldiers and possibly some of those Koans who had politically compromised themselves in the two years of Pontic occupation. The Lycians' service on Kos was actually a delicate one. They should protect a re-gained ally against any Mithridatic counterattack (the war was not over yet!) and gently seal the island's new allegiance to Rome and its camp. They obviously succeeded in this and were reasonably proud of their success.

Appendix 2:
A catalogue of the dedications to the "paternal gods" for Nikias[7]

1. *PH* 76. "Small basis built into a wall," 58x20 cm.

2. Ibid. 77. "In the house of Tsinias."

3. Ibid. 78. Reported at that time on Symi, "small stele with aedicula," not complete on the left, 27x27 cm.

4. Ibid. 79. "In a wall on the road to Lampe."

5. Ibid. 80. "Near the cemetery."

6. Herzog, *KF*, 17. "Blauer Kalkstein (μαύρη πέτρα), in die Brunneneinfassung im Garten des Sarrara Jussuf verbaut," left edge missing, 42x16cm.

7. Ibid. 18 (=Segre, *I.Cos*, EV 57). "Marmor, im Haus des Γεωργαρᾶ(ς), im Stadtviertel Aspa," 30x19x11 cm. "Schrift flüchtig."

8. Ibid. 19. "Marmor, eingemauert im neuen Haus des Δαμιανός," upper part preserved, 17x34 cm.

9. Ibid. 20 (= Segre, *I.Cos*, EV 295). Fragment of the lower right part of a similar (marble) monument, in the house of "Achmet im Stadtviertel Jeni Kape," 37x29x8 cm.

10. Ibid. 192 (republished here after the *editio princeps* in *MDAI(A)* 20, 506). Found "beim Bau eines Hauses in der Gegend Ἁγ. Νικόλαος." Herzog (ibid., p. 67) estimated on the ground of the reported dimensions of the stone (175x50 cm) that this should be a small altar or base of a votive offering or something similar.

11. Maiuri, *NS*, 479 (= Segre, *I.Cos*, EV 310). White marble base transported "dalla via Aspa al Museo del Castello," 49x21x25 cm.

12. Ibid. 480 (= Segre, *I.Cos*, EV 293). Fragment of a white marble tablet (left part) found during the restoration works at the Castle. 31x21x9 cm.

13. Ibid. 481 (= Segre, *I.Cos*, EV 130). Fragment, material and findplace the same as of the previous one, 17x23x5 cm.

---

[7] The identification of the inscriptions published more than once, in this and the following lists, unless noticed in one of the more recent publications itself, has been made after a close comparison of the texts in question and all other data on them available. As a rule, references to earlier publications than the main one/s here cited are not repeated. Only what seemed to me to be rather significant details about the inscriptions or noteworthy aberrations from the standard text are noticed. Dimensions of the stones (height, width, thickness) are given to help form an idea about the size of the original monument. Segre's measurements have been always preferred.

14. Wilhelm, *Beiträge*, no. 148 (p. 171). "Block weißgrauen Marmors," 76x21,5x28 cm, "im Hofe des Nationalmuseums zu Athen." The only known such document for Nikias where ἥρωος has not been added.

15. Sherwin-White, *Cos*, p. 142, n.324. Another such plaque for Nikias reported by P.M.Fraser to exist in the Museum of Rhodes.

16. Segre, *I.Cos*, EV 74. White marble stele from demolitions in the city, 40x22x10 cm.

17. Ibid. 283. Small white marble base from demolitions in the city, "in alto presenta un piccolo intaglio rettangolare per l'inserzione di una statua," 23x25x17 cm.

18. Ibid. 285. White marble base broken above, from demolitions in the city, 41x27,5x11 cm.

19. Ibid. 291. Fragment (left part) of a white marble stele, from demolitions in the city, 38x24x7 cm.

20. Ibid. 309. White marble block from demolitions in the city; it should have been previously "adoperato...come capitello di pilastro o come mensola," 42x29x20 cm.

21. Ibid. 312. White marble altar "con cornice in alto e in basso," from demolitions in the city, 47x26x13 cm.

22. Ibid. 340. Left part of a white marble tablet, from demolitions in the city, 29x13x5 cm.

23. G.Pugliese Carratelli, "Epigrafi del demo Coo di Isthmos," *PP* 24(1969), 130 (no. 9). A small altar of white-bluish marble, found in Herzog's excavations at Kephalos (1902). This is probably one of the four similar documents for Nikias mentioned by Herzog, *N&X*, 208, n.3 as unpublished. We cannot know yet whether the remaining three are to be identified with some of the previous documents of this catalogue or not.

Appendix 3:
A catalogue of the dedications to the "paternal gods for C.Stertinius Xenophon

1. *PH* 84. "Under the plane tree...stele surmounted by an aedicula, within which is a snake."

2. Ibid. 85. "At Symi," 43x28 cm.

3. Ibid. 86. "At Symi," 45x27 cm. The formula ὑπὲρ τᾶς...σωτηρίας instead of the regular one ὑπὲρ ὑγείας.

4. Ibid. 87. "In the house of the painter Theodoros," left part preserved, 30x24 cm.

5. Ibid. 88. "In the garden of Sherif-Bey...width about 33 cm." Εὐσεβοῦς is here omitted.

6. Ibid. 89. "In a wall near the theatre," upper part preserved, 33x30 cm.

7. Ibid. 90 (= *CIG* IV.6844).

8. Ibid. 91. A small fragment.

9. Herzog, *KF*, 21. Marble block, undecorated, at the "Museumsplatz," 32x22 cm. Writing style as "in PH 87, etwas schief und nicht ganz sorgfältig."

10. Ibid. 22. Marble tablet in the house of Katol Hussein, 30x25 cm. Writing style as in *PH* 85, "nicht sehr sorgfältig."

11. Ibid. 23. Fragment of a marble tablet at the "Museumsplatz," careful writing style.

12. Maiuri, *NS*, 476 (= Segre, *I.Cos*, EV 43). White marble tablet, "rinvenuta...entro la periferia della città," 43x30x8,5 cm.

13. Ibid. 477 (= Segre, *I.Cos*, EV 299). Upper part of a marble stele with an upper cornice preserved, from demolitions near Παναγία τοῦ Φόρου, 27x24x7 cm.

14. Ibid. 478 (= Segre, *I.Cos*, EV 68). Upper part of a white marble tablet found during the restoration works at the Castle (1916), 29x30x6 cm. As Segre notes: "in alto è raffigurato in rilievo il serpente di Asclepio."

15. Ibid. 485. Fragment of a white marble tablet built at that time into the wall of N.Nikolaidis' vineyard, thickness: 7 cm.

16. *SEG* III.740 (based on a report by G.Patriarca). Marble tablet in the Museum of Kos, found "in praedio quodam," 40x36 cm.

17. Benedum, 240 with pl. 3. A marble tablet at the Castle.

18. Segre, *I.Cos*, EV 22. White marble tablet with a relief cornice at the upper and lower ends, from demolitions in the city, 49x33x6 cm.

19. Ibid. 25. White marble stele, rounded above, from the excavations of the city inside the fortifications, 39x31x5 cm.

20. Ibid. 46. Left part of a white marble tablet, from demolitions in the city, 37x21x9 cm.

21. Ibid. 70. Fragment of white marble, from demolitions, 24x26x11 cm.

22. Ibid. 83. White marble tablet, from the excavations of the Great Thermae, 32,5x31x7 cm. "In basso è rozzamente inciso il serpente di Asclepio." Cf. Benedum, 240 with pl.2.

23. Ibid. 97. Upper right part of a white marble tablet from the excavation of the Odeum, 24x26x8 cm. The surface of the inscription has been given the form of a *tabula ansata* with a surrounding relief cornice. In his original publication in *Historia* 8(1934), 444 Segre also reported traces of red colour in the letters.

24. Ibid. 112. Left part of a white marble tablet from the excavations of the Great Thermae, 37x33x7 cm. "In alto è rozzamente figurato il serpente di Asclepio."

25. Ibid. 117. Fragment (upper part) of a white marble tablet, from demolitions in the city, 24x31x7 cm.

26. Ibid. 124. White marble tablet "ornata in alto di frontoncino spezzato," from demolitions in the city, 48x27x8 cm. Superfluous letters inscribed in ll. 2,9.

27. Ibid. 126. Fragment of bluish marble from demolitions in the Castle, 22x15x23 cm. The fragments of words preserved are those of the standard text of these dedications but the thickness of the stone might also suggest some sort of honorary base for Xenophon. Cf. Segre, ibid.

28. Ibid. 143. White marble tablet from Amygdalona, 46x38x8 cm.

29. Ibid. 286. White marble stele from demolitions in the city, 23x25x7 cm.

30. Ibid. 288. Upper part of a block of white marble, from demolitions in the city, 18x20x11 cm.

31. Ibid. 289. White marble stele broken on the right and below, from demolitions in the city, 34x26x7 cm.

32. Ibid. 290. Lower part of a white marble stele, from demolitions in the city, 16x23x6 cm.

33. Ibid. 294. Lower part of a white marble tablet, from demolitions in the city, 28x51x9 cm.

34. Ibid. 296. Upper part of a white marble block, from demolitions in the city, 30x28x16 cm.

35. Ibid. 297. White marble stele from the excavations of the Roman Thermae at Amygdalona, 44x32x10 cm.

36. Ibid. 298. Fragment of a white marble tablet (ca. one third on the right is missing), from demolitions in the city, 43x24x7 cm. As Segre notes, at the end of the lines the words are divided in an often "asyllabic" way. The coarse writing style very probably completes the picture of an amateur's work.

37. Ibid. 300. Lower part of a stele of bluish marble, from demolitions in the city, 20x28x5 cm.

38. Ibid. 301. White marble stele with an upper cornice, from the excavations of the Great Thermae, 58x38x13 cm. The erasion in l. 7 could not have previously accommodated φιλονέϱωνος (see the photograph, ibid.): as Segre notes, both here and at the end of l. 3 (a superfluous N) we should rather recognize errors of the stone-cutter.

39. Ibid. 302. White marble base with a cornice at the upper and lower ends, from demolitions in the city, 53x39x21 cm. On the upper surface the dowel holes for two small feet are visible. Segre noted: "La base sosteneva probabilmente una statua di Asclepio." It seems at least equally possible to assume that a small statue of the actually honored, Xenophon, crowned the small monument (cf. esp. the votive monument no. 17 for Nikias above, and here no. 27).

40. Ibid. 311. White marble base, from demolitions in the city, 48x28x25 cm.

41. Ibid. 314. White marble base, from the excavations inside the fortified city, 41x30x27 cm.

42. Ibid. 315. Upper part of a white marble stele from the same area, 21x23x5 cm.

43. Ibid. 316. Right part of a white marble stele, from demolitions in the city, 22x12x5 cm.

44. Ibid. 317. Fragment (upper right part) of a white marble stele, from demolitions in the city, 18x12x4,5 cm.

45. Ibid. 318. Fragment of similar data, 26x15x5 cm.

46. Ibid. 319. Small marble fragment with ca. the middle part of the standard text, from the excavations of the Great Thermae, 10x15x2 cm.

47. Ibid. 320. Fragment of the lower right part of a similar monument, from demolitions in the city, 17x24x14 cm.

48. Ibid. 321. Left part of a white marble stele, from demolitions in the Castle, 38,5x19,5x7 cm.

49. Ibid. 322. Small fragment of a similar monument, from demolitions in the city, thickness: 4,5 cm.

50. Ibid. 324. Fragment of the lower left part of a white marble tablet, from the Odeum, thickness: 6 cm.

51. Ibid. 325. Fragment of the lower right part of a white marble stele, from demolitions, thickness: 6 cm.

52. Ibid. 327. Fragment of the upper part of a white marble stele, from demolitions in the city, thickness: 6 cm.

53. Ibid. 337. White marble stele, preserved in two joined fragments, from demolitions in the city, 45x31x6 cm. Above the inscription "è figurato in rilievo il serpente di Asclepio."

54. Ibid. 341. Fragment of the upper right part of a white marble stele, from demolitions in the city, thickness: 12 cm.

55. Ibid. 344. Small white marble fragment of unknown provenience, thickness: 4,5 cm.

56. Ibid. 347. White marble tablet, from the locality Buzuktá, 40x20x14 cm.

57. Ibid. 365. Small marble fragment, from the Great Thermae, thickness: 8 cm.

58. Ibid. 366. Three joining fragments of the upper part of a white marble tablet, from the houses of the Roman period at the "Via di Circonvallazione," 38x39x5 cm.

Appendix 4:
A catalogue of the dedications to "the paternal gods" for M.Aelius Sabinianus and M'.Spedius Rufinus Phaedrus

I. For M.Aelius Sabinianus

1. *PH* 95 (= Segre, *I.Cos*, EV 84). White marble tablet from demolitions in the city, originally "in the house of Antonios Stamatiades," 31x24x6 cm.

2. Ibid. 96. "Now at Symi, blue marble," 20x15 cm.

3. Ibid. 97 (= *CIG* 6843), "in Oxford."

4. Herzog, *KF*, 26. Upper right strip of a marble tablet "im Besitz des Demarchen Herrn Joannidis."

5. Maiuri, *NS*, 482. White marble tablet (below not completely preserved), found in a house of the previous Turkish district and deposited "al Museo del Castello," 25x24x9 cm.

6. Ibid. 483 (= Segre, *I.Cos*, EV 308). Fragment of a white marble tablet, found in the city of Kos, thickness: 4 cm.

7. Ibid. 484 (= Segre, *I.Cos*, EV 313). White marble base decorated with cornices on three faces (see Segre, ib., pl. 142), from the surroundings of the city, 39x35x24 cm.

8. Segre, *I.Cos*, EV 71. Small block of white marble, from demolitions in the city, 26x24x14 cm. The only inscription so far preserved where Sabinianus is also styled as δάμου υἱὸς (cf. p. 112 above). Segre notes: "in alto...una cornice in rilievo non interamente conservata, in cui si riconosce però la figurazione di un serpente." On his dating of this inscription cf. p.114.

9. Ibid. 86. Small Doric capital with the inscription on the upper part of the abacus (right part missing), from the excavations of the Great Thermae, 28x21,5x11 cm.

10. Ibid. 88. Tablet of bluish marble, from demolitions in the city, 32x29x7 cm.

11. ib. 281. White marble tablet "col margine superiore arcuato," from the excavations of the Great Thermae, 32x36x3 cm. Segre adds: "In basso è rozzamente inciso il serpente di Asclepio."

12. Ibid. 282. White marble tablet, from the excavations of houses of the Roman period by the "Via di Circonvallazione," 17x40x2,5 cm. Segre adds the details: "il margine sinistro appare sollevato e quello superiore è risegato nella parte posteriore." These data, the height and

thickness of the inscription and a comparison of the photograph given ibid., vol. II, pl. 135 with Benedum's, no. 5 (p. 239), pl. X have convinced me that the latter is just the left part of the same document, meanwhile broken, as Benedum found it in the Castle of Kos some time before his publication (1977).

13. Ibid. 287. Upper part of a white marble stele, from demolitions in the city, 16x19x5 cm.

14. Ibid. 292. Small block of white marble, from demolitions in the city, 21,5x17x10 cm. Segre explains that the stone must have been reused to engrave this inscription and remarks: "ciò prova il carattere occasionale di questo tipo di documenti, per cui spesso furono riadoperati marmi già destinati ad altro uso..."

15. Ibid. 304. Right part of a white marble piece that had been worked "in forma di pàtera" (where the inscription was engraved), from the excavation of the Great Thermae, 22x15x4 cm.

16. Ibid. 305. Upper part of a white marble piece worked as a triangular prism (preserved height: 19 cm) the big side of which bore the inscription (see ibid., vol. II, pl. 140), from demolitions in the city.

17. Ibid. 306. Fragment (upper right part) of a white marble stele, from demolitions in the city, 13,5x13x2 cm.

18. Ibid. 307. Upper left part of a white marble piece, from demolitions in the city, 13,5x18x10 cm. According to Segre it had been probably rounded for a previous use (capital or small table).

19. Ibid. 323. Upper left part of a white limestone piece, from demolitions in the city, 15x12x8 cm. "In alto al centro è figurata una patera."

20. Ibid. 336. Two joining fragments of a white marble tablet, from demolitions in the city, 31x26x3,5 cm.

21. Ibid. 338. Three fragments (two joining, one not) of a white marble stele, from the Great Thermae, 29x29x2,5 cm.

22. Ibid. 342. Upper part of a white marble tablet found in the excavations of houses of the Roman period by the "Via di Circonvallazione" (1939), 15,5x14x2 cm.

23. Ibid. 343. Upper part of a white marble tablet, from the city inside the walls, 13x15x4 cm.

II. For M'.Spedius Rufinus Phaedrus

1. *PH* 98. "Outside the house of Sherif-Bey," 60x30 cm. The complete form of the name is given.

2. Segre, *I.Cos*, EV 81. Upper part of a white marble tablet, from the excavation of the Odeum, 21,5x17,5x3 cm. Complete form of the name.

3. Ibid. 303. Left part of a white marble piece (the inscribed area has been given the form of a "tabula rilevata"), from demolitions in the city, 24x18,5x6 cm. The name appears as [Μανίου Σπε]/δίου Φα[ίδρου...

4. Ibid. 339. White marble block, from the vicinity of the Odeum, 24x35x4,6 cm. The name in the form Μανίου/[Φαί]δρου Σπ(ε)δ(ί)ου, the latter written on the stone as ΣΠΡΔΟΥ. The stone-cutter was also unable (as in the previous case) to keep the lines of his text horizontal, the whole writing style (cf. Ibid., vol. II, pl. 147) makes a late-antique impression.

Bibliography[1]

Accame, S., *Il dominio Romano in Grecia dalla Guerra Acaica ad Augusto.* Roma 1946 (Accame)

Ager, S.L., *Interstate Arbitrations in the Greek World (337-90 B.C.).* Berkeley 1996 (Ager)

Bagnall, R.S., *The Administration of the Ptolemaic Possessions outside Egypt.* Leiden 1976 (Bagnall)

Baker, P., *Cos et Calymna, 205-200 a.C. Esprit civique et défense nationale.* Québec 1991 (Baker)

Benedum, J., "Inschriften aus Kos," *ZPE* 27(1977), 229-40 (Benedum)

Bernhardt, R., *Imperium und Eleutheria. Die römische Politik gegenüber den freien Städten des griechischen Ostens.* diss. Hamburg 1971 (Bernhardt, *I&E*)

Bernhardt, R., "Die Immunitas der Freistädte," *Historia* 29(1980): 190-207 (Bernhardt, *IF*)

Bernhardt, R., *Polis und römische Herrschaft in der späten Republik (149-31 v.Chr.).* Berlin 1985 (Bernhardt, *Polis & RH*)

Berve, H., *Die Tyrannis bei den Griechen,* I-II. München 1967 (Berve, *Tyr.*)

Bowersock, G.W., *Augustus and the Greek World.* Oxford 1965 (Bowersock, *A&GW*)

Braund, D.C., *Rome and the Friendly King. The Character of Client Kingship.* London 1984 (Braund)

Brulé, P., *La piraterie crétoise hellénistique.* Paris 1978 [Annales Litteraires de l'Univ. de Besançon/Centre de Recherches d'Histoire Ancienne, 27] (Brulé)

Buraselis, K., *Das hellenistische Makedonien und die Ägäis.* München 1982 (Buraselis, *HM&A*)

Burnett, A.-Amandry, M.-Ripollès, P., *Roman Provincial Coinage, vol.I: From the Death of Caesar to the Death of Vitellius (44 BC-AD 69),* I-II. London 1992 (Burnett, *RPC*)

Campanile, M.D., *I sacerdoti del Koinon d'Asia (I sec. a.C.-III sec. d.C.),* Pisa 1994 (Campanile)

---

[1] Only books and articles cited more than once above are listed here; the abbreviation used each time is appended in parenthesis. The remaining literature is fully cited in the footnotes.

Carratelli, G. Pugliese, "Nuovi documenti della romanizzazione di Cos," in: *Synteleia V.Arangio-Ruiz*, II (Napoli 1964), 816-9 (Carratelli, *Rom.Cos*)

Carratelli, G. Pugliese, "Il damos Coo di Isthmos," *ASAA* 41/42, n.s. 25/26 1963/64), 1965: 147-202 (Carratelli, *Isthmos*)

Chaniotis, An., *Historie und Historiker in den griechischen Inschriften. Epigraphische Beiträge zur griechischen Historiographie*. Stuttgart 1988 (Chaniotis, *H&H*)

Chaniotis, An., *Die Verträge zwischen kretischen Poleis in der hellenistischen Zeit*. Stuttgart 1996 (Chaniotis, *KV*)

Corbier, Mir., "Usages publics du vocabulaire de la parenté: *patronus* et *alumnus* de la cité dans l'Afrique romaine," in: *L'Africa romana* VII (1989), a cura di Att.Mastino. Sassari 1990, 815-54 (Corbier, *Parenté*)

Crawford, M. (ed.) et al., *Roman Statutes*, I-II. London 1996 (Crawford, *RS*)

Cucuzza, N., "Artemis *Toxitis* a Coo. In margine alle guerre rodio-cretesi e ad Aglaos di Coo," *PP* 52(1997): 13-31 (Cucuzza)

Degrassi, At., "Iscrizioni latine inedite di Coo," *Clara Rhodos* 10(1941): 203-13(Degrassi, *ILIC*)

Demougin, S., *L'ordre équestre sous les Julio-Claudiens*. Rome 1988 (Demougin, *OÉ*)

Demougin, S., *Prosopographie des chevaliers romains julio-claudiens...* Rome 1992 (Demougin, *Pr.*)

Devijver, H., "Suétone, Claude, 25 et les milices équestres," *AncSoc* 1(1970): 70-81 (Devijver, *C&MÉ*)

Devijver, H., *Prosopographia militiarum equestrium quae fuerunt ab Augusto ad Gallienum*, I-II. Leuven 1976-77 (Devijver, *PME*)

Dobson, B., "The Praefectus Fabrum in the Early Principate," in: *Britain & Rome. Essays Presented to Er. Birley...* (ed. by M.G.Jarrett & B.Dobson). Kendal 1965, 61-84 (Dobson)

Durrbach, F., *Choix d'inscriptions de Délos*, Paris 1921-23 (Durrbach, *Choix*)

Ferrary, J.-L., *Philhellénisme et impérialisme. Aspects idéologiques de la conquête romaine du monde hellénistique*. Rome 1988 (BÉFAR, 271) (Ferrary, *P&I*)

Fraser, P.M., "The Kings of Commagene and the Greek World," in: *Studien zur Religion und Kultur Kleinasiens (Festschrift F.K.Dörner...)*, hrsg. von S.Sahin u.a., I. Leiden 1978, 359-74 (Fraser, *Kings of Commagene*)

Fraser, P.M., *Ptolemaic Alexandria*, I-III. Oxford 1972 (Fraser, *PA*)

Fraser, P.M., *Rhodian Funerary Monuments*. Oxford 1977 (Fraser, *RFM*)

Fraser, P.M.-Matthews, E., *A Lexicon of Greek Personal Names, Vol. I: The Aegean Islands, Cyprus, Cyrenaica*. Oxford 1987 (Fraser-Matthews)

Gauthier, Ph., *Les cités grecques et leurs bienfaiteurs*. Paris 1985 [*BCH* Suppl.XII] (Gauthier, *C&B*)

Gow, A.S.F.-Page, D.L., *The Greek Anthology. The Garland of Philip and Some Contemporary Epigrams*, vols. I-II. Cambridge 1968 (Gow-Page, GA)

Graf, F., *Nordionische Kulte*. Rom 1985 (Graf, *NK*)

Habicht, Chr., "Athens and the Ptolemies," *ClAnt* 11(1992), 68-90 (Habicht, *Athens&P*)

Habicht, Chr., "Neue Inschriften aus Kos," *ZPE* 112(1996): 83-94 (Habicht, I.Kos)

Hatzfeld, J., *Les trafiquants italiens dans l'Orient hellénique*. Paris 1919 (= New York 1975) (Hatzfeld)

Head, B., *Historia Nummorum*. Oxford 1911 (Head, *HN*)

Herzog, R., *Koische Forschungen und Funde*. Leipzig 1899 (Herzog, *KF*)

Herzog, R., *Das Heiligthum des Apollo in Halasarna*, Sitzungsberichte Berlin, phil.-hist.Kl., 1901, XXI (Herzog, *Hal.*)

Herzog, R., *Heilige Gesetze von Kos*, Abhandlungen Berlin, phil.-hist.Kl., 1928.6 (Herzog, *HG*)

Herzog, R., "Nikias und Xenophon von Kos. Zwei Charakterköpfe aus der griechisch-römischen Geschichte," *HZ* 125(1922): 189-247 (Herzog, *N&X*)

Höghammar, K., *Sculpture and Society. A Study of the Connection between the Free-standing Sculpture and Society on Kos in the Hellenistic and Augustan Periods*. Uppsala 1993 [Boreas, 23] (Höghammar)

Holtheide, B., *Römische Bürgerrechtspolitik und römische Neubürger in der Provinz Asia*. Freiburg 1983 (Holtheide)

Huß, W., *Untersuchungen zur Außenpolitik Ptolemaios' IV*. München 1976 (Huß, *Pt.IV*)

Kader, Ing., "Heroa und Memorialbauten," in: M.Wörrle & P.Zanker (Hrsgg.), *Stadtbild und Bürgerbild im Hellenismus*. München 1995, 199-229 (Kader)

Kallet-Marx, R.M., *Hegemony to Empire. The Development of the Roman Imperium in the East from 148 to 62 B.C.* Berkeley 1995 (Kallet-Marx)

Kroll, J., "The Late Hellenistic Tetrobols of Kos," *ANSMN* XI(1964): 81-117 (Kroll)

Kromann, Anne, "The Greek Imperial Coinage from Cos and Rhodes," in: *Archaeology in the Dodecanese* (ed. by S.Dietz & Io. Papachristodoulou). Copenhagen 1988, 213-217 (Kromann)

Labarre, G., *Les cités de Lesbos aux époques hellénistique et imperiale.* Lyon 1996 (Labarre)

Levick, B., *Claudius.* New Haven 1990 (Levick)

McGing, B.C., *The Foreign Policy of Mithridates Eupator King of Pontus.* Leiden 1986 (McGing)

Magie, D., *Roman Rule in Asia Minor.* Princeton 1950 (Magie)

Maiuri, Am., *Nuova silloge epigrafica di Rodi e Cos.* Firenze 1925 (Maiuri, *NS*)

Marek, Chr., *Stadt, Ära und Territorium in Pontus-Bithynia und Nord-Galatia.* Tübingen 1993 [Istanbuler Forschungen, 39] (Marek, *PBNG*)

Mason, H.J., *Greek Terms for Roman Institutions. A Lexicon and Analysis.* Toronto 1974 (Mason)

Millar, F., *The Emperor in the Roman World.* London 1992[2] (Millar, *ERW*)

Münsterberg, R., "Verkannte Titel auf griechischen Münzen," *JÖAI* 18 (1915), Beibl., 307-324 (Münsterberg)

Nawotka, K., "The Attitude towards Rome in the Political Propaganda of the Bosporan Monarchs," *Latomus* 48(1989): 326-38 (Nawotka)

Neppi Modona, Aldo, *L`isola di Coo nell`antichità classica*, Memorie pubblicate a cura dell`Istituto Storico-Archeologico di Rodi, vol. I (1933) (Neppi Modona)

Nigdelis, P.M., *Πολίτευμα καὶ κοινωνία τῶν πόλεων τῶν Κυκλάδων κατὰ τὴν ἑλληνιστικὴ καὶ αὐτοκρατορικὴ ἐποχή.* Thessaloniki 1990 (Nigdelis)

Oliver, J.H., *Greek Constitutions of Early Roman Emperors from Inscriptions and Papyri.* Philadelphia 1989 (Oliver, *GC*)

Paton, W.R.-Hicks, Ed.L., *The Inscriptions of Cos.* Oxford 1891 (reprint Hildesheim 1990) (*PH*)

Patriarca, G., "Iscrizioni dell'Asclepieo di Coo," *Bullettino del Museo dell'Impero Romano*, vol. III (1932) [appendice al vol. LX (1932) del *Bullettino della Commissione Archeologica di Roma*], 3-34 (Patriarca)

Pflaum, H.G., *Les carrières procuratoriennes équestres sous le Haut-Empire romain*, I-III. Paris 1960-1961 (Pflaum, *CPÉ*)

Pflaum, H.G., "Une inscription bilingue de Kos et la perception de la vicesima hereditatium," *ZPE* 7(1971): 64-68 (Pflaum, *I.Kos*)

Pleket, H.W., *The Greek Inscriptions in the Rijksmuseum van Oudheden at Leyden*. Leiden 1958 (Pleket, *I.Leyden*)

Pohl, H., *Die römische Politik und die Piraterie im östlichen Mittelmeer vom 3. bis zum 1. Jhdt. v.Chr.* Berlin 1993 (Pohl)

Price, S.R.F., *Rituals and Power. The Roman Imperial Cult in Asia Minor.* Cambridge 1984 (Price, *R&P*)

Quaß, F., *Die Honoratiorenschicht in den Städten des griechischen Ostens. Untersuchungen zur politischen und sozialen Entwicklung in hellenistischer und römischer Zeit.* Stuttgart 1993 (Quaß, *Hon.*)

Quaß, F., "Zur Verfassung der griechischen Städte im Hellenismus," *Chiron* 9 (1979): 37-52 (Quaß, *Verf.*)

Reger, G., "The Political History of the Kyklades (260-200 B.C.)," *Historia* 43(1994): 32-69 (Reger, *Kyklades*)

Reynolds, J., *Aphrodisias and Rome.* London 1982 [*JRS*, Monogr. 1] (Reynolds)

Rizakis, A.D. (ed.), *Roman Onomastics in the Greek East. Social and Political Aspects.* Athens 1996 [ΜΕΛΕΤΗΜΑΤΑ, 21] (Rizakis, *R.Onomastics*)

Saddington, D.B., "Praefecti Fabrum of the Julio-Claudian Period," in: Ek.Weber & G.Dobesch (Hrsgg.), *Römische Geschichte, Altertumskunde und Epigraphik. Festschrift für Arthur Betz...* Wien 1985, 529-546 (Saddington)

Salomies, O., *Adoptive and Polyonymous Nomenclature in the Roman Empire.* Helsinki 1992 (Salomies)

Schazmann, P., "Das Charmyleion," *JDAI* 49(1934): 110-127, with figs. 1-11 (Schazmann)

Segre, M., "ΚΡΗΤΙΚΟΣ ΠΟΛΕΜΟΣ," *RFIC* n.s. 11(1933): 365-392 (Segre, *ΚΡ.ΠΟΛ.*)

Segre, M., *Tituli Calymnii.* Bergamo 1952 (*ASAA* vol. 22/3, n.s. 6/7: 1944/45 (Segre, *TC*)

Segre, M., *Iscrizioni di Cos*, 1(Testo)- 2(Tavole), redazione di Dina Peppas-Delmousou e M.A.Rizzo. Roma 1993 [Monografie della Scuola Archeologica di Atene..., VI]   (Segre, *I.Cos*)

Sherk, R.K., "Cos and the Dionysiac Artists," *Historia* 15(1966): 211-16 (Sherk, *Cos*)

Sherk, R.K., *Roman Documents from the Greek East. Senatus consulta and Epistulae to the Age of Augustus*. Baltimore 1969   (Sherk, *RDGE*)

Sherwin-White, A.N., *Roman Foreign Policy in the East (168 B.C. to A.D. 1)*. London 1984   (Sherwin-White, *RFPE*)

Sherwin-White, S.M., "A Note on Three Coan Inscriptions," *ZPE* 21(1976): 183-8   (Sherwin-White, *Note*)

Sherwin-White, S.M., "Inscriptions from Cos," *ZPE* 24 (1977): 205-17 (Sherwin-White, *I.Cos*)

Sherwin-White, S.M., *Ancient Cos. An Historical Study from the Dorian Settlement to the Imperial Period*. Göttingen 1978   (Sherwin-White, *Cos*)

Sokolowski, F., *Lois sacrées des cités grecques*. Paris 1969 (Sokolowski, *LSCG*)

Stavrianopoulou, Ef., "Die Wiederverheiratung auf Kos," *Historia* 43(1994): 119-125   (Stavrianopoulou)

Syme, R., "Who was Vedius Pollio?," *JRS* 51 (1961): 23-30   (Syme, *Vedius Pollio*)

Tuchelt, K., *Frühe Denkmäler Roms in Kleinasien. Beiträge zur archäologischen Überlieferung aus der Zeit der Republik und des Augustus, Teil I: Roma und Promagistrate*. Tübingen 1979   (Tuchelt)

Wilhelm, Ad., *Beiträge zur griechischen Inschriftenkunde*. Wien 1909 [Sonderschriften des österr. archäol. Instituts in Wien, VII] (Wilhelm,*Beiträge*)

INDICES

A. Index of persons, places and terms

B. Index of sources

a. Literary sources

Aelian

Ποικίλη Ἱστορία (I.29) : 38f., 53

Aelius Aristides

Ῥοδίοις περὶ ὁμονοίας (Keil XXIV) : 139[84]

Aeschylus

Pers. (Broadhead), 401 ff. : 49f.

Appian

Mith.

4.22 : 16

4.23, 115: 15

9.62 : 123[5], 129, 136[75]

9.63 : 128[28]

BC

I.102, V.6 : 136[75]

Apuleius

Met.

IV.26.3 : 52[118]

Aristophanes

Frogs

1431-3 : 38

Knights

724, 769-70, 1215 : 54

Wasps

1465 : 51

Aristotle

Ath. Pol.

55.3 : 47

Aulus Gellius

III.16.8 : 119

Cassius Dio

48.40.6 : 53

51.2.1 : 134[64]

51.8.3 : 131

54.30.3 : 147[120]

56.27.2-3 : 135

60.19.2-3: 73

60.20.2-6; 21; 23 : 71f.

60.24.4 : 139[84]

Cicero

Ad Att., XII.26.2; Ad. Fam.IX.10.1-2 : 55

Ad Qu. fr., I.1.26; V.21.7 : 56[137]

In Verr.

II.1.89 : 126[17]

Off.

3.87 : 136[75]

CJ

VI.4.1 : 119[45]

Dig.

27.1.17.1 : 136[75]

Diodorus

17.114.2: 103[172]

27.3; 28.1 : 9[14]

Eusebios

Chronik (Schoene)

II.145 : 147[120]

Herodian

1.17.3 : 107

Herodotus

V.56.1, 92β.3; VI.131.2 : 38

Homer

Od.

I.371 : 58[147, 148]

IX.3-4 : 131

IX.34-35 : 50

Josephus

Ant. Jud.

13.13.1 :   15

14.111-113 : "

14.233 : 115f.

16.10.2 : 42

20.183 f. : 120f.[52]

B.J.

1.26.5 : 42

Krinagoras

AP VII.633 (= Gow-Page, AG, I.208f. (no.XVIII) :
    40

AP VII.645 (= Gow-Page, AG, I.210f. (no. XX) "

AP IX.81 (=Gow-Page, AG, I.210f. (no.XXII) : 39f.

AP IX.235 (= Gow-Page, GA, I.212f. (no.XXV) :
    40

Livy

per. LXXXIX : 146

Lucian

Peregr.

15 : 105[188]

Lysias

XIII.91 : 54

Nepos

Att.

6 : 69f.

Pausanias

2.26.3-8 : 33

Philo

De leg. ad Gaium

37 : 106

Pindar

Pyth. III

7 : 33

Plinius Sen.

NH

29.5.7 : 77[57]

29.5.8 : 78

Plinius Jun.

Ep.

7.22 : 71

b. Inscriptions

INDICES

N&X
214, n. 4 : 37[48]
246, n. 2 : 77, 110[210]

inedita (L. Hallof's catalogue), no. *0573 : 17[44]

Höghammar
no. 4 : 89[118]
no. 36: 7
no. 48 : 7
nos. 49, 50 [= PH, 134[2]] : 17[46]
no. 69: 90[119], 137[76]
no. 70 : 60[155]
no. 81: 62

IBM
893 : 128[28]
894 : 102[169]

IC
I.xviii.55: 58[147]
II.xi.3, 9f. : 38[51]

IG
I[3] 857: 60
II[2] 3546: 70[27]
   4351, 4365, 4367, 4372, 4374, 4400, 4403: 60
IV.205 : 103[172]
IV.1[2].121.96, 99-100 : 20[54]
V.1.559 : 100[160]
   970 : 133[60]
   1449 : 102[169]
XI.1.58 : 143[100]
XII.1.2 : 14[28], 139[84]
XII.2.154 : 100[159]
   246 : 121[52]
   549 : 100[160]

XII.5, 143 (+ add., p. 309) : 29[14]
XII.8, 207.15 : 79[71]
XII.8.260 : 45[86], 125f.[17]
XII.9.947 : 118[35]
XII Suppl. 7.3-4 : 99f.
XII Suppl. 250.11 : 61

IGRR
III.87 : 51
   91 : 57[143]
IV.292, 293, 293a : 56
   963 : 57[143]
   984 : 104
   991 : 108[203]
   1302: 57[142]
   1724 : 76[55]
   1732 : 104

I.Ephesos
13 : 142
27 : 85[97], 104
3801 : 102[169]

I.Mylasa
341, 410 : 57[143]
534, 535, 536: 132

I.Stratonikeia
I, p.67 : 118
II.1, 1018 : 58[147], 132[48]
   1024 : 102[169]

IvOl
53 : 91, 134

Lykia_II. 9ff.: 151ff.

364 : 106[20]
373 : 113

TC
111 : 95[135], 107, 110
146 : 74[44], 77[59], 96[138]
167-172 : 86[99], 117[27]
181 : 86
193, 194 : 45[85], 86[100], 96[140]
197 : 79
202 : 111
Test. XII: 10[18]

Sherk, RDGE
18, 20, 21 : 123[5]
22 : 26, 29, 123[6]
23 : 123[5]
49 : 126ff.
57 : 129[34]
58 : 26, 28[12]
67 : 129[32]

SEG
7.825 : 102[169]
14.529 : 49[106]
17.596 : 102[169]
26.1817: 153
32.1982: 106[189]
33.155 : 61[159]

33.1038 : 61f.
34.307, 313 : 102[169]
34.1067 : 64[176]
40.739, 763 : 63f.[168]

Syll.³
67 [= Meiggs – Lewis² 49.5] : 60f.[156]
144.25 : 61[157]
215 : 60[154]
473.11f. : 61[157]
567: 9
685.107 : 11[22]
693 : 135[72]
748: 130
753 : 57[141]
755 : 55[127]
766 : 131[46]
793, see **Herzog,** Hal., no.4

806, see **Segre**, TC, 146
814.45 : 103[174]
819: 143[100]
820.9 : 103[174]
854 : 51[117]
1023.29ff. : 55[129]

c. Papyri

P.Fay. 137.2 : 19

P.Lond. VII, 2188.32 : 11[21]

P.Oxy. 1021 [= Sel. Pap., II.235] : 93[127]

P.W.**Pestman, Chronologie** égyptienne d' après les textes démotiques (332 av J.-C. – 453 ap. J.-C.), Leiden 1967, 50 : 11[21]

d. Coins

Burnett, RPC

no. 2724-2731 : 30ff., 44f.

no. 2732 : 32, 42, 91

no. 2734 : 32, 44

no. 2735 : 44[78]

no. 2740-2742 : 45

no. 3508, 3533 : 31[24]

no. 3871 : 31[24], 64[175]

no. 4778-4779 : 107[195]

no. 5210, 5219, 5230, 5240, 5249, 5260 : 93[127]

BMC Caria

no. 165-169, 177, 192-193 : 30[17]

no. 212-215 : 94[131]

E. Christiansen, The Roman Coins of Alexandria,

Aarhus 1988, I. 38ff. (passim) : 93[127]

M. Crawford, Roman Republican Coinage,

Cambridge 1974, 499f. (no. 490), 740 : 31[20]

H.V.Fritze, Die antiken Münzen Mysiens (1913)

no. 355-356, 358-359 : 37

Head, HN

607 : 136[75]

634 : 30[17]

NC 1990, 224f.: 132

PH N 134 : 21

SNG Copenhagen

nos. 106-107, 109-114 : 37

SNG v.Aulock

no. 2440-2444 : 36

M. **Thompson** et al. (eds.), An **Inventory** of Greek
Coin Hoards, New York 1973, no. 1308 : 21.-